The Terrain of Comedy

The Terrain of Comedy

edited with an introduction by
LOUISE COWAN

The Dallas Institute of Humanities and Culture
Dallas

With gratitude to
The Dallas Institute of Humanites and Culture
and
The Women's Board of the University of Dallas

Copyright © 1984 by The Pegasus Foundation
All rights reserved

Cover: Jean Baptiste Camille Corot, *The Muse—Comedy*
Copyright © 1979 by The Metropolitan Museum of Art
Bequest of Mrs. H. O. Havemeyer, 1929.
The H. O. Havemeyer Collection.

Cover design: Patricia Mora and Maribeth Lipscomb

Library of Congress Cataloging in Publication Data
Main entry under title:

The Terrain of comedy.

  Includes index.
  1. Comic, The, in literature—Addresses, essays, lectures. I. Cowan, Louise, 1916–
PN56.C66T47   1984   809'.917   84-22667
ISBN 0-911005-05-6 (pbk.)

The Dallas Institute of Humanities and Culture
2719 Routh Street / Dallas, Texas 75201 / (214)698-9090

Contents

Editor's Preface		vii
Introduction: The Comic Terrain *Louise Cowan*		1
1	Against the Belly of the Ram: The Comedy of Deception in *The Odyssey* *Glenn Arbery*	19
2	The Bible as Genesis of Comedy *Daniel Russ*	41
3	Aristophanes' Comic Apocalypse *Louise Cowan*	61
4	Dante, Hegel, and the Comedy of History *Bainard Cowan*	89
5	*Commedia dell'Arte*: The Image of Comedy *Mary Lou Hoyle*	111
6	The Communal Action of *The Winter's Tale* *Kathleen Latimer*	125
7	Carnival and *Don Quixote*: The Folk Tradition of Comedy *Marilyn Stewart*	143
8	The Copious Inventory of Comedy *Robert S. Dupree*	163
9	The Icon and the Spirit of Comedy: Dostoevsky's *The Possessed* *Dennis Slattery*	195
10	Faulkner's Bachelors and Fertility *Mary K. Mumbach*	221
Index		253

Editor's Preface

This book issues from what might be called a long collective obsession. My students at the University of Dallas from 1960 (the year I first taught Dante) on were drawn into participation in a relentless preoccupation with genre theory. Many of them, because the generic approach I suggested seemed perfectly obvious after it had been enunciated and applied, went on to refine and enlarge and modify it until it became, for some of us at least, an unconsciously governing figure in the background of our thought. Something of the variety and scope possible within a general theory of genre is displayed in the present essays. To most of us writing in this volume it seems that genre patterns are patterns in reality which the poet apprehends and then imitates in language. The images and forms he produces take their place in the creation of a poetic universe which, though seemingly complete in itself, is constantly, throughout the centuries, under construction.

The authors of these essays might be said to constitute something of a school of criticism. They all studied at one stage of their careers at the University of Dallas, all of them with two exceptions having taken their doctoral degrees there in the Institute of Philosophic Studies. They have spent years in conversation with each other, and though they have gone their separate ways and followed their own lines of thought, still they exhibit an underlying kinship in sharing a universe of discourse and a coherent set of images which they can take for granted. Their focus here is comedy, primarily because it has received less critical attention than the other "kinds," but also because its general nature is most often misconstrued. They hold a common view of comedy in considering it less an extrinsic structure than an interior organizing principle that places a work in a certain world—a world that we have agreed to call the terrain of comedy.

I am grateful, first of all, for the opportunity of working with such students and colleagues as these in numerous literary ventures—primarily, with most of them, in a splendid and noble, if short-lived, graduate program, one that undertook its task, as I think of it now, with the zest and elevation of high comedy. My husband has shared this comic vision—no doubt engendered it—and helped this literary endeavor in word and deed. I am indebted to The Dallas Institute of Humanities and Culture and the Women's Board of the University of Dallas for encouraging the production of this book, to the Metropolitan Museum of Art for permission to use a reproduction of Corot's "The Muse—Comedy," to Mary Vernon for suggesting the Corot painting, to Patricia Mora and Maribeth Lipscomb for designing the cover, and in large measure to Susan Dupree for editorial help and patient and intelligent typesetting.

Louise Cowan
Dallas, 1984

Introduction
The Comic Terrain

LOUISE COWAN

THE paradigms of comedy are manifold, outwardly disparate and even refractory in their refusal to yield to generalities. Far more than other genres, comedy invites a skeptical attitude toward any effort to isolate out of its multiplicity a single principle of classification. Yet a serious attempt at comic theory can hardly escape the conviction that works customarily designated as comic, despite their variety, do indeed participate in some sort of community. If the tie joining them is something like the "'gold to airy thinness beat'" of Donne's superlunary lovers, undiscernible to those "whose soul is sense," it is nonetheless binding. Such dissimilar specimens as many-turning Odysseus's long voyage home, Aristophanes' fantastic obscenities, and the worldly intrigues of New Comedy are upon examination found to be capable of coming together in an unlikely harmony with the churchly art of the mystery plays, the spiritual writings of Dante, and Shakespeare's benevolent deceptions for love. Something links together in one category works that are outrageously different, requiring anyone thinking about comedy to confront on all sides the most perplexing contradictions.

And apparently these troublesome antinomies contained within the phenomenon of the comic are ineradicable by any process of simple reduction: the notion of comedy seems by its very nature to include all aspects of human life, the darkest as well as the brightest elements in the entire literary spectrum. In fact, upon observation comedy shows itself to be the least exclusive of all literary forms, able to accommodate structures at once simple and complex, treating both the natural and artificial and reconciling the grossest bodily indecencies with the most rarefied spiritual and intellectual refinements. Yet despite a puzzling breadth and variety, any single comic specimen is likely to manifest a discernible characteristic that proclaims its identity. Critics and audiences alike have almost without fail been able to recognize a work of comic art, and not necessarily by its possible incitement to laughter. Comedies have been designated comedies even when their atmosphere is melancholy and depressing, as in the plays of Chekhov, or even painful and disgusting, as in those of Ben Jonson and Samuel Beckett.

Thus one might hazard that an encompassing image lies beyond mere appearances in comedy, capable of being recognized in countless situations, with varying characters, on different strata of life, with emphasis on many possible segments of the large central action. Such an image could be said to be expressive of a fundamental aspect of human feeling and, as such, to elicit a response less acquired than innate, less reasoned than instinctive. In fact, the comic sense seems to suggest to its audience a hidden current in the flow of life, intelligible to all members of the human race, at its most basic level what Susanne Langer has called "the pure sense of life,"[1] and at its highest the river of living water spoken of in the Scriptures. Well before apprehending plot, character, or theme, spectators or readers are able to observe clues pointing the direction in which their imaginations are impelled; they can almost unconsciously gauge from angle and speed the implied destination—the completed curve, one might say, of which only an arc is visible. Audiences and readers are hence not likely to mistake comedy: they are able with little difficulty to distinguish it from tragedy or epic. Further, comedy might be said to belong to the people as community even more than do the other genres. No culture has lacked some manifestation of it, and it is often so much woven into the patterns of a social order that it is taken for granted and comes to be disregarded as serious art by intellectual members of society. And yet comedy might be thought of as an expression of the communal unconscious of a people—its yearning for a more liberated life—and, as such, a binding

Introduction: The Comic Terrain

force among its members. But if as viewers people apprehend comedy without much conscious effort, as critics, when they come to analyze the comic effect, they tend to mistake accidental properties of individual comedies—for instance, satire, farce, wit, and humor—for the comedic image itself.

But comedy, as a handful of authorities have pointed out throughout the ages, is not necessarily the laughable. W. K. Wimsatt's remark—that a comedy that does not provoke laughter seems to be "an odd success"[2]—is applicable only if one can discern no other, more compelling, purpose for the comic vision. Perhaps Plato began the oversimplification when, in the *Philebus*, he assumed comedy to be about "the ridiculous" and ascribed the audience's mixed feelings on viewing a comedy to a combination of pleasure and envy (that is, we are delighted at the misfortune of our friends). Aristotle continued this misconception when he viewed comedy as "an imitation of characters of a lower type," particularly the "ludicrous [which] consists in some defect or ugliness which is not painful or destructive." Medieval theorists, largely following the lead of Aristotle and Horace in an analysis of the formal parts of comedy and its ethical nature, gave their chief concern to the comic catharsis, which they deemed to be laughter, and to the comic moral responsibility of teaching. The immense body of Italian Renaissance literary criticism had no trouble reconciling the still-dominant medieval didacticism with the new humanism, and the subsequent result, later expressed in neoclassical theory, led to the widespread conviction by the eighteenth century that comedy teaches the sensible attitude toward life (*raison*) by ridiculing the rigid, extreme, fanatical, and pretentious. That interpretation has prevailed, with some exceptions, to the present.

A few critics and philosophers in our time—Susanne Langer, Albert Cook, Northrop Frye, Nevill Coghill, among others[3]—have given their attention to what is "behind" comedy, that invisible meta-form which I have been speaking of as the image. But in the main the bulk of comic theory today as in the past has tended to develop around the idea of social melioration—largely deriving from Greek and Roman new comedy. And though over the years criticism has clarifed formal elements and distinguished between such strains as wit and humor, burlesque and satire, farce and comedy of manners, it has chiefly remained concerned with constitutive elements rather than with the entire phenomenon of comedy, its governing outlook, one might say, that which makes it a single imaginative mode and animates its specific parts. Further, comic theory as it now stands seems to have made little effort to apprehend the way in which a particular instance of comedy, even when it represents only a portion of the complete comic action, evokes —and fits into—a full imaginative world of comedic possibilities.

The task of understanding the nature of comedy, then, is to be pursued less by analysis than by vision. Consequently comic theory poses a problem that can hardly be solved by empirical methods—by juxtaposing or even superimposing art works generally designated comedies and attempting to ascertain their common structural or thematic constants, however much such a strategy may constitute a beginning. It is by necessity an ontological question that the literary critic poses in seeking to know the essential nature of comedy. And though a satisfactory apparatus for resolving ontological questions may not be readily at hand in our time, nonetheless the serious critic of comedy must at least make the attempt to engage the issue.

Admittedly, one can know the nature of comedy only through the immediate thing—the individual work. But the fictional whole, the play or the novel, presents to the imagination an intuition of an invisible form which, from a glimpse, may be apprehended in its entirety. It is here that the underlying form of comedy is to be found, not so much in an abstraction as in an image that the mind seizes upon with delight. The task of the critic, however, is not to stay with this superactual realm but rather to return to the work at hand, better equipped to explore its true nature. In such a process, a specific representation of human action is able to reveal the universal image of comedy that has rendered countless dramatic works of art comic and, as such, recognizable to their audiences throughout the years.

One does not have to eat the entire pudding to know that it is flavored with vanilla—or that it is a pudding and not a cheese soufflé. All that is required is a taste. Similarly, the character of comedy is so definitive, its reality so unquestionable, that one can discern its nature even from a brief experience of the work. Its qualities permeate it, as the vanilla permeates the pudding and thereby modifies its component parts. For it is not the separate features of an art product that make it

Introduction: The Comic Terrain

comedy; rather it is the purpose, the form-making principle of the entire work that welds all its elements into a single unit. One should be able, I maintain, to choose any page of a work—not necessarily the beginning or the end, but any portion of it—and discern from a reading of that segment whether or not the work is comic. Even though tragic elements may be present in comedy or comic elements in tragedy, the reader—or hearer—can still detect the general character of the work as a whole.

In *Hamlet*, for example, the word-play, punning, levity, wit, Hamlet's "antic disposition," his wild and disconcerted action are devices that one associates with comedy rather than tragedy. And in point of fact the young prince does behave for a while like a comic protagonist—as in his baiting of Polonius:

> *Polonius.* Do you know me, my lord?
> *Hamlet.* Excellent well. You are a fishmonger.
> *Polonius.* Not I, my lord.
> *Hamlet.* Then I would you were so honest a man.
> (2.2.173-76)

And, later, in the same conversation, he purposely misunderstands Polonius's inquiry, "What is the matter, my lord?" and answers it with a pretended innocence:

> *Hamlet.* Between who?
> *Polonius.* I mean the matter that you read, my lord.
> (2.2.196-97)

Hamlet responds with the verbal "patter" that marks the Fool or the Clown in Shakespeare's comedies:

> *Hamlet.* Slanders, sir, for the satirical rogue says here that old men have gray beards, that their faces are wrinkled, their eyes purging thick amber and plum-tree gum, and that they have a plentiful lack of wit, together with the most weak hams. All which, sir, though I most powerfully and potently believe, yet I hold it not honesty to have it thus set down; for you yourself, sir, should be old as I am if, like a crab, you could go backward.
> (2.2.198-206)

The undertone to this essentially comic routine is not only a dark irony, but a deathward pull, so that one is not surprised at Hamlet's reply to Polonius's solicitous question:

> *Polonius.* Will you walk out of the air, my lord?
> *Hamlet.* Into my grave.
>
> (2.2.208-09)

The entire passage with the foolish old courtier has all the earmarks of comic repartee, as does the coarse jesting with Ophelia, the sparring with Rosencrantz and Guildenstern, the ironic exchange with the gravedigger. Yet it is clearly recognizable that in *Hamlet* one is not in a comic but a tragic realm, no matter how foolishly people may conduct themselves in it.

In counterposition are many of the comedies—*All's Well that Ends Well, Much Ado about Nothing,* along with *The Merchant of Venice,* and the later plays, particularly *The Winter's Tale* and *Cymbeline.* All contain dark, painful, and unpleasant elements—the raw materials of tragedy, one could say—and most of them have less to do with laughter than with shock and grief. In both *The Winter's Tale* and *Cymbeline,* for instance, the action begins in utmost malice and destruction: a husband turned against a wife, a father against a daughter. In both plays violence and betrayal increase until the entire action seems to be moving toward death. Hermione and Imogen are both falsely accused and thus separated from the beloved; but both behave not as a Gertrude or a Juliet would behave, but with staunch and enduring hearts. Hermione waits, for all of sixteen years, until her husband's jealousy has run its course. Imogen, unlike Juliet, when she awakes in a grave beside what seems to be the dead body of her husband, trusts in an ultimate power to work things out and joins the army of Romans marching through Wales. In both plays friends and guardians do what they can to avert catastrophe, and yet catastrophe does occur: after the death of the king's son from grief, Paulina attempts to persuade Leontes to reinstate his wife and baby daughter, and, failing, must take Hermione surreptitiously under her care. Antilochus, commanded to kill the child, leaves her instead on the seacoast of Bohemia before himself being overtaken by a bear. Pain, anguish, deception, jealousy, calumny, hatred, injury—these are the materials of comedy as well as tragedy. If we were to place *Hamlet* beside *The Tempest,* for instance, seeking to ascertain their respective genres by a comparison of elements, we should find some striking similarities. Both plays are about usurpation, betrayal, assassination, revenge, the perils of the father-

Introduction: The Comic Terrain

daughter relationship, the grief of a son for a father, death by water, rebirth out of the sea. Yet one play is quite definitely a tragedy and one a comedy.

Comedies are perceptibly governed by the comic image—not simply by virtue of their happy endings or their discursive structure, but by their very being—the way in which characters and plot develop, the manner in which people speak, the course that events take, the apparent incidentals that incorporate themselves into the action. Over and above these single works appear universal features, complex structures or qualities and values that are discernible in life only through having been given form in the realm of comedy. As Dante says (or, at least, as Barbara Reynolds has him say), "... my sight by seeing learns to see."[4] Those things that are all about us are noticeable only by being fitted into a different kind of totality—in this instance, a comic universe.

Such reflections on comedy give rise to fundamental questions concerning the meaning of literary genre. Poetic works, one could say following Aristotle, tend to aggregate in four moderately distinct segments of the poetic universe, tragedy, comedy, epic, and lyric. These are the genres of literature that express the basic gestures—the actions—of the soul. In his book *The Formal Method* (written with or without his colleague Pavel Medvedev) the Russian critic Mikhail Bakhtin indicates that, far from being an abstract description of devices, genre is a fundamental orientation toward reality. "One might say," he writes, "that human consciousness possesses a series of inner genres for seeing and conceptualizing reality."[5] And he goes on: "A particular aspect of reality can be understood only in connection with the particular means of representing it."[6]

It is with the "inner genre" of comedy that this volume is concerned—and with the reality of which it speaks. "The particular means of representing it" is, if we use Aristotle's terms, the comic *mimesis*, the artistic representation, whereas the "particular aspect of reality" revealed by the art-form is the *praxis*, the action that is imitated. For the genres are not external structures governed by rules and conventions but internal forms, perspectives upon life that indicate the kind of response called for by a particular work. Not to know their nature is like being deaf to the tone of voice in which a comment is spoken and blind to the face and gesture that express it. To be oblivious of the large generic metaphor governing the climate of a work and hence the very atmosphere in which its characters live and breathe is to remain unaware of its deepest meaning and hence its power. The different contexts result, if we are to believe Aristotle, from the fact that different genres "imitate" different actions, different "movements-of-spirit," in Francis Fergusson's phrase, to which all the elements of a work conform.[7] An entire world lies in and beyond the plot and characters—a tragic, comic, epic, or lyric world—and each act within it corresponds to the actual world only when the viewer or reader is aware of its mimetic distortion. It may be more profitable here, however, to be concerned with the genres as representing not so much particular kinds of action as actions that can fittingly take place in certain kinds of realms. A work is tragic, for instance, not because any of its analyzable elements make it so but because the action it imitates—that which animates its inner being—takes place in the region of tragedy.

Such a generic territory is ruled by its own laws, analogically related to life yet different from daily experience. The vision of the individual work emerges in this space, and the warping of the space that typifies the genre governs the kind of art through which it may be expressed. As Susanne Langer has written, "In any work of art, the dimensionality of its space and the continuous character of it are always implicitly assured. Perceptual forms are carved out of it and must appear to be still related to it despite their most definite boundaries."[8] Hence the particular distortions of its elements identify it as belonging to a particular genre. In a sense a knowledge of genre might be thought of as a guide to the laws of the land, if one is willing to grant the existence of a territory of the imagination. Our attempt to ascertain what gives a single work of art a comic identity, then, leads us to the necessity of distinguishing the image of a world—the comic terrain—lying behind the action of the work and presupposed by it. And what we find first of all in such an endeavor is that comedy, any comedy, seems to be enacted in an identifiable and familiar world, so familiar that anyone, whether prince or pauper, can walk about in it and find it home.

When we speak of a comic terrain, we must locate it somewhere within what we might call an entire cosmos of imagined forms. This virtual cosmos, like what Adolf Hildebrand calls "total space," can be visualized "as a body of water into which we may sink certain vessels,

Introduction: The Comic Terrain 9

and thus be able to define individual volumes of the water without, however, destroying the idea of a continuous mass of water enveloping all."[9] The *mundus imaginalis* is not a mere mental replica of the world in which we have our daily existence, though it resembles it in many ways and derives from it through poetic vision. This cosmos of the imagination is a realm not of pure spirit, but of matter permeated by spirit, a realm of "ontological splendor," in Jacques Maritain's phrase.[10] It possesses an order that guides interpretation of individual works and of whole families of works. The large forms of lyric, tragedy, comedy, and epic make up this universe, embodying certain complex attitudes of the soul, constituting complete worlds in themselves. No work therefore stands entirely alone, but takes its place within both the genre to which it belongs and the complete cosmos that makes up the whole of man's image of himself. If one seeks to visualize this image in its totality, one must resort to some sort of schematic diagram, one that is more an aid to reflection than a literal representation or a prescription. My own such diagram would consist of a circle, with lyric at the summit, tragedy following clockwise after lyric in a descending fall, comedy continuing in the lower arc directly opposite to lyric, and epic following after comedy and rising toward lyric (see below).

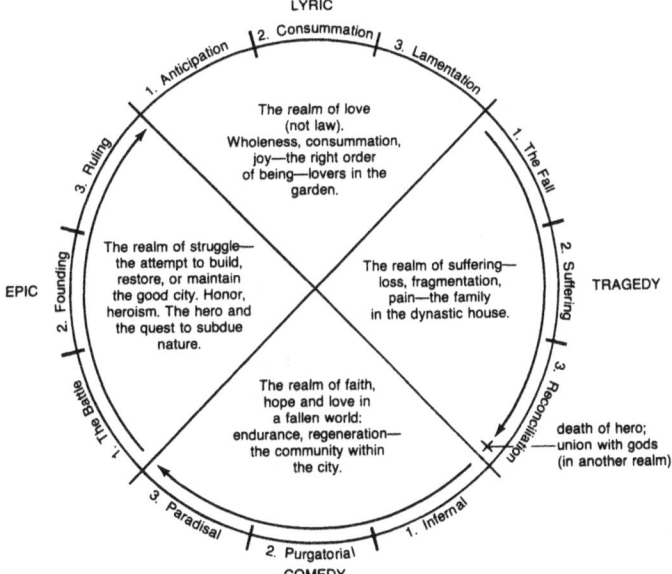

The lyric realm is the place of origins and sources, the land of heart's desire, symbolized by the garden. Tragedy, marked by the sudden catastrophe of the loss of a garden state, takes place most often in a palace or a great dynastic house. Comedy endures and perseveres in a fallen world, occurring in city streets or drawing rooms, escaping sometimes to a world of fantasy, making its way by mutual helpfulness toward a community of love within the larger order of society. Epic, though taking place in some sort of natural surrounding, struggles to build or cleanse or govern this larger order, the just city. Hence the epic goal, as it presses to complete the circle, is no longer Eden, but the New Jerusalem, the major human enterprise redeemed and made new.

It is by simultaneous contemplation of several examples of a genre that one can discern, in a kind of visionary form, its large, invisible patterns: for the lyric, one puts together Donne's love poems, Keats's odes, the Hebrew Psalms, and The Song of Songs; for tragedy, the dramas of Aeschylus, Sophocles, and Shakespeare; for epic, Homer, Virgil, the Anglo-Saxon poets, Milton. For comedy, the concern of this volume, the paradigms, as I have earlier maintained are numerous and widely diverging. The work of two poets, however, seem to me most fully to establish the large pattern of the comic genre: Aristophanes and Dante. Both evoke expansive images of the comic terrain, images that remain in the realm of imagination, available to all of us after they have been given form.

For Aristophanes access to the fullness of the comic vision was available only potentially, through an apocalyptic vision of final fulfillment. Dante, coming at a time that endowed him with what Maritain calls "luck,"[11] found the philosophic and theological presuppositions of his poetic vision ready at hand to give his poem the completeness of an intellective as well as an imaginative act. Hence Dante provides the clearest image of the comic terrain. Further, his art is incarnational, finding in the very makeup of the world the radiant play of spirit. His figural design of the possible states of soul after death represents, as every reflective reader recognizes, something hidden but nonetheless present in the depths of the soul during life. Thus Dante envisions three possible conditions for the individual and for the community, each located in a realm where the laws explicitly reflect an inner spiritual state. These three quite different "places" objectifying the three states of soul can consequently be seen to represent the three possible regions of the comic terrain.

The first, infernal comedy, is a state in which grace is utterly absent and where selfishness and malice prevail. The community has accepted its fallen condition and cynically attributes its corruption to "the way of the world." Love cannot dwell in such society; everyone is fundamentally alone, though hypocrisy and self-serving may give the appearance of friendship. None of the virtues is present: only a sinister "double" of each prevails. The style of a comedy portraying this darkness may be light and witty; nevertheless grotesque and bestial forces are not far underneath its surface—and may, in some comedies, be openly present, testifying to the deformation of forms and the hideousness of the soul when it attempts to establish itself as autonomous. This is the prevailing moral climate of such a world; not everyone in it however is in the infernal state. Like the pilgrim Dante, someone may find himself trapped in an infernal society without participating in its malice. If innocence or truth does wander into this no man's land, it is preyed upon and virtually destroyed. I use the word "virtually" because the real destruction of tragedy is alien to the comic muse. In this totally fallen world, her "humanely malign" light, to use George Meredith's phrase, is grantedly merciless; but she stops short of evoking pity or terror.

In the infernal state the pretty girl, who is one of the chief identifying marks of comedy, is either absent or, if she does enter the boundaries of this dark region, victimized. Lust, avarice, hypocrisy, and treachery are the vices most prevalent in this doleful city. Irony and wit govern the utterance of its characters. The intellect is supreme in its own self-love. The body is debased, ill, deformed, or totally ignored in favor of abstract and over-systematic rationality. Natural pleasure, such as feasting or love-making, is diseased or distorted. The comic hero, whom Cedric Whitman in his study of Aristophanes characterizes as a *poneros*—the rogue who puts survival above all else and whose inventiveness is constantly turned to that end[12]—becomes, in this realm, really wicked, like Mosca or Tartuffe, or naughty like Face or Mak; if he is good-hearted, he is either willing to compromise with the world, like Callimacho or Mirabell or he finds escape as quickly as possible, like Dikaiopolis or Yossarian. He cannot, while remaining in this region, win the lovely lady. For marriage, ordinarily the goal of all comedy and its chief good, is maligned in dark comedy: old husbands tyrannize young wives, spouses are unfaithful, maidens are linked by opportunism to unsuitable mates: society has allowed its codes to degenerate to the falsest of conventions.

Deception and disguise, characterizing marks of comedy, are used in infernal society for the purpose or gaining advantage, usually to the harm of others. Even the guardians, those figures of disinterested benevolence who manifest themselves from time to time within the comic tradition, realize their helplessness to change the general situation and either withdraw as does Alceste or concentrate their efforts on the rescue of the feminine victim, as do Ligurio, Paulina, Sir Henry Harcourt-Reilly and Julia, and Gavin Stevens and Ratliff. The wicked are in control of the city, though frequently in the end they are outwitted by someone even more tricky than they. Face is outfaced; Shylock is outlegalized; Flem Snopes is destroyed by something within Snopesism itself. The biter bit, the gull gulled—these eventualities are often the outcome of infernal comedy, since wickedness multiplies incrementally and gives the appearance of infinite resource. Yet there is usually a reckoning, in which the community is reaffirmed, even if in the sternest possible way; justice is meted out to offenders, and the innocent are vindicated.

This is the realm of dirty jokes, of harmful trickery, of cruel deceit. The Greeks were only imperfectly aware of it as a human possibility, the Old Testament portrays it but seldom, for it is less the world of sin than of abomination—Sodom and Gomorrah, the false prophets in Pharaoh's court, Jezebel, the Tower of Babel. But the medieval world, fully aware of its implications, found it in daily experience: Chaucer's pardoner and his friar inhabit this world, as do the characters in the miller's and the merchant's tales. Piers Plowman's vision of the seven deadly sins is in this infernal mold. Machiavelli continues it into the Renaissance in his *Mandragola*, Ben Jonson in his *Volpone* and *The Alchemist*, Shakespeare in *Troilus and Cressida*, and the characters of Shylock, Lucio, Cloten, and Iachimo. Moliere and Restoration comedy are in this mode also, a fact that explains the frequent charge of "immorality" leveled against them. Blake's "London," Flaubert's *Madame Bovary*, Gogol's *Dead Souls*, Swift's *Gulliver's Travels*,

Introduction: The Comic Terrain

Dostoevsky's *The Possessed*, Eliot's *The Waste Land*, Katherine Anne Porter's *Ship of Fools*, O'Connor's *Wise Blood* exhibit its dark and malevolent lineage. William Faulkner, as one can judge from his early drafts of the Snopes saga, gradually turned from tragedy to comedy in conceiving his trilogy over the years, coming to see the evil engulfing the human enterprise as contemptible and ultimately defeatable.

I have gone into this first stage at such length because it is the most misunderstood mode of comedy, least considered in any comic theory. In practical criticism, it is frequently confused with tragedy or considered to be a kind of "tragi-comedy," and often interpreted as nihilistic when, on the contrary, at least traditionally, it has been the most severely moral of all the guises of comedy. The other two comic worlds—the purgatorial and paradisal—are less misconstrued, since they more naturally tend toward the "happy frame of mind," to use Hegel's phrase,[13] that is ordinarily associated with the comic. In fact, many theories of comedy are based almost entirely on the second, or purgatorial, stage and thus fail to take account of the entire comedic scope.

This middle stage of comedy is, as we have indicated, the purgatorial realm. Its mood is pathos: in it the community hopes and waits, powerless to save itself. This is by far the broadest region of comedy; a large part of the literature that is generally considered comic inhabits this terrain: the Old Testament, *The Odyssey*, most of Aristophanes, Chaucer, and Shakespeare, Cervantes, Fielding, Jane Austen, Dostoevsky, Henry James, Chekhov, Beckett, Flannery O'Connor's *The Violent Bear It Away*. In it people, though lost and in need of delivery from something outside themselves, are not really wicked. Neither are they positively good, but most of the characters in this kind of world do the best they can and patiently endure. Imperfection and weakness rather than malice and evil are the obstacles to happiness in this realm of middle comedy; the pretty girl is yearned for, though not to be possessed; and deception and disguise are undertaken to make bad situations work out better. Time, in this realm, stretches out its lengthy wait; but time is benevolent and will eventually permit things to be healed. In the realm of space, too, this middle region has greater largesse. This is the stage in which the "second world" of comedy accomplishes its effects most beneficently—a community may locate itself in a place where things can work out according to laws other than those that have gone astray in civilization. The "worlds" of Circe, Queen Arete, Calypso, in particular for Odysseus, aid him in understanding and undertaking his task. For Aristophanes' solitary little hopeful figures, the heavens, or the underworld, or the bedroom are places of strength to be used against the corruption and decay of the city. For Shakespeare, Belmont, the Forest of Arden, the woods outside Athens, and Milford Haven are places of sanctuary and healing. For Henry James, Europe; for Melville, a sea-voyage; for Mark Twain, the river; for Faulkner, the big woods—these other "places" shelter the realities that the world has forgotten and offer an experience of renewal, allowing the time and space necessary to keep the protagonist and other members of the community from despair or some irrevocably hasty action. In this stage, the action ends with mercy rather than justice; its mood is wistful sadness, or muted joy. In it, love is beginning to be apprehended, if not as the power that "moves the sun and the stars," than at least as that which can change and modify human existence.

The highest realm within the comic terrain is the paradisal: here grace and forgiveness supplant even mercy. Man is lifted up into a realm beyond himself, one that he has not gained by his own effort. Aristophanes' *Birds* portrays this realm symbolically; Dante's *Paradiso*, Shakespeare's *Tempest*, Faulkner's *Reivers* body it forth. Its mood is merriment and joy, its motive pleasure and freedom. Deception and disguise are revealed to be what they are in reality: magic, grace, art. Here love is supreme; one is not required by one's own efforts to save the day—the natural tendency of things is upward. The pretty girl has become the vessel of reality and grace: Basileia, Beatrice, Portia, Miranda. In the modern world she has been victimized and injured, but the quality of which she is the bearer remains undamaged: Sonya Marmeladov, Mme. de Vionnet, Everbe Corinthia, and Linda Snopes. Very few literary works take place entirely in this realm —perhaps only Dante's *Paradiso*—but many make their way to it, stumblingly and feelingly. The mark of it is not simply romantic love, the attainment of the beautiful lady, but the movement beyond her to that of which she has borne witness: universal love.

* * *

Introduction: The Comic Terrain

What is the terrain of comedy? What is the slant of light, the curving of space that identifies it? One might attempt to visualize it, though the actual image remains elusive, revealing itself only to an interior sense. But the intuition of *place* is unmistakable; and perhaps only a metaphor can do justice to it. The image has the largesse, the "room" of a land, a terrain. There is darkness in that land, we might begin by saying; but in its mellow atmosphere shadows move before the protagonist and shorten in the course of the day. The path cutting through the hills and valleys, crossing the wide plains, and winding upward in a gentle slope is one that various characters trudge upon for only partially completed journeys, stopping along the way for retreats in woods or caves, or gathering together at intervals for festivity. Homer, Aristophanes, Dante, Chaucer, and Shakespeare have given us specific metaphors for this constant image. But the geography of this terrain informs all comedy, whether dark and bitter or full of mirth and delight, whatever the local territory or temporal code. It informs each genuine work of comedic art not as a map or an outline would do, but as an image. The image is complex, containing an order and an interplay of values which in each comedy must be worked out by mutual accommodation. The comic terrain, then, is a figure of the permanent laws of being as seen under a single aspect, a governing figure that provides the most humble comedy with its power. It is a correlative for the hope—and then, finally, one realizes, the experience—of being loved, of being cared about and guarded and showered with "tender mercies." If the high peak of lyric is insight into knowing and loving, then the corresponding high point of comedy lies not in knowing, but in being shown, being led into the harmony of the cosmos to receive better than one deserves. Not revelation, then, but receptivity leads to its summit, its permitted high vista.

What are the laws and customs of its land, acknowledged even by those who flout them? Its supreme law, of course, is love; its concern is with *physis*, the flow of being that animates and connects all things. Comedy takes place in a fallen world; it begins in established disorder, usually with an old regime in control, where people have lived by law, by reason, or by custom, neglecting wholeness, pleasure, and love. It moves toward the recapturing of those qualities by ingenuity and audacity. It may resort to the fantastic in order to effect a needed break with routine, and it pulls others along with it in a creative recapturing of community, with friends and helpers serving as guardians and counsellors. Its justice is mercy and forgiveness. Its supreme fiction is the journey of the soul; its virtues, faith, hope, and charity, its vices the seven deadly sins. Its mode of action is deception and delay, since if Fortune and not Fate is to be the governing authority, one must do whatever is necessary to stave off the ultimate fatal defeat. Life must go on, at any cost, since in comedy life can blossom again even out of impossibility if only the final, unthinkable event does not occur. Life, the *élan vital*, is far more important than established morality, since the very continuance of the human species is in question. In the end, however, the comic seeks to reestablish morality and to reanimate the life of moral and spiritual forms. The terrain of comedy is, in fine, an image of the world as organic rather than mechanic—as living, interrelating, aspiring, growing, and healing. It is a vision of matter participating in spirit, of grace permeating nature, of the body being lifted up, like Bottom, in an overwhelming and irrational joy.

The authors of the essays in this volume would conceive of this comic territory, I think, as having, like Gaul, a tripartite division and would see each comedy as positioned chiefly in one of the three regions. They would agree that comedy represents one of the major spatializations of reality of which literature is capable, would not limit its presence to drama, and would view individual examples of comedy as representations of an order in reality, images of which may recur throughout history without need of direct influence between writers. And, finally, these critics might agree, though I am making perhaps an ungrounded assumption here, that the action of all comedy possesses that polysemousness that Dante attributed to his *Commedia*: that (if we translate the medieval exegetic schema into our own terms) archetypally, the comic action is the psyche moving out of stasis into the rhythm of the life force; culturally, it is the flexibility of the community prevailing over rigid and oppressive custom; psychologically, it is the heart finding its right order, its abundance, in love; and anagogically, it is the soul's participation, through the *komos*, the marriage feast, in universal blessedness.

But though there lies behind these essays a more or less shared theory of comedy, the essays themselves are, in general, exercises in practical rather than theoretical criticism. That is, they examine specific comic elements or themes and specific comic literary works or groups of works. They make no attempt at completeness. What the essays do, however, is to adumbrate the comic terrain: they show it as a world in which people must keep going, must "endure." And they show that if they do keep going, whether in hope or desperation, they finally, so to speak, catch the bus. When they have caught it, even if they have fallen and skinned their knees and made fools of themselves in the process, they are as surely on it and going with it to its destination as if they had arrived a couple of hours before departure and decorously available themselves of the best possible seats. The point of arrival is the same; and, at least for those comedies that take us the whole distance, or even imply it, the end is nothing short of joy, transcendence, and love.

Notes

1. Susanne K. Langer, *Feeling and Form: A Theory of Art* (New York, 1973), 327.

2. W. K. Wimsatt, Jr., "Introduction: The Criticism of Comedy," in *English Stage Comedy*, ed. W. K. Wimsatt, Jr., English Institute Essays, 1954 (New York, 1955), 3.

3. The best of these, besides Langer, are Albert S. Cook, *The Dark Voyage and the Golden Mean* (Cambridge, Mass., 1949); Northrop Frye, "The Argument of Comedy," in English Institute Essays, 1948 (New York, 1949) and *Anatomy of Criticism* (Princeton, N.J., 1957); Nevill Coghill, "The Basis of Shakespearean Comedy," in *English Association Essays and Studies* 3 (1950): 1-28; and more recently Robert Heilman, *The Ways of the World: Comedy and Society* (Seattle, 1978). Of course such classic nineteenth-century studies in comic theory as Charles Baudelaire's *On the Essence of Laughter*; George Meredith's *An Essay on Comedy*; Henri Bergson's *Laughter*; and Sigmund Freud's *Wit and Its Relation to the Unconscious* attempt to get at the nature of the comic and succeed in illumining at least an aspect of it.

4. Dante, *Paradise, The Comedy of Dante Alighieri* 32, 1, trans. Dorothy L. Sayers and Barbara Reynolds (Hammondsworth, Baltimore, and Victoria, 1971): 112.

5. P. N. Medvedev and M. M. Bakhtin, *The Formal Method in Literary Scholarship: A Critical Introduction to Sociological Poetics*, trans. Albert J. Wehrle (Baltimore, 1978), 129-30.

6. Ibid., 134.

7. Francis Fergusson, "Introduction," in *Aristotle's Poetics*, ed. S. H. Butcher (New York, 1961), 4.

8. Langer, 75.
9. As quoted in Langer, 75.
10. Jacques Maritain, *Art and Scholasticism, with Other Essays*, trans. J. F. Scanlan (New York, 1930), 28.
11. Jacques Maritain, *Creative Intuition in Art and Poetry*, The A. W. Mellon Lectures in the Fine Arts (Cleveland and New York, 1965), 274.
12. Cedric Whitman, *Aristophanes and the Comic Hero* (Cambridge, Mass., 1964), 29-50.
13. G. W. F. Hegel, *The Philosophy of Fine Art* 4, trans. F. P. B. Osmaston (London, 1920): 302.

1

Against the Belly of the Ram:
The Comedy of Deception in *The Odyssey*

GLENN ARBERY

"MUCH has been talked of the melancholy of Virgil," writes C. S. Lewis, "but an inch beneath the bright surface of Homer we find not melancholy but despair. 'Hell' was the word Goethe used of it. It is all the more terrible because the poet takes it all for granted, makes no complaint."[1] The fact that Homer refers to the deepest miseries of war, not in his straightforward narration but in his similes, convinces Lewis that for Homer the horror of the world is simply accepted, not opposed. For one example, Lewis quotes this passage from book 8 of *The Odyssey*:

> As a woman throws herself weeping over her warrior husband, who fell fighting before his city and people... she sees him dying and gasping for breath and embraces his body keening loudly, while the enemy behind strike her on back and shoulders with their spears and lead her off into slavery to bear hard work and sorrow....(8.523–27)

"This is a mere simile," Lewis remarks, "the sort of thing that happens every day."

A world characterized by such matter-of-fact despair, it would seem, precludes the possibility of comedy, but *The Odyssey* stands at the beginning of Western literature as a great comic paradigm, the counterpart of the paradigmatic tragic action of *The Iliad*. Its fundamentally purgatorial movement away from error through suffering to homecoming and reconciliation establishes the characteristic pattern of human life as a comic mode of being, and its hero, the "man of many turns" (or tropes), anticipates the Aristophanic *poneros* who can always find an out through imagination, tricky speech, and bravado. Above all, Odysseus is a superb deceiver, so skilled in the manipulation of appearances that Dante, who received him only at second or third hand, honored him among the false counselors in hell. For Odysseus, the prime agent of all human deception is language, with which he can cast a persona on or off as easily as changing clothes. He has many likenesses, and through most of the poem he thinks of himself as the master of ceremonies, the man who controls the similes under which he is perceived. But the comedy of the poem as a whole depends upon a movement away from the human despair that leads him never to trust others and toward a divine view which allows him to believe in the entire action as one great likeness. Odysseus must overcome the idea that, as Lewis puts it, "this is a mere simile."

Lewis's phrasing ("an inch beneath the surface" and "mere simile") reflects a common belief that Homer's comparisons reveal the way the poet sees the quotidian world behind his stories of gods and heroes; according to this view, similes make visible the real background that Homer accepts without reflection. But to read Homer in this way is to do him an injustice. There is horror in the world called up by the simile Lewis quotes, but it is deliberate horror, measured, understood, accepted so that it can be overcome in a mode different from war. Lewis's misreading, to use a term that has become honorific, is nevertheless the right one to make; he inadvertently (perhaps with Homer's blessing) touches on exactly the right problem, for the poem depends throughout on the difference between what appears to be and what in fact is. Indeed, the poem's own surface might be as substantially deceptive as the back of the ram that the Cyclops felt while Odysseus was escaping from his cave. If this difference between the surface and what is an inch beneath it did not exist, *The Odyssey*'s comedy of purgation and reunion could not take place.

The approach to Odysseus, according to the poem itself, must be made through a careful attention to the difference between the thing that points to a meaning or gives rise to an assumption and the meaning or assumption itself—the difference in what linguists call signifier and signified. When Telemachos asks Menelaos at Sparta about his father, Menelaos tells him a long story meant to prepare both Telemachos and the audience of the poem for the indirection involved in answering questions about Odysseus. At the heart of Menelaos's story lies his struggle with Proteus, the Old Man of the Sea. In order to capture him and force him to answer questions, Menelaos and his men must lie for hours under stinking sealskins so that they can deceive the old man into thinking that they are among the number of his seals. Proteus feels their backs and accepts the surface as the reality, whereupon the men spring up and lock him in their arms. Not to be outdone, the old man turns into a lion, a serpent, a leopard, a boar, water, and finally a tree. But the men hold him fast. In order to learn anything from Proteus, Menelaos must keep in mind what the god's nature is despite the many dangerous illusions that appear. The heroes in *The Iliad* are often described as lions or boars; Menelaos himself is once compared to a serpent. But Proteus incarnates these figures of speech. He becomes what the signifier "lion" signifies; the new wrinkle is that even the thing itself does not signify him.

Only at the end of his speeches—and then almost as an aside—does Proteus mention the plight of Odysseus. Menelaos addresses Telemachos's direct question about his father in a tale of over 250 lines, of which only six, reported as hearsay, directly refer to Odysseus's detainment on the island of Kalypso. Odysseus is hidden in speech. It is Homer's particular genius to have Telemachos, who needs to learn about his father in order to achieve his own authority, set out in search of this eclipsed hero, for Odysseus can be disclosed only by those who steadfastly endure the protean turns of metaphor to discover him.[2] Telemachos's questioning (instigated by Athene) begins to release Odysseus from his obscurity; after the visit to Menelaos, Athene convinces Zeus to send a message to Kalypso: let Odysseus go. His gradual reappearance, as we shall see, reveals that he has been abandoned for ten years in a wonderland where tropes loom in the configurations of things as well as in speech; this world is accessible to others only through the speech that re-presents it. It is difficult to discern where the boundaries of signifier and signified lie, but out of this difficulty Odysseus makes his comedy of homecoming. To see, in part, how this comedy unfolds, let us look at three linked episodes: Odysseus's presentation of himself to the Phaiakians, his escape from the Cyclops's cave, and his self-revelation in Ithaka.

* * *

Twenty sleepless days after leaving Kalypso's island, Odysseus crawls naked from the sea in Scheria. He finds a protected place under two bushes (one a wild olive), covers himself with leaves, and goes to sleep. Fourteen books later, Homer uses the same description for the lair of the great boar who gave Odysseus the distinctive scar that Eurykleia recognizes on his first night back in Ithaka. Homer does not stress the comparison: he simply puts it there. Out of the likeness, however, much can be made. Odysseus unobtrusively becomes the boar that gives him the sign which ultimately discloses his identity; in some sense he has come to mark himself by the time he crawls ashore in the land of the Phaiakians. The way he has signed himself comes to light slowly in the events that follow. All of his difficulties, we discover, result from his disastrous self-naming after he blinds the Cyclops. The simile for Odysseus's sleep under the leaves both anticipates (in the poem) and recalls (in the actual chronology of events) this feat of blinding and the obscurity that Odysseus is forced to undergo as his punishment for claiming the deed in his own name. Homer compares Odysseus's burial of himself under the leaves with the burial of "a burning log in black embers in an isolated place in the country, where there are no neighbors near." By exercising such foresight, a man isolated from any community can save "the seed of fire, having no other way to get a light" (5.488-93). When Odysseus was similarly isolated in the cave of the Cyclops, he kept a sharpened beam in the ashes of a fire to harden and heat the point so that he could blind Polyphemos with it. On the island of Kalypso that he has recently left, he was the only mortal, and he had to save the seed of his name from being extinguished in the obscurity of Kalypso's offered immortality. Life is fire is seed. There is much to keep alive: existence, fame, and, not the least, his seed, Telemachos. An inch beneath the leaves slumbers a plexus of tropes.

Odysseus's first problem in Scheria is to gain control of his own appearance. He wakes on his first morning, naked, not knowing where he is, and hears the cries of young women. He has, in one sense, all the helplessness of a new baby, but in another, all the menace of wild beast. He covers his body with a leafy branch and moves forward like a hungry lion whose "belly urges him on." He comes upon the young ladies "covered with dry spray," terrifying them so that they flee "first one way and then another across the jutting beaches" (6.127–38). The graceful comedy of the simile emphasizes the rapacious sheepishness of Odysseus's situation. He is desperately hungry, but his needs will not in themselves win him sympathy. He has no way to influence what he seems to signify because he has no clothing; appearing simply as a man, naked and ungroomed, he is as terrifying as a lion to the Phaiakian maidens, and they will not stay to hear the blandishing words that can transform his significance. Only the intervention of Athene can embolden Nausikaa to stand her ground and listen. Odysseus says to her that he cannot tell whether she is a goddess or a mortal woman. What she signifies is unclear, but the respect with which he treats her, and his comparison of her to a beautiful young tree that he saw once, win her loyalty. She clothes him and takes him back to her city. It would have been better for the Phaiakians if she had not.

The Phaiakian people provide a crucial contrast with Odysseus because they are unaccustomed to any sort of deception. When the king, Alkinoos, meets Odysseus, he wonders at first if the man before him might not be a god, but then he reasons that "the gods have always shown themselves openly to us in the past." Gods traveling alone "do not conceal themselves," and if one of them has now come down in disguise, then it must be "something new the gods are devising" (7.200–05). The Phaiakians are usually uncivil to strangers. They feel that they can depend upon the visibility of the truth; they have no experience of the sort of thing that Heidegger means when he writes that "What must be thought, turns away from man. It withdraws from him."[3] For the Phaiakians, the gods manifest themselves without concealment, and there is no need to wonder whether a stranger is a god in disguise. No difference exists for them between signifier and signified. This unexamined trust in signs inaugurates their undoing. Already

Athene has disguised herself to lead Odysseus into the city—evidence that the gods are indeed devising "something new." Moreover, in Odysseus the Phaiakians encounter a mortal who has more subtlety than they had ever imagined in a god. They know the name "Odysseus" because of the divinely inspired songs of Demodokos, but they do not know yet the many-troped reality to which it refers.

Odysseus's means of revealing his identity to the Phaiakians bears close attention. After dinner on his second night among them, Odysseus asks Demodokos to sing of the wooden horse, "the stratagem great Odysseus once filled with men and brought to the upper city; it was these men who sacked Ilion" (8.494-95). Odysseus asks, we notice, for the story of the sack of Troy, which he had caused with his deceptive stratagem. Tears begin to drench his cheeks as he listens. At this point occurs the simile that Lewis cites as evidence of Homer's matter-of-fact despair: Odysseus weeps in the pitiful manner of a bereaved woman shedding tears over her fallen lord. Homer is careful to associate Odysseus's weeping with that of a woman in a city being ravaged; propinquity in the narration marks the city as Troy. His tears signify a desperate sorrow like that of a woman in the city his deception destroyed. This is no "mere simile."[4] This particular likeness softens Odysseus's first acknowledgment of his name, as if he can utter the word that signified him only after he has felt in his own heart and spirit the grief he has caused others. His tears lead Alkinoos to ask what name can explain who this man is.

Finally the man announces, "I am Odysseus son of Laertes, known to all men for my many wiles, and my fame reaches to the heavens" (9.19-20). Homer does not describe the reaction of the Phaiakians, but he has prepared us to imagine it. Most mortals hear tales of the gods they have never seen; the Phaiakians are accustomed to undisguised immortals and to an easy blessedness in all that they do. But when they hear tales of great heroes, they are fascinated by the trouble and difficulty other men encounter. Here the greatest figure of mortal difficulty, the man of whom they have heard the most wonders, suddenly announces himself among them: he discloses to the Phaiakians a man, a mode of being they had not considered significant in itself. Among them, telling his own story, sits a being who has lived, and lives still, in the perilous interval between godlike intelligence and a mortal body that a sharp spear or a little sea water could kill. The fact that he is alive and speaking must awe the Phaiakians; they are confronted for the first time with the misleading character of the insignificant sign, man.

Even now they do not suspect how misleading it can be. They listen to Odysseus's story unreflectively. Halfway through his account of the underworld, Odysseus stops, saying that it is time for his sleep, and adding, "but you, and the gods, will see to my homeward journey" (11.330-32). In their desire to hear the rest of his story, the Phaiakians fail to recognize what Odysseus is doing to them. He calls attention to his own fatigue. Gluttonous for the story, Arete and Alkinoos move their people to offer great gifts if only he will continue. They had rather hear the story than go to bed; therefore, they can be deceived into excessive generosity by Odysseus's admissions of weakness. "I could remain in this hall until the bright dawn" Alkinoos says, "as long as you could bear to tell me of your sufferings" (11.375-76). Odysseus can bear it. He knows suffering better than Alkinoos. He has learned to use it, in fact, so that in person he can appear to signify a sleepy man entirely different from the clever, deceitful, and powerfully enduring hero of the tale they pay him to continue telling. He can best deceive those who do not pursue the reality behind his tropes. His capacity to reveal who he is, then to disguise his nature even in the revelation, enables him to come home with supernatural swiftness and a ship full of gifts. He uses the fact that he is merely a man as his supreme comic device.

* * *

Nowhere is this device more important than in the episode with the Cyclops. One thing keeps Polyphemus from taking Odysseus seriously: the fact that Odysseus is a man. The full importance of the relation between appearances and names does not emerge until after Odysseus has blinded the Cyclops and is safely out to sea, but the entire episode involves the difference between what words and things seem to and actually do signify. The Cyclops's cave, in fact, is the first *place* in the poem that Odysseus must learn to interpret as a trope; with this cave and its inhabitant, the whole cosmos in which Odysseus is trapped becomes a language of dreadful significance.

The cave in itself is a confusing sign. Civilized beings do not live in caves because they prefer the order, the rectitude, of buildings that are made according to the artifice of straight lines. Natural dwellings follow rounded contours like those of the mouth, the stomach, and the womb—all associated with the appetites of the body rather than the accomplishments of the mind. Those contented to live in caves would be unlikely to imagine the possibilities of craftsmanship and work. Odysseus points out to the Phaiakians that the Cyclops have no agriculture, no institutions, no buildings, and "no ships with vermilion cheeks among them, nor builders of ships." When Odysseus approaches the cave of Polyphemos, he brings a goatskin full of divine wine because he suspects that he will encounter a man "wild and prodigious in strength, who disregarded both laws and human custom" (9.214-15). However, the cave does possess an order and abundance that Odysseus and the men he has chosen to accompany him find they can admire. They find baskets full of cheeses, pens crowded with lambs and kids which had "been placed in separate pens, the firstlings in one, and then the summer lambs, and again the newborn" (9.219-22). Milk pails and pans overflow with whey. Throughout *The Odyssey*, animal flocks are metaphors for human and divine communities; one hardly expects flocks so expertly ordered to surround Polyphemos, who is perhaps the most lawless member of a race which already rejects any communal law. The cave seems to signify two different things: a lazy or untutored orientation toward bodily appetite and the ordered soul of a good ruler.

Odysseus convinces his unwilling companions to remain in the cave to see if the inhabitant of it will give them gifts. But Polyphemos closes off the mouth as soon as he returns, and the natural dwelling becomes self-contained. It is completely under the control of the Cyclops's one great eye and the enormous appetite it serves. Once he sees Odysseus and his men, he begins to demonstrate his contempt for the signs by which men and gods order themselves. Odysseus asks him to remember that any injury to guests and suppliants is likely to be avenged by Zeus, who is himself the guest god. Polyphemos scoffs,

> The Cyclops do not heed Zeus of the aegis, nor any of the rest of the blessed gods, for we are better than they. Nor, out of fear of Zeus' hatred would I spare you or your companions if my spirit moved me to

do otherwise. But so that I may know, tell me where you put your well-made ship when you arrived? Hard by or far off? (9.275-80)

He explicitly scorns the name of Zeus and what it signifies—the highest divine power, the ordering principle of the cosmos, the god who blesses kings and protects strangers. The Cyclops further abuses the purposes of speech by attempting, clumsily, to trick Odysseus into revealing where his ship is.

Although Odysseus is not fooled by the attempt to get information, he is much deceived in his interpretation of the Cyclops's reason for wanting it. Odysseus thinks, correctly, that he should protect his ship, but he does not consider the poverty of his own reading of the Cyclops's appearance or his cave. He tells a lie about the destruction of his ship and emphasizes again the helpless character of those present in the cave. Polyphemos answers nothing. Instead of sharing food and conversation with the men, the Cyclops silently catches up two of them and devours them whole, after dashing them "against the ground as though killing puppies" (9.289-90). His cave is an anticity, a great belly, where the order of community is inverted. The architectural spaces of a city arrange the passions and needs of men within the structures of imaginative reason, whereas the cave subsumes reason to the belly. The most horrible aspect of Odysseus's description of the monstrous meal is the fact that Polyphemos "cut them up limb by limb," for in this act one can see the truly terrifying cooperation of reason with lawless appetite. Men come to signify mere food. No dignity remains in the human form. Intelligence, hope, love—all the godlike things of man not apparent on the surface—are consumed by the indiscriminate hunger of the monster, who sees one thing with his one eye: meat for the belly.

Killing Polyphemos would be simple. Odysseus could have done it on the first night after the single-minded giant ate his men and fell asleep, but the "second thought" stops him, for he remembers in time that he and his men could never push away the boulder Polyphemos had propped in the mouth of the cave. He prevents disaster by acting with two thoughts instead of one; there is the present deed to consider, and there are the consequences of the deed. Two times coexist in thought. This doubling capacity of mind, which the Cyclops lacks as thoroughly as a second eye, is the same one used in making similes. For instance, Odysseus tells the Phaiakians that the Cyclops drove his flocks out of the cave the next morning, "lightly moving away the great doorstone, but then setting it in its place again, like a man replacing the lid on a quiver" (9.313–14). He can see the action itself and he can see what the action is like. The importance of this capacity to see double lies in the reasoning that it initiates. Odysseus invites us to follow his train of thought: if the doorstone is like the lid of a quiver, then the cave itself is like a quiver, and a quiver contains arrows. Without this simile, Odysseus might not have seen the significance of the things lying about in the cave.

> Lying there beside the pen was a great club of olive wood belonging to the Cyclops, which he had cut. Still green, it was drying out until he could carry it with him, and we looking at it thought it about the size for the mast of a broad black merchant vessel of twenty oars which crosses the open sea, so huge it was in length and thickness. I went up to it and cut off a piece about a fathom long and gave it over to my companions and told them to plane it down, and they smoothed it while I, standing by them, sharpened it to a point and immediately put it over the bright fire to harden. (9.319–28)

For Polyphemos, the wood is simply itself, a thing to carry about. It is not a sign of anything else. But Odysseus sharpens the great bludgeon into a pointed weapon, and the cave becomes a quiver. His doubling of thought does not stop with this likeness, however. He is the man of many tropes: even as he makes his great arrow, he reflects that the wood is the size of a mast. The Cyclops, who does not build ships, would never make this comparison, the significance of which we shall see shortly.

Odysseus hides the weapon under some dung. To men who cultivate land, dung has great importance as fertilizer, but for the herding Cyclops, it is merely waste matter with no significance. As such, it fittingly hides the weapon that will blind him. When he returns with his herds, he performs his habitual chores and again snatches up two men for his dinner; he does not notice anything out of the ordinary. Neither does he suspect Odysseus of guile when the little man offers him wine. Tasting this "ambrosia and nectar," the Cyclops speaks for the first time since he found that Odysseus had no ship nearby. This time he feigns civility, asking for more and requesting the name of his "guest," ostensibly so that he can offer Odysseus a gift (9.355–59). It occurs to him to ask for a name only after he has drunk the divine wine; the small man he sees with his eye has no importance to him except as the bringer of this intoxicating pleasure. Odysseus pours him more and more until the giant is befuddled with it, then he tells Polyphemos that his name is "Nobody." The Cyclops, with his single vision, does not foresee the consequences of using the name to refer to someone not visible; the word seems accurate enough to him as he looks drunkenly down at the diminutive and powerless being who offers him wine. How could such a nobody do him harm?

Odysseus's use of the name reflects his keen understanding of the Cyclops's strange literalism. Everything in the cave suggests that Polyphemos has no respect for the relation between a signifier and what it signifies. His speech, when he speaks at all, is reckless; he blasphemes Zeus without thinking, and he lies without taking care to make his lies plausible. Words are nothing to him because he lives alone, without laws or companions. All the things that surround him are, for him, merely things. He rarely has occasion to name them, thus to treasure the names as signifiers of the things; certainly he would not make the leap from single names to the heady doubleness of similes. It is Odysseus who finds the cave's significance and who therefore uses the name Nobody: a signifier that signifies nothing. The comedy of this name stems not only from its cleverness but also from the fact that it allows Odysseus his eventual homecoming. He becomes Nobody, and he wins his escape. The name "Odysseus" would be as inappropriate in the anticity of Polyphemos as it is appropriate in utopian Scheria.

The process of blinding the one eye of Cyclops develops, appropriately, the simile suggested when the men found the great bludgeon: shipbuilding. In telling the story, Odysseus finds it necessary to use similes; each relates in some way to the art of building ships. The procedure for building a ship is outlined in the description of raft-building earlier in *The Odyssey*. Kalypso gives Odysseus tools when the gods order her to release him:

> he started cutting timber and quickly finished his work. He felled twenty in all, and trimmed them well with his axe of bronze, then planed them skillfully and made them straight to a line. Kalypso, the fair goddess, came back then with an auger, and he bored through each and jointed the raft together with dowels and cords. (5.243–48)

Curiously, this normal sequence of actions is reversed in the similes used to describe the blinding of the Cyclops. When Odysseus and his men first discover the bludgeon, they consider it to be about the size of the mast on a "cargo-carrying broad black ship of twenty oars." But as they begin to blind Polyphemos with it, the wood becomes a tool used in building a ship that is not yet complete:

> They seized the olivewood beam, sharpened at one end, and drove it into his eye, while I from my place about put my weight on it and twirled it, like a man with a brace-and-bit who bores a ship beam while his men, grasping the strap on wither side, whirl it from beneath and it drills ever more deeply. (9.382–86)

Craftsmanship informs this blinding. It is not a matter of one panicked stab, but of a deliberate and resolute application of techniques unknown to the Cyclopes as a people. Furthermore, the craft of shipbuilding is exercised on an eye which becomes, in the simile, "a ship beam" the more it is blinded—that is, Odysseus and his men regain their own ship as they blind the Cyclops. We notice, however, that the sharpened bludgeon itself has regressed from a mast to a tool used on ship timbers. The next simile continues this regression: "As when a blacksmith dips a hissing axe blade or plane into cold water, tempering it, since this is what makes steel strong, just so Cyclops' eye hissed around the olive stake" (9.391–94). This comparison speaks of an art prior to shipbuilding as such—metallurgy. This art, too, is unknown to Polyphemos and thus proper to evoke the sound of his blinding. One must know how to make axe blades and planes before one can cut down trees for ship timbers and plane them. The transformed bludgeon sizzles in the liquid of the eyeball like hot metal being made into the tools necessary for starting to build ships.

It is strange that Odysseus should begin by speaking of the untouched bludgeon as the mast on a completed ship and end by referring to it in terms of the precondition for cutting down trees. If we follow the tropes, we find that Odysseus is speaking of two things at once: the fact that the irrevocable blindness of the Cyclops is like the state of not knowing how to build ships (or lacking the tools); and the fact that the art of shipbuilding required to blind Polyphemos and escape from his cave dismantles Odysseus's own ships and eventually leaves him stranded on Kalypso's island. Part of the hard comedy of the poem centers on Odysseus's inflated opinion of himself as the man famous for his wiles and craft, and this incident contains his tacit acknowledgment that sometimes it would be craftier not to insist on fame. It is true that Polyphemos is blind not to see that the small and insignificant-looking Odysseus is no Nobody; it is also true that Odysseus errs in cleverness when he fails to recognize that the brutal and blasphemous Cyclops might be the son of a god. The acknowledgment of his error becomes more explicit when he gloats over the success of his ruse. Blinded, Polyphemos bellows that Nobody has tried to kill him by treachery, and the other Cyclopes answer that, if no one is to blame, he would do well to accept the sickness: "then pray to your father, Poseidon." Odysseus appears not to hear the significant part of their comment. "So they spoke as they departed," he reports, "and my heart within me laughed to see how my name and my crafty planning had deceived him" (9.413-14). The next nine years will be spent learning what the signifier "Poseidon" signifies.

Odysseus, we cannot tell ourselves too often, is the man of many tropes. One of the most significant is one that he does not make explicit at all: the relation between his means of escape from the cave and his desire to be known by his true name. After his blinding, the Cyclops removes the great stone from the cave entrance and sits, his scorched eye-socket dripping gore, with his arms spread wide in case the men try to escape. Odysseus once again uses the Cyclops's deficiencies against him. The name Nobody has done its work of failing to signify; now Odysseus will employ the giant's beloved sheep in a parallel deception. He lashes his companions under the male sheep, saves the largest ram for himself, snuggles under the wool of its belly, and clings fast (9.432-35). The backs of his own sheep will disguise the escaping men from Polyphemos. Even his sense of touch misleads him. As dawn comes, the male sheep hurry out of the cave toward pasture. The cave resounds with painful female urgency as the ewes bleat, unmilked; this sound, this painful sense of needed release, is the simile for Odysseus's own feeling at being Nobody. An intense inner pressure persists even after the escape. He and his men make it safely to their ship and steal the sheep. They row out to sea. But Odysseus cannot endure the anonymity and the disrespect he has suffered in the cave. He shouts to the Cyclops that "it was no weakling's companions you were to eat violently." But still Odysseus is unsatisfied. Nothing will do, after the brilliance of his escape and the devastation he has wrought on the monster, but that he give the deception a name; an almost female urgency overcomes him. He cries that he is "Odysseus, sacker of cities." The name fails to impress the Cyclops with Odysseus's greatness. Polyphemos groans and says that a prophecy had foretold his blinding at the hands of Odysseus, but that he was always "on the watch for a man handsome and tall, endowed with great strength," whereas in fact the name turned out to signify "a little man, worthless and feeble." As in so many comedies, it is the lowly man of stratagems and wiles who triumphs. All that the proud revelation of Odysseus's true name provides Polyphemos is a means for cursing him.

By the time Odysseus crawls ashore in Scheria ten years later, "Odysseus" no longer means the same thing. It no longer signifies a "sacker of cities"; indeed, Odysseus speaks his name to the Phaiakians only after he has wept with the female urgency of a Trojan woman who has watched her own husband die. The disguise and verbal ambiguity that eventually allow Odysseus his homecoming undergo a long chastening as he loses all his men and spends seven years in complete obscurity. The deceit made possible by the difference between signifier and signified is not in itself comic. The order of Zeus—the whole order—is the point, not the individual name, and Odysseus has made the entire Cyclops episode into a self-serving feat by insisting on his name as its meaning. The arrogance that makes him endanger his men is as irresponsible and uncivil as the cannibalism of Polyphemos. But his years of penance instruct him rightly, so that by the time Telemachos seeks news of his father in Sparta, Odysseus has learned his lesson: deception in service of the kingly civil order must be the basis of Odyssean comedy.

* * *

Odysseus's homecoming, of which his joyous reunion with Penelope is the central event, depends upon deception. Uncivil suitors fill his house. Once again, as in the cave of the Cyclops, he must be Nobody. This time he adopts the disguise of a beggar. He spends his first night at home watching the unfaithful women of his household leave the palace to sleep with the suitors. All day he has beheld the arrogance of

Antinoos and the others. Because of his low appearance, they have abused him and taunted him in his own house; they have paid no more heed than the Cyclops to the demands of piety toward strangers. They have destroyed his flocks in sacrifices meant not to honor the gods, but to provide the suitors with meat for feasting. All these things they have done as they competed with one another in lusting for his wife. To see the women of his household corrupted by such men tests him severely, but he endures the sight by remembering the significance of the episode that caused all his trouble:

> And as, when facing a stranger, a bitch stands over her tender puppies growling and eager to fight, so Odysseus's heart growled within him as he looked in anger on these wicked deeds. He struck his chest and rebuked his own heart, saying: "Endure, my heart. You have endured worse before this on that day when the unrestrained and furious Cyclops ate up my mighty company, but you endured it until craftiness got you out of the cave, though you thought that you would die."
> (20.14-21)

Again the simile is the clue. In the cave ten years before, Polyphemos had smashed out the brains of the men "as though killing puppies" (9.289). This time feminine urgency serves Odysseus in good stead. The protectiveness he felt too little when he was so concerned about his name emerges only now when he is among his own people. Odysseus now sees that the suitors as a group comprise "an unknown man" as blind to significance as Polyphemos and even more estranged from Zeus. Yet the trope has still another turn: a bitch faces strangers with distinct inhospitality; she does not participate in the order of Zeus, guardian of suppliants. The suitors have made the women of the house into bitches who greet their master as an unknown man. Other things also point back to the Cyclops's cave. Uppermost on the bed that the women make for Odysseus in his house are "many fleeces of sheep" —a sure tactile reminder of his night snuggled against the belly of the ram. All these signs establish a great simile. Getting the suitors out of his house is like getting himself out of the Cyclops's cave.

The worst problem Odysseus faced in that episode was how to keep his own pride from overcoming him. He failed; he shouted his name to Polyphemos. But already in his own house, Odysseus has been recognized by signs, for his old nurse Eurykleia knows the scar given to him by the boar. This recognition emphasizes again the relation between signifier and signified. At first, before she sees the scar, Eurykleia comments that this stranger resembles Odysseus in feet, voice and appearance more than anyone she has ever seen. In denying who he is, Odysseus tells her that those who have seen Odysseus and him "say the two of us are very similar" (19.384)—he makes himself his own simile. He is like Odysseus: this is his homecoming trope. In order to keep Eurykleia from seeing his scar, he turns to the dark side away from the fire, and Homer relates the story of Odysseus's naming. First Autolykos gave him the name Odysseus, "distasteful," because the land of Ithaka is itself distasteful to many. Later Odysseus kills the boar with Autolykos's sons and receives the scar that is the physical sign of his identity. Eurykleia washes his leg and sees the scar: immediately she knows the name. "'Then you are truly Odysseus, dear child. I did not know you before, my lord, until I had touched you all over'" (19.474-75). Here an almost sacramental buckling of likenesses occurs. No longer is this stranger like Odysseus; he is Odysseus. Name and scar rush together. But the recognition does not gladden him at all, for ten years of suffering for it have given his name a sour taste in his own mouth. He is marked: distasteful.

The puzzling and apparently ignoble comparison that Homer uses to describe Odysseus's worry over the unfaithful women and the suitors later that night is also distasteful—a sign that the great comic resolution is about to begin:

> And as a man takes a paunch pudding filled with blood and fat and turns it this way and that over a great fire while trying to get it cooked rapidly; so he tossed from side to side, meditating how, only one against so many, he could lay his hands on the shameless suitors. (20.25-30)

Why would Homer think of a paunch pudding? Earlier in the day, Odysseus had been in a fight with a fat beggar named Iros, and the suitors had offered paunch puddings as the prize for the victor. When he won, Odysseus received the almost totemic organ that should remind him of his ten-year penance: a belly. However, as he lies on the fleeces meditating, he seems to read the pudding simply as another instance of his dishonor. No doubt he has indigestion. As yet he does not see that once again the simile contains the solution: trap the suitors in the belly; that is, do what the Cyclops did with his guests.

Against the Belly of the Ram: The Comedy of Deception in The Odyssey

Athene, who sees Odysseus's anxiety, visits him in "the shape of a woman." Her appearance is another sign, for Odysseus must learn the feminine trust and patience that characterize his wife. "She came and stood above his head, and spoke a word to him: 'Now why are you awake again, O most unfortunate of all men? Is this not your house, and is your wife not in the house, and is not your son here? Is he not the sort of son any man would want?'" (20.32-35). Her question borders on cruelty. She is quite aware of the difficulties Odysseus faces, but she wishes to turn his mind away from the affront given his honor—his name—by the suitors, and back toward an appreciation of the goods in his life: home, wife, son. She emphasizes the order of Zeus so that he will not forget himself (by insisting on himself) and commit the same mistake twice.

> Then resourceful Odysseus answered her in his turn: "Yes, goddess, all that you say is right and just; even so, here is something my heart still nurses, how, all alone against so many, I can lay my hands on the shameless suitors. But they always come here in a body. And an even greater problem to worry my heart is that, even if, by the grace of Zeus and yourself, I do kill them, how shall I myself escape? That is what I want you to think about." (20.36-43)

The phrasing points back to the problem of escaping from the Cyclops: How can he deal with "a body" so much larger than he? How can he get out of the cave blocked by so huge a stone? Yet there is a new question, too. How can he escape the retribution of those whose sons these men are? The urgency in man for vengeance is the real cave; it consumes the possibility of comedy and disallows a trusting, patient inquiry into the whole action of one's life as a complex signifier, indeed, a kind of simile.

Athene's reply makes it clear that Odysseus has not yet understood what she, a goddess, signifies:

> Perverse man! Many would trust a friend weaker than I, a mortal with none of my craft. But I am a god and I shall guard you to the end. And now I will tell you plainly: even though there were fifty battalions of mortals surrounding and eager to kill us in battle, you could still drive away their cattle and fat sheep. So let sleep overcome you. It is vexatious to lie away awake and on watch all night. Soon you will be out of trouble. (20.45-53)

Nothing could be clearer. Athene has been the hidden poet providing him with tropes. Because she is a goddess, she can use physical realities as signs, so that, by means of their transportation first into language, then into simile, they can become the means of unifying a whole action in one moment of insight. With this epiphany, comparable in its way to Christ's revelation of himself as the meaning of the text under discussion on the way to Emmaus, or to Beatrice's severe correction of Dante at the top of the mountain, Odysseus can see the whole great weave shimmer, his hard lessons transfigured into a profound comic pattern. Suffering becomes purgation just at the moment the curse of justice ends. Odysseus has come home to find troubles in his household: the Cyclops's curse is over, and the blessing of Athene is beginning.

Athene has a great deal more freedom to act in the action of *The Odyssey* then she did in *The Iliad*, where her deeds were always linked to those of Hera. She was bound to a pattern of vengeance ultimately based on wounded vanity, and the essentially intellectual and comic bent of her inspiration was constrained to the severely fated pattern of events surrounding the honor of Achilleus. Similes in *The Iliad* reflect this sense of fate; for instance, Achilleus compares himself to a mother bird in his reply to Odysseus's report of Agamemnon's offer of great prizes in book 9. The simile recalls the great divine sign and Kalchas's prophetic interpretation of it years before at Aulis, which Odysseus had recounted in book 2: a serpent coming up from under the altar had eaten eight baby birds, then the mother. Kalchas had predicted that after the ninth year passed, the Achaians would capture Troy; thus, the mother bird is Achilleus, who must die, and the nine years are necessary in order to bring about his necessary honor. Athene has no control over the pattern of unfolding events or over the weave of likenesses that is gradually revealed, for it is by no means a comic pattern. In *The Odyssey*, however, Achilleus is dead (he himself declares that his honor was not worth its cost), and the human arena is thus cleared for Athene's characteristic gifts of wisdom, courage, endurance, and wit. *The Odyssey* is, in many ways, the record of her difficult generosity in establishing the new comic paradigm for mortals.

On the day after Athene's self-revelation, Odysseus, still disguised as a beggar, privately reveals who he is to Eumaios and a few other trusted servants. His first move, once he sees what Athene intends, is to close off the entrance to his house and trap the suitors at their feasting. Instead of a "wall of cliff sky-high" to stop the doorway, Odysseus's oxherd uses a "byblus-fiber cable for a twin-galleyed ship" (21.390–91) to secure the door. This substitution of seamanship for brute force marks the difference between Odysseus's act of divine purgation and the Cyclops's deed of gross impiety. Both prey on their "guests," but Odysseus does so at the urging of a goddess. Moreover, Odysseus uses the humble disguise of mere man, unenhanced by wealth or divine favor, to fool the suitors. Once again he deliberately appears to signify less than what he actually is so that he can accomplish more. Had he approached the suitors undisguised and said, "I am Odysseus, sacker of cities," he would have been killed at once; he is careful to avoid using his own name even when he tells his own true followers who he is. He wants to be known only as a beggar, for a beggar poses no problem to proud men, those who cannot see what is true because they think that they are in themselves, at the present moment, the signifiers of all that is worth signifying. It would no more occur to Antinoos than to Polyphemos that a nobody might be his undoing.

Certainly not one of the suitors suspects that the beggar will be the only one to string the bow that none of them could manage. They are insulted that he should even be given the chance. Still less, in their astonishment, do they heed the simile that suggests itself when he strings the bow:

> but now resourceful Odysseus, having taken up the great bow and looked it all over, as a man who is skilled in the lyre and singing, easily stretches the strongly twisted cord of sheep's gut, after tying it at both ends, and slips it over a new peg, so, effortlessly, Odysseus strung the great bow, plucked the bowstring, as he held it in his right hand, so that it gave him back a sweet sound like the song of a swallow.(21.404–11)

A man who "is skilled in the lyre and singing" sees the relations between all his tropes and knows the form of the whole work. The whole form of Odysseus's action is present to him in this moment: it is one note "like the song of a swallow," the bird whose form Athene takes in the midst of the killing. The first killing recapitulates the blinding of Polyphemos. After shooting an arrow through the twelve axes, Odysseus strips off his rags and calls to the suitors: "'Here is trial ended without any deception. Now I shall aim at another mark, one that no man has yet struck, if I can hit it and Apollo gives me the glory.' He spoke and pointed the bitter arrow at Antinoos'' (22.5-8). The shooting itself involves no deception; indeed, it reveals identity in a way better than self-naming. It signifies. Everything here signifies. The word translated "pointed" is a form of the verb *ithyno*, which refers to the steering of ships and the planing of wood "true to a line." In beginning to kill the suitors, Odysseus uses the art of the straight line; he makes straight what nature had left in the rounded contours of the cave, the womb, the belly. He had employed the rudiments of this art in sharpening the "arrow" to blind Polyphemos; here he uses its finer points. The arrow is driven "through the fleshy part of the throat." This killing throws the body of the suitors into a blind, groping panic, and it is fitting that this blindness should come through Antinoos's throat. His words have led the other suitors in bad deeds; he has presented to them, like the Cyclops's one eye, the uncivil counsels of expediency. The neck, through which speech comes, is also the way to the belly, and Antinoos's speech has been driven by appetite. Odysseus demonstrates on Antinoos the deadly art of homecoming, the art that attends to similes.

After the slaughter, the problem of escape remains. Again, it is not simply a matter of getting out of the house, but of avoiding the wrath of the dead men's relatives. Phemios, the singer whom Odysseus spares in the killing, provides the inspired means. When Odysseus had first begun the killing, he said, with an irony made possible by Athene, "Now is the time for supper to be prepared for the Achaians while it is still light, then followed with other amusements, the dance and the lyre; for such things come at the end of the feast" (21.428-30). Now that they are dead he orders a more festive music:

> First go bathe and put on your tunics and tell the women in the palace to take out their clothes. Then let the divine singer take up his loud lyre, and lead us in a festive dance, so that if anyone is outside—a neighbor or a person on the street—and hears us, he will say that we are having a wedding. (23.131-36)

The whole household celebrates the killing with comic festivity, as if Penelope had finally married one of her suitors. The trope for the slaughter is a wedding feast. The difference between what this celebration appears to signify and what it actually means is great, but it allows the poem its greatest comedy. The happy music that disguises the absence of the suitors from the townspeople gives Odysseus a night of wedding celebration. He lies once again with his own wife, in their own chamber, in the bed built around an olive tree (mast, arrow, lair of boar) rooted in the earth. That night they enjoy "their old rite." The comedy of homecoming is complete.

What makes the difference between despair and hope? For Odysseus, it is the capacity to turn, to become a trope, to think in similes so well that his whole life becomes a likeness of what he now is. Identity is a sudden joyous piercing of the remote similitude by the imaginative present. In order to see the past and present as one action, Odysseus must hope that the similes of things—based on experience—are trustworthy. The trust makes them significant, but the very fact of similes precludes despair. Language, with its difference between signifier and signified, ultimately reflects the doubleness of what man is—godlike intellect, unpromising appearance. Once this doubleness, not clever duplicity, becomes the conscious principle of Odysseus's action, he gives over the distasteful insistence on the significance of his own name. For Dante, who establishes the complete comic paradigm, the doubleness will become that between eternity and time: man acts in time with eternity as the hidden unity of his deeds. This same disparity between human time and divine presence underlies the true comedy of The Odyssey. It is the comedy of trust in the gods, hope in the pattern of experience, and hospitality toward strangers: the theological virtues of Ithaka.

Notes

1. *A Preface to* Paradise Lost (London, 1956). Line numbers throughout this essay refer to the Greek text, from which the citations have been directly translated.

2. See George E. Dimock, Jr., "The Name of Odysseus," in *Homer: A Collection of Critical Essays*, ed. George Steiner and Robert Fagles (Englewood Cliffs, N. J., 1962), 106-21. My reading of Kalypso and my treatment of Odysseus's name owe a good deal to this essay, surely one of the most brilliant and delightful ever written on the poem.

3. *What is Called Thinking?* trans. J. Glenn Gray (New York, 1968), 8.

4. See Cedric Whitman, *Homer and the Heroic Tradition* (Cambridge, Mass., 1963) for a treatment of this same simile. Whitman argues that in this case the simile, which would usually rise "like a prismatic inverted pyramid upon its one point of contact with the action," is controlled by the demands of the larger action. He is certainly right to remark that "with the simile of the captive woman, Homer suddenly injects a graphic and terrifying vision of the world from which Odysseus comes, a world of burnt cities, slain men, and women dragged to slavery, the old turbulent Achaean world, which to the Phaeacians is just a song for an evening's amusement" (116). John H. Finley, Jr., *Homer's* Odyssey (Cambridge, Mass., 1978) comments upon this same simile to show that "Odysseus as a sorrowing woman is parted from home and marriage" (29). The difficulty I find with both Whitman and Finley is not in what they say, for they are right, but in what they do not grant to Homer—that is, the capacity to use reversals of expectation deliberately as part of his whole meaning. We are forced to imagine a Homer who rather clumsily wedges in a comparison without paying much attention to the distracting elements. I would argue that, because the simile has a point of likeness, Homer can introduce a broadening unlikeness in which the more difficult dimensions of the comparison are refracted. Odysseus is not a woman: a wealth of speculation (in this poem about women) *therefore* becomes accessible, especially since Odysseus elicits this comparison when he is in the company of the woman-led Phaiakians, since he breaks off his story to them at the point when the famous tragic women of the underworld were clustered about him (thereby winning from Arete the promise of more gold), and so on. More is at stake here than what Finley, in his remarks on Homer's reversals of sex, age, or condition, calls "common categories of experience in which an individual shares and by sharing becomes illustratively human" (29).

2

The Bible as Genesis of Comedy

DANIEL RUSS

READERS of literature have little difficulty in identifying a long line of comic writings stretching from Homer to Beckett. Such a lineage would be most unlikely, one may be fairly certain, to include within its boundaries the Old and New Testaments. And yet, improbable as it may seem at first glance, when the Scriptures are viewed from the perspective of comedy they may be seen to constitute the fullest achievement of that genre in Western literature.

The widespread blindness to the comic form and structure of the Bible can hardly be attributed to a narrow conception of the comic art. On the contrary, the generally accepted canon embraces an astonishingly broad diversity of modes and styles. What critics call comedy spans the range from the dark and grotesque journey of *The Odyssey*, exemplifying a harsh code of justice, to the light-disclosing pilgrimage of *The Divine Comedy*, its punishments tempered by mercy and love. The comic scope includes such dissimilar types as Greek Old Comedy, Roman satire, medieval liturgical drama, carnivalia, Renaissance love comedy, neo-classical comedy of manners, Romantic melodrama, and contemporary drama of the absurd, as well as countless permutations of the novel. But biblical comedy, though it shares many of the features of these various kinds and sheds light on the form of comedy in general, is unlike related examples of the comic art in one basic aspect.

These others locate the comic spirit in the vices or *faux pas* of human beings, clumsily caught within mortal time, failing to live up to their own best standards. By contrast, biblical comedy arises out of divine action itself: a God creates the world with comic possibilities before time, wrestles and sups with His people, enduring their rebellion and scorn in the midst of time, and plans a wedding feast on earth at the end of time.

The assertion that the Bible, that most sacred of texts, is comic could no doubt lead to a misunderstanding. The biblical canon is certainly not a formal drama, nor does it profess to be a fictional narrative, the two poetic modes in which comedy is most often encountered. On the contrary, the Bible presents itself as an anthology of history, biography, poetry, prophecy, and epistle carefully formed to reveal God's purposes for and among His creation. In short, the Bible is about historical events shaped by the divine imagination through its human counterpart. William Lynch has written:

> We have watched men constructing poems, and have taken it for granted that the poetry ends in and gives us insight... let us now make a not-too-violent mental transfer and suppose that God, in the two Testaments, is describing a construction of his own which he has carved out in history and which leads to increasing insights for the human race, finally indeed to the insights of the resurrection. What are some of the simple methods and laws we can discover about this divine construct? How does God "imagine" through the lines of this poem, through the lines of this history he has made and is making.[1]

To discover the patterns and design of the biblical stories is to recover history as comedy. We first apprehend this "divine construct" in the Bible's characters and themes. Its heroes are created in and called out of communities, particularly the family, as it gives birth to the larger community. Even at the moment of creation man is the divine *creature*, neither God nor animal, both spirit and dust: "God created mankind in His own image, in the image of God He created him: male and female He created them" (Gen. 1:27).[2]

That this fathering God stubbornly persists in His attempts to redeem humanity through and for a community resounds throughout the Old and New Testaments. He calls Adam and Eve, Noah and his family, Abraham and Sarah, Isaac and Rebekah, Jacob, Leah, and

Rachel, Moses, Zipporah, Aaron and Miriam, Elijah and Elisha, Hosea and Gomer, the Twelve Apostles, as well as Paul with his assorted cohorts. The autonomous self-sufficient hero of classical epics and tragedies has little place in the biblical stories. True, there are those such as Samson, Saul, Solomon, and Judas, who represent tragic moments peripheral to the comedy of grace. But for the most part, whether called children of Abraham, Israel, the remnant of Jacob, the bride, followers of the way, or the Church, God's heroes are a comic lot of redeemed rascals and rogues, from creation to apocalypse.

The archetypal comic plot—order to chaos to order—is the form of the scriptural canon. God's people begin in a garden in right relationship with Him, fall through their foolish pride, attain redemption by the unlikely incarnation of God Himself, and come finally to a city which contains the original garden. It is a movement from the calling out of one tribe, Abraham's, to the gathering of a people from every nation. Its comic heroes identify with the folly of the fragmented community rather than stand apart from it. The biblical story of salvation is about an old order passing away in a new vision of things, old wineskins burst by new wine, and an old life upset by an infant born to die and rise from the grave. It is a story of scandalous success, of triumph over outrageous obstacles, of prevailing against all odds. As Northrop Frye describes it, the action of both comedy and the Bible moves "from law to liberty."[3] This liberty cannot be destroyed by human stupidity or evil because God gives it, preserves it, and promises its triumph in the end. How he does so reveals his character and the distinct character of biblical comedy.

The Bible not only reverberates with life when read as comedy, but speaks to the life of people through whom and for whom its revelations were given. This comic movement can be discerned in the book of Genesis, which may be said to be the proto-comedy of the Bible. For Genesis is not only the first book of both the Jewish and Christian canons, but the seminal history founding the hope of Jews and Christians alike. This hope is rooted in the covenant relationship established by God with Adam and Eve, Abraham and Sarah, and their descendents. These characters are not merely founders of the community but living symbols in its subsequent literature. God's people in both covenants are called the seed of Abraham, Jacob, and Israel. So Genesis begins the plot, introduces the characters, founds the ideas, and sets the tone for the entire story of redemptive history—the comedy of grace.

This comic tone is evident in the opening chapters, which report God's shaping a world abounding in concrete, humble things in "the dense reality of time."[4]

> And God said, "Let there be light"; and there was light. And God saw that the light was good.... God called the light Day, and the Darkness he called Night. And there was evening and there was morning, one day....
>
> Then God said, "Let us make man in our image, after our likeness; and let them have dominion over the fish . . . the birds . . . the cattle . . . all the earth . . . and every creeping things that creeps. So God created man in his own image.... male and female . . . and said to them, "Be fruitful and multiply, and fill the earth and subdue it...."
> And God said, "... I have given you every plant yielding seed . . . and every tree with seed in its fruit . . . for food.
>
> And to every beast . . . and to every bird . . . and to everything that creeps . . . [and] has the breath of life, I have given every green plant for food." ... And God saw everything that he had made, and behold, it was very good. And there was evening and there was morning, a sixth day.
>
> And on the seventh day God finished his work . . . and he rested. (Gen. 1:3-2:2)

The delight of this description of creation is to be found in this God who moves the world to an order throbbing with living things. He is concerned not only about light and darkness but about small, concrete particulars: "trees bearing fruit in which is their seed" and "Beast, birds, and creeping things" as well as plant and fruits. He shapes the cosmos, even to its tiny details within the confines of six days, pauses to congratulate himself for his good work, then rests on the seventh. Such a description is a scandal to literalists who would save God through invoking anthropomorphisms or rationalists who would mock this God so out of conformity to Darwin. Both are reductionistic responses which balk at acknowledging that this transcendent God, who simply was "in the beginning," lovingly fashioned time and space and creeping things and man, male and female, calling everything he made very good. But the account unmistakably indicates that He created a world pregnant with comic overtones.

Unlike Hesiod's *Theogony*, the Bible does not pretend to explain God's origin. Rather, he is described as "hovering over the face of the waters" as a mother eagle "flutters over its young" (Deut. 32:11). He hovers over an earth that is formless and void ("tohu" and "bohu"), a phrase used elsewhere in the Old Testament to describe the tragic destruction and ruin of Israel by Babylon. The image is one of a cosmos without the order of life: old ruins that God rejuvenates. Thus God is the force of life, the creator of the new, and not the patriarch, the *senex* as one might expect. He hovers over chaos, the garden, the flood, Abraham and Sarah, Canaan, Isaac and Rebekah, Jacob, Leah and Rachel, Joseph and Egypt, constantly redeeming them from the dead inhumanity of the old orders, creating a new thing. Man, the blocking character of the Genesis comedy, does not frustrate this creator God (Elohim), whose personal presence (Yahweh) keeps infusing new life in this old world.

Not only is God constantly forming a new and fuller order of things, but He does so through diversity. We are told that the world He calls into being is teeming with diverse things, "after their kind." Such diversity is one of the marks of the comic vision, rendering a world of complex plots and motley characters, teeming always with life. Comedy acknowledges death but not as the end, the eschaton of life. As Lynch comments, "The comic is par excellence the greatest enemy of the univocal mind," his term for the reductionistic mentality which "wishes to reduce and flatten everything to the terms of its own sameness, since it cannot abide the intractible differences, zigzags and surprises of the actual."³ Adam and Eve attempt such a reduction—to be like God rather than man, "Original sin" keeps on originating this monstrous sameness whether in the animal-like debasement of Noah's culture or the urban monomania of the Babel society. This lifeless imitation is against God's character and design. Beginning with the broad strokes of light and darkness, earth and heaven, land and sea, He animates the cosmos with living things after their kind. Then, without hesitation or apology, He takes up the dust of the earth and fashions His consummate creation after its own kind and in His image. In dust and spirit, male and female, all the elements of life's comedy are present prior to the fall.

Moreover, the God who founds a world by His word is more in

keeping with the garrulous world of comedy than the laconic universe of tragedy. As we have seen above, God even talks to Himself as He pauses to remind Himself that what He makes is good. The word founds creation, assures the covenant, exacts judgment, lays claim to a strange land, and wins Joseph a strategic position in Egypt. Four centuries after Jacob, God tells Moses to liberate His people from the most powerful ruler on earth, armed only with speech. Moses founds the tradition of Old Testament prophets, whose sole power over tyrants and depraved nations is the word. And the Church in the New Covenant faces the impregnable force of Rome armed with good news. This parade of God-breathed dust daring to challenge and transform empires by the word has produced some of the great comic moments of history: Moses before Pharaoh, Elijah with Baal's prophets, Daniel and Nebuchadnezzar, Jesus with the Pharisees, Paul before Agrippa, and many others. These moments, found throughout Scripture, grow out of the God-talkers of Genesis. There is Noah telling a world which has never seen rain that God has instructed him to build a boat for a flood. And his neighbors, like us, cannot imagine how he is to persuade the animals to join him on the voyage. Nor can we forget Abraham, the father of the covenant, bargaining with God over the destiny of Sodom. And Joseph, the supreme man of words, precociously babbles his way into slavery and graciously and wisely talks his way into power. The comic turn in each episode grows out of the character's faith in God and His word. A God who would rather talk than fight does not make for great tragedy, but is replete with comic possibilities.

Such possibilities grow out of what He creates as well as how He creates. This manifold creation is crowned by mud and spirit—mankind. A creature made of dirt and God's breath is formed, in highly unlikely fashion, in God's image, male and female. To ponder these paradoxes suggests the visible and priceless images which are the inexhaustible source of comedy. The boundary between man as dirt and spirit gives rise to the ridiculous: Adam and Eve hiding from God behind leaves; the Babel craftsmen building a tar and brick tower to heaven; Jacob, the youth, with sheepskin on his arm to deceive his father, Isaac; and Jacob, the man, wrestling with God. No less rich is the endless joke embodied in sexuality: Abraham playing the patriarchal panderer in bartering for his life with Sarah; Sarah jealously having second thoughts about Hagar; Laban and Leah deceiving Jacob into marriage; and Rachel deceiving her father Laban with the ambiguous apology, "Let not my lord be angry that I cannot rise before you, for the way of women is upon me" (Gen. 31:35). While Genesis does not diminish the effects of sin and death on this God-breathed/God-sexed dust, the darkness never overwhelms the wit and humor.

God, the ever-originating force of diversity and creativity, overturns the ossified codes of his creatures turned *senex*—Noah, Abraham, Isaac, Jacob, Laban, and Pharaoh. In the tragic times of Noah, God looks upon mankind declaring, "... the earth is filled with violence through them; behold, I will destroy them with the earth" (Gen. 6:13). God sees moral chaos and judges it after its kind: i.e., he withholds his restraining power so that the chaos of "the fountains of the great deep burst forth, and the windows of the heaven were opened" (Gen. 7:11). The waters of the sea and the heavens are the physical analogue to moral chaos in the Hebrew imagination. As with Adam and Eve, Lot, and Esau, God judges by letting the rebels live out the consequences of their choices. True to the comic spirit, just punishment is a consequence of despicable human actions, not the fate of divine whim. It is this biblical sense of human beings choosing to stew in their own juices that later characterizes the hell of Dante's *Commedia*. This God of diversity will grant man the right to serve himself for time and eternity. But He will not allow the diversity of his creation, human and animal, to be leveled to the chaos of sameness.

Comic justice characterizes the Babel story, for example, as a redemptive and recreative act. The people gather with one language to build a city to give them an identity in earth and heaven. We are told that they gather in one place to avoid being "scattered upon the face of the whole earth" despite God's design that they should multiply and subdue the earth. But they are not merely frightened; they are arrogant, desiring fame. Such fame is based, as the history of such cities reminds us, on the oppression of the many for the exaltation of the few. In short, implicit in the Babel enterprise is the destructiveness which comes of despotism and empire building. God's solution is to divide the single language and so deny the people of Babel their means to monolithic tyranny while restoring his original design of a diverse creation. That the flood and Babel are pregnant with comic undercurrents is evident in the way they are retold in sources as diverse as the Wakefield mystery plays and contemporary stand-up comedy.

These early chapters of Genesis develop God's character more fully than those of his people because the comedy of history originates in Him. In chapter 11 the focus moves to human comic heroes as God re-creates history by calling a man, a family, and a people to himself. He begins by calling an old man and woman out of an old world to do a new thing—"to become a great nation . . . by which all the families of earth shall be blessed" (Gen. 12:2-3). The contrast with the monomania of Babel is stark. And the picture of Abraham and Sarah is a bit absurd. Called at seventy-five years from the ancient city of Ur, Abraham leads his wife and household up and down a strange land for a quarter of a century making two preposterous claims: he and his sixty-five-year-old bride would soon have a son and that they, in fact, own the land. His first heroic act to this end is to flee to Egypt during a famine and negotiate for his life by giving Sarah to Pharaoh (Gen. 12:10-20). Fearing that Pharaoh would kill him to obtain Sarah, Abraham schemes, "Say you are my sister that it may go well with me because of you, and that my life may be spared on your account." He repeats this tomfoolery years later (Gen. 20), as does his son Isaac with Rebekah (Gen. 26). In these moments, Abraham and Isaac are the very personification of Bergson's comic man who lives by rigid formulas and foolish repetitions.[6] They instinctively retreat to the misogynous customs of the pagan cultures out of which God is redeeming them.

There is more to the story of Abraham and Sarah than these humiliating scandals, however. Between the ugly episodes in Abraham's and Sarah's life occurs one of the high comic moments of all literature. They have awaited the promised child for a quarter of a century, and, finally, a messenger from God tells them that the baby will come soon. Behind the door, Sarah laughs. Frederick Buechner allows his imagination to envision the scene:

> The place to start is with a woman laughing. She is an old woman, and, after a lifetime in the desert, her face is cracked and rutted like a six-month drought. She hunches her shoulders around her ears and starts to shake. . . . She is laughing because she is pushing ninety-one hard and has just been told she is going to have a baby. Even though it was an angel who told her, she can't control herself, and her husband

can't control himself either. He keeps a straight face a few seconds longer than she does, but he ends by cracking up, too.... They are laughing because the angel not only seems to believe it but seems to expect them to believe it too. They are laughing because with part of themselves they do believe it. They are laughing because with another part of themselves they know it would take a fool to believe it. They are laughing at God and with God....[7]

God commemorates this tender and hilarious exchange (Gen. 17:15-8:15) by instructing Abraham to name his son Isaac, which means in Hebrew "he laughed." In that name God captures for all time the absurd, ridiculous, and joyous moments which were inseparably bound to awaiting this promised miracle child and to his ensuing life. Kierkegaard reminds us in *Fear and Trembling* that Abraham's is a comedy of faith without which tragedy is imminent. It is the certainty of this faith, in fact, which redeems Abraham's story from being, at best, pathetic.

The romantic comedy of Isaac and Rebekah serves as a transitional episode to reveal the roots of Jacob's character (Gen. 24-27). These two so divinely matched in youth are at odds with each other in old age. The battle is over favored children: Isaac loves Esau and Rebekah loves Jacob. Both know that God favors Jacob for the promised line, but Isaac, the *senex*, apparently believes that even God cannot disregard primogeniture. One cannot say that Rebekah is any more faithful to God, however, since she never claims His promise as a reason for favoring Jacob. In true comic femininity she simply chooses the right man with the wrong motives and then trusts her womanly wiles to win Jacob his place. "Upon me be your curse, my son," she says to Jacob as she orders him to help her counterfeit the wild game stew his father relishes and winds sheepskin on his hands and neck so that he will feel like his hairy brother Esau if old blind Isaac touches him. By means of such comic devices of deceit Jacob obtains the formal blessing from Isaac, though he must flee for his life because of Esau's rage. This is a comedy of the battle between the sexes which shows eros in old age working out its tensions through two spoiled sons. Isaac and Esau are slaves of their bellies while Rebekah and Jacob stoop to conquer without regard to their own dignity, much less that of others. But it is a comedy of grace in that God's purposes are worked out despite the ludicrous acts in this domestic charade.

Of all the episodes revolving around these patriarchal rogues, Jacob's story is most fully comic. He is a spiritual picaro who needs a conniving uncle, two scheming wives, and a wrestling match with God to teach him that God's promises are not won by intrigue. Laban pulls one of the funniest deceptions in all literature. Aided by the ancient custom of veiling the woman's face, he manages to give in marriage his older homely daughter Leah instead of the younger beauty Rachel, a fact not discovered by Jacob until the morning after. Jacob then proceeds to marry Rachel as well and spends two decades working off the bride prices and building his estate. Having paid his debt by hard work, finagling, and unacknowledged grace of God, he is ready, now a rich man, to leave Laban. But he is a rich man pursued by an angry father-in-law who has lost much of his estate, a rich man awaited back home by a vengeful brother whose blessing he had stolen twenty years before. It is in this predicament that Jacob wrestles with God's messenger all night, finally winning a blessing and a game hip by dawn. Because of his undaunted struggles, the messenger tells him "Your name shall no more be called Jacob, but Israel (Hebrew, 'He who strives with God'), for you have striven with God and with men and have prevailed" (Gen. 32–38). We are reminded for all time that this God chooses a most preposterous and undignified episode as an occasion to rename Jacob, through whom He would name His people Israel —God wrestlers. Unlike Adam and Eve who wanted equality, God delights in the tension and diversity between man and Himself.

Joseph, Jacob's younger son, takes up his father's picaresque behavior in a comedy of errors that brings the book of Genesis to a climax. Joseph's preferment and precocious attitude enrage his half-brothers and incite them to plan his murder. Even Jacob is incensed that his favorite son dreams of rulership over his family. The young men's contempt for the "dreamer," as they call him, is appeased only by his brother Reuben's suggestion that they throw Joseph into a pit so that his blood will not be on their hands. Reuben secretly intends to rescue him from the pit. But just as certainly as Reuben's plot reverses Joseph's fortunes, so does another event reverse them once more: when a caravan of Ishmaelites happens by, another brother, Judah, persuades the others to pull Joseph from the pit and sell him into slavery, an act which both saves them from bloodguilt and enables them to turn a profit. Surely we have here a depiction of avarice, hatred, and deceit transformed, by the comic spirit, into "some mistake or a piece of ugliness which is not painful or destructive to life," as Aristotle describes a characteristic of comedy.[8] Joseph's brothers move from blood vengeance to voluntary manslaughter to profiteering. And their greed saves his life. Joseph's guileless character leads him from one misadventure to another until he ends up, by God's design, a ruler in the house of Pharaoh.

The memorable scene between Joseph and Potiphar's wife (Gen. 39) further establishes the comic bent of the story: "And although she spoke to Joseph day after day, he would not listen to her, to lie with her or to be with her" (Gen. 39:10). This is not a romance as with David and Bathsheba. It is an undignified tale of a rustic youth pursued by a stereotyped love-starved female who shamelessly goes after what she wants. Joseph is not tantalized by his master's wife and remains utterly loyal to his master, even to the point of pulling himself out of his coat and leaving it behind in the predatory woman's hands. The master is a bit of a cuckold not because he trusts Joseph but because he trusts his wife. The story does not play upon these comic overtones but simply records them, leaving to our imagination the difficulties Joseph encounters in his efforts to manage Potiphar's household and politely avoid its mistress.

Finally we are told that Joseph is put in prison, where he again becomes an overseer, while poor Potiphar is left to live with his wife. In this situation the story reveals the ends toward which God is working in order to redeem His people, manifesting the comic nature of that redemption. In prison Joseph naively interprets the dreams of the royal baker and butler. With a guileless curiosity, he asks these new prisoners, "Why are your faces downcast today?" What appears to be open-hearted small talk is actually prophetic insight revealed in the prisoners' reply, "We have had dreams and there is no one to interpret them." Joseph's priceless reply reminds us of why his brothers hated him: "Do not interpretations belong to God?" he asks artlessly. "Tell them to me, I pray you." The butler has dreamed that a vine matures before his eyes from which he crushes grapes into Pharaoh's cup and serves him. Joseph boldly declares that the butler will be restored and politely requests that the servant remember him before Pharaoh. The baker has dreamed of baking bread for Pharaoh, which is eaten from the basket on his head as he attempts to deliver it. Joseph forthrightly tells him that Pharaoh will hang him in three days. Needless to say, Joseph makes no special request of the baker. The baker dies and the butler is restored. But the butler forgets to mention Joseph before Pharaoh, as he had promised, until God, the comic manipulator, disturbs Pharaoh with a dream that begs for an interpreter. The wily butler seizes the moment to commend Joseph to his lord (Gen. 40:1-41:14).

Finally in power, in the court of Pharaoh, Joseph uses the classic comic deceit to test his brothers' character, discover their attitude toward his younger brother Benjamin, and finally offer a refuge to Jacob and his people, Israel. He pretends to suspect that they are spies and imprisons them for three days. He then permits them to buy grain but holds Simeon as a hostage and commands them to return bringing Benjamin, Joseph's full brother, the only other son of Rachel. Old Jacob grieves over this demand but yields to it, reminding his sons concerning Benjamin, "If harm should befall him on the journey you are to make, you would bring down my gray hairs with sorrow to Sheol" (Gen. 42:38). When Joseph later plots to keep Benjamin with him, their half-brother Judah intercedes, invoking Jacob's grief and offering himself as a substitute for Benjamin. This gesture breaks Joseph's heart, and he ends the intrigue.

Joseph has finally matured beyond the gullible rustic to become a true comic deceiver. These final scenes render a recognition of the highest comic order, as Frye describes the phenomenon:

> The "cognito" in comedy, in which the characters find out who their relatives are . . . is one of the features of comedy that has never changed much. . . . The watcher of death and tragedy has nothing to do but sit and wait for the inevitable end; but something gets born at the end of comedy, and the watcher of birth is a member of a busy society.[9]

Later, Jacob would memorialize Judah's sacrifice by declaring that "the scepter shall not depart from Judah." Through Judah's tribe will come Messiah, the great *cognito* of history. What gets conceived at the end of Genesis is born in Exodus: Israel. It is not the nativity of the concept of abstract hope of Israel but of the very character and conflicts of the Israel which unfolds in history. The favored son of Israel tests the character of his brothers not to reduce the other brothers to ashes but to insure the diversity that will become the twelve tribes. Jacob himself foretells the destiny of the tribes that will arise from the various characters of his sons. When this diversity is reduced by Israel's desire for a king such as the "goyim" have, the situation inevitably leads to a diminished Israel. But there is that remnant *led* by Joseph, Moses, Daniel, Ezra, and Nehemiah who recover for the people of God the rich, complex, busy society which is their genesis. This diversity is continued even in the Christian canon, the New Covenant, where Jesus promises a Kingdom within which twelve apostles will rule over the twelve tribes of Israel—these God wrestlers.

Within this stumbling and scheming redeemed and redeeming community, women play a unique and significant role. They are inseparably part of God's embodied image, breathed into mankind. While Genesis is often called the story of patriarchs, the actual text shows inordinate concern for the matriarchs of the chosen people. Unlike Helen, Clymenestra, Dido, and other feminine characters in Greek and Roman literature, Sarah, Rebekah, Leah, and Rachel are integral to the enterprise to which God has called their people. Nor are they "feminine forces" in some romantic sense. They are fully human, like Eve, and are therefore both temptresses and virtuous wives. Sarah conceives after having used Hagar to get a child by Abraham, and then later, with God's approval, imperiously demands Hagar's and Ishmael's exile. Rebekah properly favors Jacob in accordance with God's revelation and then contrives a series of ungodly schemes to win Jacob's place from Esau. Leah and Rachel are submissive wives and competitive mistresses who drive Jacob to fatherly ecstasy and husbandly distraction.

This strategic place of women in the biblical narratives only begins with Genesis, to continue throughout the Old and New Testaments. The life of Israel's great liberator, Moses, is bounded and shaped by the courage and acumen of women. His ingenious mother places her son in a basket on the Nile to avoid Pharaoh's purge of Hebrew males; Miriam, his resourceful sister, executes the plan and watches as Pharoah's daughter finds the baby and compassionately takes him in. Miriam then offers to obtain for the infant a wet nurse, who turns out to be, of course, the baby's mother. All of this blessed trickery is possible because the Hebrew midwives deceive Pharaoh, frustrating his plans to annihilate the Hebrew threat through infanticide. Later, in Moses' adulthood, Miriam joins with him and Aaron to complete the triad of authority that God establishes over his people in the Exodus. In the regime of Joshua, one of God's gracious signs that His people will conquer the Canaanites is their reception and preservation through Rahab, a harlot of Jericho. The pious author of the New Testament epistle to the Hebrews has the audacity to list her presence in the great "cloud of witnesses" which historically surrounds God's people. Nor can it be ignored that in the dark and cruel time recorded in Judges, the most flawless Judge recorded is Deborah (Judg. 5-6). She is a wife, prophetess, and judge who resents being coerced to witness bloodshed because Barak, Israel's supreme commander, will not fight without her presence.

Sensitivity to the redeeming place of womanhood is revealed also in the final episode of Judges. Having almost annihilated the Tribe of Benjamin in blood revenge, the leaders of the other eleven tribes awaken to the need of wives for the few surviving Benjaminites. They first attempt a bloody raid on Jabesh-gilead but can find only 400 virgins. They then suggest that the men of Benjamin hide in the vineyards at Shiloh and seize Hebrew maidens at the dance of the annual festival. Since the girls will be stolen, the ruse will enable the other tribes to keep their oath not to give their daughters to Benjamin. Such a child's game, restoring to the Benjaminite community the necessary feminine presence, is played so that they can return to their inheritance, rebuild the towns, and dwell in them (Judg. 21:23). In this same period, the story of Ruth reminds the Hebrews that God is justly purging his people but mercifully preserving a remnant. He does so not only through woman, but through a gentile woman at that.

The rest of the Hebrew canon amplifies the centrality of women to the comedy of redemption. Hannah's cry to God for a child recalls God's opening the wombs of Sarah, Rebekah, and Rachel. And with Samuel a new era is inaugurated in which kings rule Israel and women counsel them. As a young man, David listens to Abigail, and as an old man, to Bathsheba. The Song of Solomon exalts the power of a wise woman, even though in his actual life Solomon failed to honor women, using his wives in his youth and being controlled by them in old age. The wisdom of women and the joy such wisdom brings is the crowning theme of Proverbs as well. The final wise saying spoken to King Lemuel by his mother describes the destructive power of a seductress and the priceless value of a good wife (Prov. 31:1). When the kingdom splits in two, the eminence of woman in Israel's golden age is lost.

But even in the ominous times leading to exile, women retain their place as a mark of God's comic actions among his people. There is Jezebel, a pagan amazon, whose diabolical powers are destroyed before God's holy fool, Elijah. But there is also Esther, through whose beauty and wisdom God saves his people in a story replete with irony. When she is merely displaced, as in the time of the Judges, God mercifully purges his people and restores the graces of womanhood through such women as Deborah, Naomi, Ruth, and Hannah. But when she cries "unsex me," when, as in the words of Isaiah,

> the daughters of Zion are haughty
> and walk with outstretched necks,
> glancing wantonly with their eyes
>
> (Isa. 3:16)

the judgments of God on the culture are as harsh as those foretold by Isaiah. This flight from and by woman leads to the lament of Jeremiah, who says of the mothers of Jerusalem:

> Even the jackals give the breast
> and suckle their young,
> but the daughter of my people has
>   become cruel . . .
> The hands of compassionate women
> have boiled their own children,
> they became their food. . . .
>
> (Lam. 4:3, 10)

The degradation of woman or of womanhood is the diminishment of God's comic design in the Old Covenant. It is very much as George Meredith has observed: "The higher the comedy, the more prominent the part they [women] enjoy in it."[10]

The place of women in the biblical stories elucidates the distinction between the comic dimensions of the Old and New Covenants. The Old Testament never reaches the heights of paradisal comedy because

God has not yet produced his ultimate comic trick—Messiah. This stratagem of disguise, which Isaiah anticipates in the suffering servant (Isa. 53) and celebrates in the fertility songs of the barren (Isa. 54) and the new Jerusalem (Isa. 65), remains a hope through the time of the post-exilic prophets. The New Covenant, however, begins with God's great deceit in choosing the humblest and weakest vessel for his scheme. As George Herbert has expressed it:

>   Mary
>   Ana   Gram
>   Army
> How well her name an *Army* doth present,
> In whom the Lord of Hosts did pitch his tent!

From the laughter of Mary and Elizabeth, full of grace and truth, to the shock and grief of women who witness the empty tomb, the New Covenant people participate in the Kingdom come. This fullness of comedy is evident not merely in woman but in the redeemed significance of the human body, the community, as well as the world's body itself. Here God does not merely create flesh in his image but becomes flesh and dwells among us. Saint Paul reminds the reader in his epistle to the Romans that the answer to the depraved body (Rom. 1) is the redeemed body (Rom. 8) and the body made available to God (Rom. 12). Because of Christ the whole human community is valued, from the "least of these" to the Pharisees, thus confounding the elitism of Roman citizenship and Pharisaic religiosity.

This recovery of the value of all embodied humanity restores the proper value to the world's body, nonhuman things. Jesus enjoys common things and common people—he is a friend of tax collectors, drunks, and sinners and a favorite guest at their festivities. But he refuses to worship mere things, and he disdains their being valued more than people: he drives money changers from the temple and tells parables about spending money to gain friends. The final vision of the kingdom is in fact a city, the New Jerusalem where God will be present, people will be in abundance, and gold will be underfoot. But this is not a different vision from the Old Covenent. It is rather the fulfillment (the filling full) of God's original design, His creative and recreative acts first spoken in Genesis.

Perhaps this understanding of Genesis and the stories it initiates

The Bible as Genesis of Comedy

reveals why comedy reached its greatest moments in the Middle Ages and Renaissance when most people held the biblical belief that man is God-breathed dust. They believed that if "things are funny,"[11] then man is undoubtedly the funniest "thing" on earth, and that we can laugh because, despite our all being simpletons and buffoons in the hands of knaves and malefactors, there is above all a God who can cause us to say with Joseph: "Fear not, for am I in the place of God? As for you, you meant evil against me; but God meant it for good, to bring it about that many people should be kept alive, as they are today" (Gen. 50:19-20). Comedy that does not grow out of such a world view tends to view man's life as hopeless or absurd, to reduce even the sacred to savagery.

By approaching the Bible from the angle of literature, we risk no violence to its essential nature. It is dominantly an anthology of stories whose laws of construction more closely resemble those of traditional genres of literature than those forms of thought imposed upon them by modern theology, archaeology, linguistics, and ancient Near-Eastern studies. The higher criticism is an inadequate instrument for interpreting the texts of scripture, as contemporary critics such as Brevard Childs recognize.[12] Nor can conservative orthodox scholars hope to defend the Bible as if it were a modern history text. As J. Gerald Jansen recently concluded,

> The function of the biblical text, then, is to transplant the mundane community into the imaginative world of the text so as to enable the community to find within the poetic energies of that text the means to become in the mundane realm, or at least, to live toward becoming, what it is called to be.[13]

One does not have to disparage the belief that the events of the Bible are historical and that the God it reveals continues to shape history when one acknowledges that the biblical texts are better characterized by universal elements of story as Aristotle listed them—plot, character, thought, diction, song, and spectacle—than by mere historical data. As biblical theologians would have it, these books are shaped more by the inspired writer's desire to reveal God's character and design for his people than to rehearse mere events. The fundamental mode of educating a people during the time of the Old Testament writers was, after all, poetic.

Our recognition that the Bible gives itself to us in forms of literature makes possible a richer and more incisive biblical hermeneutic. The act of interpreting a text, as Hans-Georg Gadamer describes it, is the bridging of the horizons between the imaginative world of the text and that of the reader.[14] The "story" that the Scriptures tell spans that gap of understanding between text and reader. To understand the story is to understand the intention behind the text. It is a literary act of interpretation, effectively approached through the genres Aristotle describes in his *Poetics*. Since his time we have extended his definitions and added new approaches (historical, psychological, linguistic), but we have yet to go beyond his seminal delineation of tragedy, comedy, and epic.

Biblical scholars fear that such an approach will permit the light of biblical revelation to be swallowed up in the twilight of Greek philosophy. This is a danger—as the Alexandrine tradition, with scholars such as Origen, reminds us. But the antidote to such syncretism is to keep the Bible the Book of books, the canon by which all other knowledge is measured. The ironic fact is that the Bible is never more clearly "revelation" than when read alongside the great epics, tragedies, and comedies of the Greeks. The Hebrew imagination is distinct from the Greek in that it renders and anticipates a comic ending to all things—inanimate, animate, and human. This comic slant begins with the Hebrew understanding of God, who is personal before things because He was in the beginning the creator of things. This concept is in stark contrast to that of Hesiod and other sources, who tell us that the old chthonic gods and the Olympian gods were born out of night and day, earth and sky. The Hebrew imagination begins with a personal being who creates impersonal things; the Greek begins with impersonal things which generate personal gods. By contrast to the rise and fall of the gods, there is no doubt in the Hebrew imagination that Yahweh is sovereign over creation, including humanity. Not only is He not threatened by man, as the Olympians were when Prometheus offered understanding to man, but He gives mankind rulership over the earth after creating male and female in His image. As Genesis shows, this God is not a *senex* and a tyrant, but a life-giver, a creator of newness and diversity, a beneficent trickster, and a covenant maker. Because He is both Elohim (creator) and Yahweh (the one "who is" in history), the world begins in comedy. In fashioning man in His image, male and female, out of dust, he enables humanity, even when fallen, to live all comically. And because this God is from beginning to end a covenant maker, betrothing himself to His people, His world will end in comedy: that marriage-feast that characterizes a "komos."

Notes

1. William Lynch, *Christ and Apollo* (Notre Dame, Ind., 1960), 188.
2. The Revised Standard Version will be used throughout the text.
3. Northrop Frye, *Anatomy of Criticism* (Princeton, N.J., 1957), 181.
4. Lynch, 92.
5. Ibid., 107.
6. Henri Bergson, "Laughter" in *Comedy* (Garden City, N.J., 1956), 51-54.
7. Frederick Buechner, *Telling the Truth* (New York, 1978), 49-50.
8. Gerald F. Else, *Aristotle's Poetics: The Argument* (Cambridge, Mass., 1957), 183.
9. Frye, 170.
10. George Meredith, "An Essay on Comedy," in *Comedy*, 14.
11. Lynch, 10.
12. Brevard Childs, *Introduction to the Old Testament as Scripture* (Philadelphia, 1979), 15-16.
13. J. Gerald Jansen, "Review: The Canonical Context of Old Testament Introduction," *Interpretation* 34 (Oct. 1980): 413.
14. Hans-Georg Gadamer, *Truth and Method* (New York, 1975), xviii-xxvi.

3

Aristophanes' Comic Apocalypse

LOUISE COWAN

ORDINARILY overlooked as one of the paradigms of comedy in its full scope is the canon of Aristophanes, whose plays are considered by common consent brilliant though limited examples of satire and farce—uninhibited but conservative, naughty but nice. Taken in its entirety, however, Aristophanic comedy is much more comprehensive than this initial judgment would indicate, much more pregnant with things to come. It is, in fact, religious drama, in the same sense that medieval drama is religious. Both Old Attic Comedy and the liturgical comedy of the Middle Ages were essentially popular theatrical productions dramatizing a divine story, with such certainty of its sacrality that they could submit its holiest mysteries to burlesque.

Drama, as Muriel Bradbrook suggests, is "the cooperative creation of author, actors, and audience."[1] At its highest realization it exists in a kind of communion among these three, "an intercourse from which it issues and on which it depends." The Greek and medieval English theaters were such cooperative creations, "Acts of Faith," she would have it, "directed to a God who might be both subject and audience of the play."

For the Greeks, the god who is "both subject and audience of the play" was, of course, Dionysus, the divinity of wine and harvest, whose presence is marked by pain and ecstasy and who testifies to both incarnation and transcendence. Walter Otto's extensive study reveals him to be "the god who comes," and emphasizes his distinction from the Olympians.[2] The Greeks knew the sudden appearance of a god, according to Carl Kerenyi, not only as *epiphaneia* but also as *epidemia*, a "divine 'epidemic'—whose kinship with 'visitation by a disease' is undeniable at least insofar as it was always the incursion of something overpowering...."[3] As the god who comes, the epiphanic and epidemic god, Dionysus is experienced not as a governing and sustaining deity, timeless, beyond change, but as one who in time suffers, reveals, destroys, and fulfills. "The evidence is clear," Kerenyi maintains, "that the core of the Dionysian religion, the essence that endured for thousands of years and formed the very basis of its existence" was the coming of the god, his "cruel death," and, as "indestructible *zoe*," his resurrection.[4]

In his humanity, as the son of a mortal mother, Dionysus traces throughout his earthly career the course of human life and hence provides for drama its subliminal subject. In his divinity, as the offspring of Zeus, he is the hidden but all-seeing audience of a theater in which a people come to self-knowledge. But it is not simply that Dionysus expresses a duality inherent in existence. More importantly, he brings about a new order. As Otto comments, "he symbolizes an entire world whose spirit reappears in ever new forms and unites in an eternal unity the sublime with the simple, the human with the animal, the vegetative and the elemental."[5] He is the "archetypal image of indestructible life," according to Kerenyi,[6] opening for man what James Hillman calls "a new psychic geography."[7]

Athenian tragedy and comedy both grew out of ceremonies dedicated to Dionysus, and in both genres, as subject and audience, he has the effect of being "the god who comes." In tragedy he appears to the proud and self-righteous ruler and to the rigidly structured city, manifesting himself to rend and destroy. Whenever men set themselves up as gods, Dionysus comes—bringing ecstasy and terror, vision and death. In comedy, by contrast, his purpose is to bring life back to a degraded and disintegrating city. In this undertaking he works by uniting a community of people in a collective exuberance, sweeping aside the barriers that divide human beings from animals, from gods, and from themselves. Intoxication and festivity give rise to inspiration and fantasy, driving out the darkness of oppression, pain, and death. Dionysus comes, bringing revelry and joy, resurrection and life.

What is traditionally called "Old Comedy" is thought to have had its origin in phallic ceremonies at the festival of Dionysus, in the carnival revelry in his honor (the komos, or processional). Although it flourished in Athens for several centuries as popular entertainment as well as religious and mythic liturgy, comedy was not officially recognized as part of the two Athenian Dionysian celebrations until the early fifth century B.C. The names of nearly 200 authors of Greek comedy have survived, dating from the sixth century B.C. to the second century A.D. But the work of only one of them has been preserved, copied, and annotated by the Byzantine scholars, admired by the Church Fathers, his texts brought into Italy after the Fall of Constantinople and rendered into Latin long before the translation of the great tragedians. It is Aristophanes of whom I speak, of course, the comic genius who has shocked the Western world ever since his translation but who is universally regarded, in Moses Hadas's words, as "the most brilliant and artistic and thoughtful wit our world has known."[8]

Nothing remains of Old Comedy except Aristophanes' extant eleven plays (out of some forty-odd he is known to have written). Hence, when we speak firsthand of this entire mode of comic drama, we address ourselves to one author whose work was considered significant enough to be kept alive, translated, and constantly read. For all practical purposes Aristophanes stands alone, with his "terrible graces" (*phoberai charites*).[9] And yet to make this admission is not necessarily to hold, with the general opinion, his utter separation from tradition. A recent director of Aristophanic comedy, Alexis Solomos, is an extreme spokesman for this position. He maintains that Old Comedy (by which he means Aristophanic comedy) had no ancestors and no progeny—that, in fact, the Western comic tradition stems solely from Greek middle and new comedy, the style and form of which were adopted by the Roman and European playwrights in an unbroken tradition of "comedy of manners":

> The Old Attic Comedy, on the contrary, does not belong to that milennial tradition; it stands apart; its style cannot be adjusted to the normal orbit of theatre history; it is a mythological monster without parents

and without seed; it resembles the satyrs and the Centaurs, the Sphinx and the Gorgons, in being half human and half supernatural.[10]

Solomos's basic insight is of course true: the comedies of Aristophanes have something fantastic, weird, and supernatural about them. Still, it seems unjustified to set them aside from the major comic tradition and to consider them a kind of monstrous, even if magnificent, eruption.

What Mikhail Bakhtin has to say about medieval carnival[11] provides some understanding of the kind of "tradition" within which Aristophanes worked and which continued on after his time, even surviving the defeat of Greece. Old Comedy was shaped, as we have said, by folk festivals celebrating the rites of Dionysus, a pattern of communal imagination much like, and no doubt one might even say a forerunner of, the kind that gave rise to the wild and festive carnivals of the Middle Ages. Like carnival, the Greek rituals emphasized food, drink, sexuality, and an overturning of official order while at the same time celebrating and deepening an awareness of cultic mysteries. According to Bakhtin, we find in Aristophanes a veritable "heroics of the comic." All the things and events of ordinary life are transformed in his plays to become "cultic acts reinterpreted on the literary plane":

> ... they lose their private-everyday character, they become significant in human terms in all their comic aspect, their dimensions are fantastically exaggerated; we get a peculiar heroics of the comic, or, more precisely, a *comic myth*.... In Aristophanes we can still see the cultic foundation of the comic image, and we can see how everyday nuances have been layered over it, still sufficiently transparent for the foundation to shine through them and transfigure them.[12]

Bakhtin's is an illuminating comment; there can be no doubt that it is something like a comic myth that Aristophanes presents or that much of the strength of his comedy derives from its being a poetic reenactment of a cultic image or, as Bradbrook has said in a more general context, an act of faith. Both of these comments imply the action of *memoria*, as indeed in part drama must be said to be. In Aristophanic comedy, a deeply pious and conservative strain goes back to ancient fertility rites and the cultivation of the earth. But what seems fully as distinctive in these plays is the reach of their aspiration toward futurity, the projection of their spiritual and phenomenal being away from the earth into poetic space. For, unlike Homer and the author of Genesis, Aristophanes does not reveal the world and history to be comic in themselves; they are only implicitly so until seen in the light of the Dionysian imagination, which in touching and altering things, brings them to a new creation.

C. G. Jung has described what he calls "primordial experiences" that are to be found in the work of some writers, experiences that characterize a "visionary mode" of artistic creation:

> The expression that furnishes the material for artistic expression is no longer familiar. It is a strange something that derives its existence from the hinterland of man's mind—that suggests the abyss of time separating us from pre-human ages.... It arises from timeless depths; it is foreign and cold, many-sided, demonic and grotesque.... the primordial experiences rend from top to bottom the curtain upon which is painted the picture of an ordered world....[13]

Jung has here described the literature that in effect tears apart the veil of the cosmos, as opposed to that which, as he says earlier in the same passage, deals with the foreground of life. His emphasis is on a primordial experience, which arises, as he says, "from timeless depths." There is another kind of visionary literature, however, which emerges from somewhere other than the abyss; it finds its material in transcendence—in the circles of light surrounding the heavenly city. It too is grotesque and strange, though fantastic and bizarre rather than monstrous, and its evocation is more of rapture and terror than of dread and horror. This is the apocalyptic, which erupts into human consciousness from above rather than below, from the future rather than the past. An apocalypse, in its root sense, is an uncovering, a disclosure, a revelation of final things, not so much at the end of time as outside time.[14] The images that rise from that realm bespeak spiritual realities through grotesque patterns loosely associated with the vivid sense experiences that arise from ecstasy and terror. Northrop Frye contrasts apocalyptic with demonic, one a desirable world, the other undesirable: "The apocalyptic world," he writes, "the heaven of religion, presents, in the first place, the categories of reality in the forms of human desire, as indicated by the forms they assume under the work of human civilization."[15] His comment is apt, though for my purposes it needs some slight amendment. For, one must object, apocalyptic seems to speak less of the "heaven of religion" than to provide strange and marvellous images of the threshold surrounding that realm. It is in the nature of apocalyptic poetic revelation for fantasy to seize upon an intuition of something incomprehensible and to shape its patterns into allegory, out of which emerges the sweet dream of peace, a vision of the new city *coming to be*, where tears are wiped away and lions and lambs lie down together.

Both archetype and apocalypse manifest themselves through images; both are collective and not private. It is as though the first emerges out of the primordial past and testifies to those aspects of the soul which were imprinted with the *imago dei*, though marred and distorted by a warp of darkness. The second appears as if refracted into the present from an unseen future and thus carries the force of revelation. Its images are of the never-experienced and hence imperfectly comprehended fields of light, a realm which when its face is turned toward time can appear as an avenging angel of destruction and judgement, but which in itself is the still point, the kingdom of peace.

The Aristophanic vision, without doubt, is apocalyptic.[16] It is concerned with images and signs of what Rudolf Otto, speaking of apocalypse, calls "the atmospheric pressure of that which is ready to break in with mysterious dynamic."[17] An apocalypse is inherently uncanny and marvellous, as Saint John the Divine shows, with his "new heaven and new earth" and his opulent imagery of renewal and re-making: two-edged swords, golden candles, beasts with eyes in their wings, trumpets, a woman clothed in the sun, and a beast with seven heads, bear-like feet, and the mouth of a lion. And the general movement of apocalyptic is comic. For, though it announces an unsparing final judgment, its tone is one of comfort and reassurance. Despite its terror, what it symbolizes is the value of the individual soul, able to find within itself, even though confronted by principalities and powers, the strength and grace to resist evil.

Far from being monstrous, then, as Solomos would have it, the comedy of Aristophanes is apocalyptic. It reveals a total pattern of imagination, apprehended in the cult and celebration of the community. For, as Kerenyi has said, "in myth and image, in visionary experience and ritual representation [the Greeks] . . . possessed a *complete expression* of the essence of Dionysus."[18] Aristophanes was thus provided by his culture with a mythic structure embracing both origins and ends; and as comic genius, his focus was upon an ultimate order manifesting itself through and in mortal life. Because of this double vision, it is in his work that comedy can first be known for what it is. Hence his plays stand at the head of, not apart from, the development of comedy. Like Homeric epic or Aeschylean tragedy, Aristophanic comedy contains within itself the lineaments of an entire genre. Nothing in the long comic tradition introduces elements not at least intimated in Aristophanes. Admittedly, in later works emphases are altered, further dimensions of meaning added; but it is not too much to say that the entire reach of the comic universe, as a possibility in itself, was first apprehended by Aristophanes.

This imaginary universe lying behind and sustaining each of Aristophanes' comedies is one that supposes and responds to the absolute audacity of the human person. It is shown to be available by aspiration and boldness, whatever one's situation. In it, comic heroes are able to outwit their opponents, to reign supreme by simple absence of malice and love of pleasure, and to conquer enemies without becoming bellicose or ill-humored. The revealed kingdom of peace is startlingly vital, manifesting the essential harmony of body and mind, flesh and spirit, age and youth, femininity and masculinity, word and deed. Laws of logic and of probability hold no sway over it; free of the limitations of time and space, improbability and contradiction are its structural modes. It contains the entire universe of comic paraphernalia: carnival, saturnalia, festivity, farce, buffoonery, satire, romance, allegory, fantasy, nonsense, absurdity, and all manner of modes and styles. It is a vision of human possibility that is at one and the same time strange and familiar, both like life and unalterably unlike it.

To ignore the apocalyptic element in Aristophanes' dramas is to miss their deepest significance; although it is certainly true that even when his plays are judged by ordinary standards for comedy they show themselves to be masterpieces of comic technique. His plots are skillfully wrought; his language is shot through with wit. His characters, if one goes by what Aristotle maintained comic characters ought to be, are far "worse" than people actually are, much engaged in vices that provoke ridicule without causing pain. But from the very start, the plays imply more than Aristotle's sketch of comedy as social corrective can account for. Underneath their surface of naturalistic detail is hidden a strange pattern which is almost, but not quite, recognizable. As it takes over, everything becomes exaggerated and distorted. The language of wit turns into a pyrotechnic of creation: the mechanics of farce are blown up into absurdly stylized fantasy; personal abuse and satire take on the lineaments of grotesque allegorical caricature; bodily appetites develop an inordinate zest. Aristophanes' "maculate muse"[19] renders his obscenity absolute: the bawdiness and outright indecency of excremental and sexual details, in language as in image and act, elevate them to a level of abstraction where they are all but stripped of realistic reference. It is as though the plays move from a commonplace situation into a kind of electric field, where events and words are charged with energy and leap the barriers separating human action from the irrational and preposterous, upsetting and exploding the order of probability.

But, as we have already indicated, there is more even than this outrageous genius in the comedies of Aristophanes. His thought is at one and the same time as visionary and as astutely political as Plato's. His concern is the actual, his remedy the imagined, city. Over and over he castigates Athens for its venality and stupidity, defending the old ways in politics, education, and morals. Along with this scolding goes a defense of comic poetry, which, as he constantly teaches, has a privileged if largely unappreciated social importance. This critical and political wisdom, expressed all through the plays, is, to be sure, worthy of being taken seriously; and admittedly a great portion of Aristophanes' genius is to be found in his social satire. But even his invective is touched with irony and the grotesque. Cedric Whitman has suggested a scale of comic techniques, all essential to the uniqueness of the Aristophanic method—satire, wit, humor, and nonsense. "Satire denounces the world," he maintains, "wit penetrates it, humor accepts it, but nonsense transforms it."[20] There can be no doubt that Aristophanes is a master of all four modes. But very often it is the nonsensical in his work that is least valued by his readers. Whitman makes a brilliant defense of nonsense, citing Baudelaire's important distinction between the "significant comic and the absolute comic," in the latter of which a nonsensical invention or creation evokes a larger sphere of meaning. But the visionary quality that I have mentioned in Aristophanes goes even further; in his comic extravaganzas fantasy becomes much more than satire, absurdity, or nonsense, more even than absolute comedy. In almost all his plays fantasy, the establishment of an imaginary realm, is a means toward transcendence and transformation. Within Aristophanes' polis of the imagination, sublime and impossible action can take place—the battle between truth and falsity can be fought out on different grounds, desire can be fulfilled, the joys and pleasures of life celebrated, language enhanced, fertility ensured, the city renewed.

Thus the Aristophanic vision consists of two worlds: one is debased and dangerously declining; the other, bright with possibility. The first is, or pretends to be, Athens—at war, taught by sophists, vitiated by pretense, racked by vanity and the love of money, rent by constant recourse to courts of law. The other is a possibility—a realm of peace instead of war, with the lowly raised high and the self-important brought low. It posits fulness instead of parsimony, fertility and potency rather than barrenness and impotence. In this vision of human fulfillment the "good things" of life, the appetites, are truly good, and the body is worthy of respect. Sex, wine, food are endowments that are meant to be enjoyed. Agrarian rather than urban life is the model, even within the polis, since city ways render people selfish, avaricious, litigious, and dishonest. Tradition and common sense are the standard for right behavior rather than any new kind of abstract and vain learning. Blessedness and celebration are the proper state of humanity, a condition to be achieved only by audacity, by what Whitman considers the chief characteristic of the Aristophanic comic hero, *poneria*, a certain goodhearted rascality and cheerful resourcefulness that ensure survival.[21] In this fantastic world that Aristophanes creates before us, one in which the invisible city, as an object of desire, has begun to assume more importance than the visible city, everything is topsy-turvy: women are put in charge of things, old men become young again, slaves outsmart masters, the lowly little Chaplinesque figures become important and powerful, and the simple become wise. It is a vision, in its own way, of the new Jerusalem.

The question of how a person can achieve blessedness in the midst of war, avarice, contention, and falsehood is the burden of Aristophanes' comedies. His three "peace" plays—*Acharnians*, *Peace*, and *Lysistrata*—are indispensable guides to his answer to this question, for they focus on the overt contrast between harmony and strife. Peace in these plays is indicative not simply of the literal peace that Athens so sorely needs but of an intuitive and revelatory vision of the ends of human life —an apocalyptic image. The state of peace is thus for Aristophanes a massive symbol of the right order of things: in the cosmos, *physis*, or the great flow of nature; in the city, harmony and freedom; in the soul joy and delight, and overall, *zoe*, everlasting life. The dominant metaphor for this ecstasy of blessedness is different in each of the three plays concerned with peace.

In the *Acharnians*, Aristophanes' earliest preserved play, it is wine that not only brings about peace, but in a daring merging of metaphor and reality, *is* peace itself. The peace treaties brought back to the lonely little farmer Dikaiopolis (Just City or Just Citizen) are three wineskins filled with five-, ten-, and thirty-year wines. He has sent his own messenger to Sparta to make a private peace for himself, his wife, and children. The messenger shortly comes running back with his "samples" of peace, pursued by the Acharnians, old warriors who fought at Marathon and now misguidedly resent any attempt at reconciliation with the other city-states. When Dikaiopolis tastes the samples, he spews out the five- and ten-year "treaties," since one smells of tar and warships and the other of military negotiations. But when he rolls the thirty-year treaties on his tongue, he exclaims:

> O Festival of Dionysus!
> These have a fragrance of ambrosia and nectar
> And suggest nothing about a three-day ration,
> But on my tongue proclaim, Go where you like.[22]

The message of the well-aged wine, the thirty-year treaties, is peace and freedom: "Go where you like." This permission is like Virgil's to Dante when, at the peak of Mount Purgatory, after the pilgrim has been cleansed, he advises: "Take pleasure as your guide"—and the implication, in both instances, is that the person so liberated will do no evil. What is suggested here is the boundless state of the soul when it is in harmony with the good and realizes its own authority. After a taste of this heady wine, Dikaiopolis feels himself released from war and war's alarms and, since the city will not celebrate its traditional festival in honor of Dionysus, he sets out on this own to celebrate the rural Dionysia.

The theme of regeneration runs through all Aristophanes' comedies, and true to that movement, this play has not only Dikaiopolis but the chorus of Acharnians as well begin as old men, impotent, ignored, unsuccessful. They have been forgotten by the people whom they have guarded. In their place, hired soldiers and ambassadors perform their duties only perfunctorily; nobody respects the men who have served the state with patriotic devotion. Citizens are vain and gullible; prominent men are notorious homosexuals and cowards; even poetry is debased, with Euripides much preferred to Sophocles or Aeschylus. Everything is for sale. In the midst of the general corruption, citizens have succumbed to venality and, under the pressures of a war with neighbors, allowed themselves to be deprived of trade with their friends. It is out of love for the delicious Beoetian eels, the pungent Megarian garlic, the delectable Prasiaian leeks that Dikaiopolis begins again the exhange of goods by trading illicitly with inhabitants of other city-states. And it is from his rejection of war as the opposite of festivity that he and the Acharnians are, in the end, rejuvenated and potent. When the old men, won over to the side of peace, make love to Reconciliation (the first of Aristophanes' lovely allegorized maidens) they declare that as good husbandmen they will plant first a row of vines next to the little green figs; and then finally the domestic olive where, despite their age, they will pursue lovemaking with the proper unction (991-99). Their festivity blends with Dikaiopolis's celebration, expressing an unaging vitality and abundance. They have learned the secret of the comic hero's inclusive attitude toward life and will no longer suffer from penury and fanaticism. Various citizens come to Dikaiopolis to obtain a few drops of his precious peace-wine, but he will yield none—except to a bride, so that she may keep her husband home from war. Even in this early play there is the implication of the *hieros gamos*, the sacred marriage which is the source of all peace.

However, though it is joyous and transformative, the revelry of Dikaiopolis and his friends stops short of changing the entire city and must exist within an alien regime, like a current flowing within a stagnant lake. In this, the first comic drama that we possess, what is remarkable is Aristophanes' recognition that the "green world," as it has been called, the kingdom of peace, is within the soul, available when all else fails.

Dikaiopolis invites everyone to a feast in honor of Dionysus; Lamachos, a blustering braggart soldier, calls everyone to war. Both leave the stage; but Lamachos soon reappears in disarray, pierced by a vinestake while leaping over a trench. In triuimphant contrast, Dikaiopolis reappears with a pretty girl on each arm (1190-1203). Thus the fertility spirit itself, the peace and plenty of wine and festivity, has the last say. The groin of war, the allegorical figure destructive of wine and the blessings of peace, is wounded by the very emblem of what it has flouted—a vinestake. The little peaceable Dikaiopolis moves on, with a growing number of cohorts, from the Rural Dionysia to the festival of wine, the Anthesteria, where he wins the drinking contest, and the blessedness of the god is copiously manifested.

If in *Acharnians* the central symbol for reconciliation, the peace that passes understanding, is wine, in *Peace* the focus for that blessedness is food. In this, Aristophanes' fifth surviving play, it is not a thirty-year-old wine, gentle on the tongue, that possesses such magical and spiritual powers, but the harvest and fertility promised by a beautiful maiden Opora (Harvest, Bounty, Fruitfulness), along with her twin sister Theoria (Mayfair, Festivity, Ceremony). By the end of the play Opora is to wed Trygaios, a little old rustic (whose name means "crop"); and her sister is to wed the President of the Athenian Council. One young woman therefore represents rural fertility, the other urban festivity—nature and art. These two maidens have been brought to earth from the divine realm, along with the goddess Peace, who has been exhumed from a cave in which she was buried when the Olympian gods departed, leaving the dread Polemos (War) in control.

That food, as a cluster of images, is in this play the key to the way in which one reaches love and joy may be discerned in the dialogue that takes place when Hermes gives Opora to Trygaios, telling him that she is to be his bride and partner in his fields. "Marry her," he says, "and generate new vines." Trygaios asks whether after his long abstinence it won't hurt him if he partakes too copiously of her abundance. Hermes replies, "Not if you take a dose of pennyroyal" (710-15). (The scholiast noted pennyroyal as a remedy for eating too much fruit.)

Food and its accompanying festivity and lovemaking embody peace in this fantasy of paradise regained, with the bountiful harvest of autumn replacing the spring Rural Dionysia of the earlier play. Hence imagery of the entire process of consuming—eating and defecation—runs throughout the play. The opening act begins, in fact, with the servants of Trygaios complaining about the dung beetle that their master is coddling; they have to pat excrement into delicate cakes for this great beast of an insect's finicky appetite. Apparently, they conjecture, their master is mad; he gazes all day long at the sky, begging Zeus not to destroy Greece. He has been muttering, "If only I could somehow get to Zeus!" (69–70) and has tried unsuccessfully scaling heaven by means of ladders. He has recently acquired a huge Aetnaean beetle, calls it "little Pegasus, my flying champion" (76)—and now, just as we're watching, begins his ascent to heaven astride his mount. His daughter vainly attempts to call him back, doubting the dignity of a flight upon so lowly a creature. Should he not harness the actual Pegasus and so in tragic rather than comic style approach the gods? "No," Trygaios answers her, "for then I would have need of double supplies" (136–39). As it is, he tells her, there is a certain excremental economy in the arrangement with the beetle.

The food imagery continues throughout the play. In heaven, for instance, Trygaios finds War (Polemos) getting ready to make a salad of the Greek city-states, to grind them in his gigantic mortar. He throws in leeks for Prasiai, garlic for Megara, cheese for Sicily, and honey for Attica. But just when he is ready to toss his salad, he finds he must leave the scene to obtain a pestle; and it is while he is away that the chorus of farmers, suddenly appearing from nowhere, "pull for peace" and extricate the goddess from the cave, along with the two accompanying maidens. When Trygaios, returning to earth, seeks for the beetle, he finds that it has been transmogrified: as part of Zeus's entourage, serving with his horses, it is now fed on ambrosia. The transformation of dung to ambrosia could be taken as a governing image of metamorphosis for the entire drama, which has begun with unsavory images and ends with delectable ones. When Trygaios pulls the goddess Peace and the two lovely girls out of the earth and kisses them, exclaiming lyrically over their delicious scent, Hermes remarks: "They don't smell much like a knapsack, do they?" to which Trygaios replies:

> Ugh! that filthy bag of filthy men,
> It stinks of rank and putrid onion breath;
> But SHE of feasts and harvests, banquets, plays,
> Thrushes, festivals, flutes, the songs of Sophocles. . . .
>
> (525–31)

Peace is everything delightful, beautiful, sweet-smelling, delicious; whereas War has been shown to be everything filthy, ugly, fetid, foul-tasting.

After Peace has been brought back to earth, Opora given to Trygaios, and Mayfair to the Council, the action consists largely of a pageantry of rejoicing, preparations for the bridal, cooking, and feasting. The last part of the play, celebrating peace and fecundity, focuses chiefly on foods. Figs, olives, wine and myrtles, barley, flowers, fruit, herbs, and spices—all are told over lovingly as coming from the goddess's blessings. At the wedding supper, everyone is exhorted to eat and chomp away with gusto: guests are admonished to use their teeth on the festive meal and to take their fill of food and drink (1306-10). In the wellwishing for the bride and groom, they are told to dwell in peace, see their figs grow ripe, and reap their yield (1339-46).

The festive imagery of *Peace* includes in its encompassing benevolence drinking and lovemaking, as well as feasting. It is, of course, an ancient combination. Eating has traditionally been considered a communal act, binding people together by nourishment, from its most basic aspects to its most refined. Archetypally, both eating and sex are acts of union hedged about with mystery, their implications spanning the distance from humanity's dark communion with matter to its spiritual capacity for delight. Linked with two of the most fundamental motives of a society, both represent powerful communal drives toward survival. In Aristophanes' comedy they emerge as poetic symbols not only of physiological goods but of spiritual grace. The return of Peace to earth, the marriage of the old farmer to fertility, and the harvest festivals bringing together song, dance, ritual, poetry, feasting, and drinking become an image of the new creation, made all the more tender by its embodiment in old and familiar things.

If, as we have seen, *Acharnians* portrays a separate small communal peace within a warring city and *Peace* a general return among the farmers to tranquil and fruitful agrarianism, *Lysistrata* shows how peace may be restored to the political life of an entire city and, in fact, all of Greece. And the way is not through wine or food (though both are present in abundance in the feast of amity and friendship at the end of the play), but through sex—lovemaking between husband and wife, within the family, in a harmonious and ordered city. And just as wine and food are complex images in the preceding plays, taking on increasingly expanded meaning (the dung becomes ambrosia, plenteous crops from the fruitful earth, an entire nonpredatory way of life, and—to go on—a spiritual blessedness), so the grossly exaggerated sexual language and sexual gesture in *Lysistrata* become the carrier for love between husband and wife, the inner life of desire, the sacredness of the home, the harmony and order of the city, and finally even the outreaching *agape* by which one loves one's enemies.

This play is the most realistic of Aristophanes' dramas, requiring no supernatural machinery to carry out the happy idea. Its plot is more clearly structured than those of the other comedies, its characters more lifelike. It may be true that within it at times, as Douglass Parker points out, Aristophanes' "linguistic exuberance deserts him"[23] but it is nonetheless a brilliant play exhibiting unmistakable marks of its author's genius. Its comic hero is a woman, less a *poneros* than a *spoudaios* (Aristotle's virtuous person who, in comedy, is a serious character around whom comedy occurs). Lysistrata, whose name means Disbander, or Ender, of the Army, is a noble and intelligent woman, much akin to an Athena. Yet she is realistic enough to be credible as a woman, undergoing the same deprivation she demands from others. When, at the beginning of the play, she summons all the women of the Hellenic city-states to hear her "happy idea," they find it, to be sure, difficult to believe—Greece saved by women! One of her friends asks in wonderment, "How could we do/Such a wonder? We women who sit/Adorning ourselves in our saffron silks?" "These are the very weapons of the contest" (36–46), Lysistrata assures her and goes on to reveal her demanding scheme: "We must give up all lovemaking" (124). The women immediately turn to go home: she calls them back and shames them into acquiescence. If they will deliberately increase their attractiveness and yet refuse to yield to their husbands unless all fighting is ended, she tells them, they can strike a blow for peace that no man has yet been able to deliver.

Lysistrata's plan initiates a general war between the sexes. The old women of the city assemble against the old men and take over the Acropolis. When the men attempt to regain it, they fight with fire in the agon that ensues, while the women fight with water, the element that frustrates fire—something the younger women must do in quite a different theater. They join the older women in the Acropolis, where they occupy the very heart of the city and hold out until finally the men surrender. Lysistrata lectures Athenian and Spartan warriors on the virtues of peace while they gaze longingly at the pretty girl, Reconciliation, and are vanquished finally by her attraction. There is a force in the ongoing of life, the drama announces, toward which even the act of generation must bow—for a time. The most demanding of desires in the domestic realm must be thrust aside if the political realm is so awry that this life-force is threatened: indeed, these very desires can be used to rectify the political order, Aristophanes reminds us in *Lysistrata*. Authority lies finally in the will, a spiritual, not an animal quality. At the end of the play a great feast unites all of Greece, with each man promised that he may take his wife home after the celebration. In their revelry, the Athenians call upon Artemis, Apollo, Dionysus, Zeus, and Hera as holy witnesses to the noble peace they have made with the aid of Aphrodite; and the Spartans call upon Athena by her Spartan cult name, goddess of the Brazen temple, and invite Helen, a Spartan, to lead the dance.

The state of peace, as Aristophanes presents it in the plays just discussed, is not at all a humanistic compromise in which people of good will learn to tolerate one another. It is not, in actuality, a literal peace at all. These are not plays about pacifism. They depict, instead, a transformed spiritual condition, requiring for its attainment an assumption, a lifting up out of oneself. Being drunk with wine, filled with good things, caught up in the delight of lovemaking—these are both metaphors and models for such a metamorphosis. Peace in Aristophanic comedy is therefore a supra-rational condition, inaccessible to wise and sober planning and available, rather, to folly, to audacity, to a loss of self in the bounty of the divine. Its reference, therefore, as I have argued earlier, is not to a primitive garden state but to a new creation, the transformed actual city. Hence, peace, as Aristophanes depicts it, is an apocalyptic image, an image from an intuited future. It is this permanent and unchanging city, as an entire guiding presence in men's minds, that is shown to be the only trustworthy model for right action in the temporal order.

In both the *Acharnians* and *Lysistrata* this city of peace and love is possible in the midst of things, by an act of imagination, courage, and bold enterprise. In *Peace*, however, with customary methods failing, what is required is an outrageous leap into the unknown. The comic hero must seek somewhere other than in ordinary life the blessedness ardently desired and even expected by the heart. Similarly, in two other comedies—*Frogs* and *Birds*—the protagonists leave the realm of history to seek elsewhere a better destiny. In this searching for the heavenly city, Aristophanes is engaging directly in the supreme act of the comic imagination, an act that governs the entire terrain of comedy. Some seventeen centuries later, Dante, a greater poet, was able, with the aid of a coherent theology, to develop a spiritual universe in consistent detail and to display the paradigmatic modes of comic existence. His *Inferno*, *Purgatorio*, and *Paradiso* are metaphors depicting possible states of souls after death—that is, possible spiritual conditions encountered in human life, seen, however, under the aspect of eternity. These realms are defined by characters who are in one of three basic relationships to the good. They are those who in the most profound depths of their wills have chosen self at the cost of all else; or the good without being able to achieve it; or the good at the expense of self. These three states represent, in a sense, the entire range of choices possible to individual persons and to human communities, and in their full scope, with all their variation, make up the comic universe. Most writers of comedy, knowingly or not, show their characters as recognizably falling somewhere in their scheme, though they most often depict them realistically, in their daily habitat, amidst familiar things. Dante was able to turn comedy inside out, so to speak, and to place his literal action within a fantastic cosmos, with a clear notion of how it related to mundane reality. In taking his actual steps in the other world, Dante's pilgrim would have behind him an entire culture that could accept the literal sense of his action without scandal. Aristophanes, however, in ascertaining these spiritual conditions, had to rely solely on fantasy, nonsense, and an intuitive vision. Nevertheless, his work displays the same governing design. The plays *Frogs*, *Peace*, and *Birds* may be regarded as the most evident examples of his infernal, purgatorial, and paradisal realms, though these states of soul may be found in his other comedies as well. These are clearly apocalyptic dramas, since in each it is necessary for the protagonist to leave the earthly city in search of another; and, further, in each of the plays the other realm, either below or above ordinary space and time, is related to human action and even follows from it as a spiritual outcome and judgment rather than being entirely separate and independent of human history.

In *Frogs* the *poneros* is Dionysus himself, desirous of a poet to save Athens and aware that all the good poets have long since departed this life. His yearning takes him on an arduous and hilarious journey to the underworld, in search, as he thinks, of Euripides, whom he longs for as one might crave pea soup, or strawberries. On his journey across the river Styx, a chorus of frogs engages him in a singing contest. These creatures, for whom the play is named, are appropriate to the region of the dead, the chthonic world of darkness, containing the past and human history. Beings of earth and water, the heaviest and most base elements in the cosmos, the amphibian frogs are fitting conductors to a realm totally lacking in inspiration or grace. In it the order of the day is every man for himself; the accustomed course of action is based on trickery, lying, deception, rivalry, envy—all the devices of the ego to preserve itself. Even Aeschylus and Euripides are quarreling, in competition with each other over the place of honor at Pluto's table, which Aeschylus had held in uncontested splendor before Euripides' arrival. Pluto has decided to settle the issue with a contest: lines from the plays of each dramatist are to be weighed, with Dionysus serving as judge, and the tragedian he chooses will be taken back with him to earth. From here on, the action serves to reverse Dionysus's opinion of Euripides: he begins to reevaluate what this latter-day playwright has done to the art of tragedy and to the city. According to every literary criterion, Aeschylus is the superior poet; but Dionysus is still undecided. "I must not lose the love of either," he declares: "One I think wise [*sophos*], the other delights me" (1411-13). He recalls that he came after a poet so that the city could keep its choral festivals and thus be saved; hence he changes his standards of judgment from purely aesthetic criteria to ethical ones: "Whichever has the best advice for the city is the one/I mean to take back" (1420-21).

There follows a rigorous examination in which a remarkable thing occurs: whereas Euripides' answers are all extreme, sophistical, and ingenious, Aeschylus answers with the moderation and even compromise that seems characteristic of a *comic*, not a tragic outlook. When asked for his advice concerning the problem of Alcibiades, Aeschylus replies that it would be best not to raise up a lion in the city but that once one has been raised up, it is best to yield to its ways. This is the answer comedy gives: life itself is worth something; in charting the course of an entire city, one should not take an extreme stand which might possibly endanger the whole populace. To endure is to hope that somehow conditions may change of their own accord and that time can remedy a predicament seemingly beyond help. In a longer questioning, Aeschylus manages to make Dionysus see that things are not simplistically black and white: the city does not hate the good, nor does it love the bad; it simply uses those whom it must. When pressed for a remedy, Aeschylus first demurs, saying that he will speak when he is there, not here. But he is finally forced to prescribe. The city and its citizens will be saved, he says,

> When they think of their land as enemy territory
> And the enemy's possessions as their own; their ships as real wealth,
> Their only resource hardship and poverty. . . .
>
> (1460-65)

Dionysus has made his decision: "I'll choose him for whom my soul yearns" (1468). And when reproached by Euripides for not selecting the poet he had sworn to reclaim from Hades, Dionysus replies that it was only his tongue that so swore, vanquishing Euripides with a line from his own *Hippolytus*. In an atmosphere of rejoicing, Aeschylus and Dionysus begin their journey home, blessed by Pluto and the holy torches of the initiates, taking with them wisdom and poetry, as well as a more sinister gift—a rope for the necks of Kleophon, Nikomakos, and others, along with an invitation to join the troops in Hades with no delay. These concerns seem more the domain of the comic than the tragic poet. Perhaps Aristophanes is indicating that to rescue someone from the other world is to come back with a changed person, one who has learned the value of life and who is less likely to be concerned with absolute principles than with a genial acceptance of everything human except those forces that, destroying life and goodness, belong in the infernal realm. The underworld is shown to be a place of absence of life—darkness, selfishness, and ignorance. For Aeschylus to be delivered from that region is a kind of harrowing of hell.

In *Peace*, as we have seen, yearning and anguish over the fate of the declining city arise in a heroic bosom much like Dionysus's, not, however, out of desire for a vanished mortal or any hope of retrieving the city's noble past. Instead, Trygaios recognizes that divine aid must be obtained if the city of man is to endure; the heavenly image of Peace herself must be retrieved for a city that has forgotten her visage. He therefore leaves the earthly realm, storming heaven by the strength of his desire. He brings back to earth the goddess's statue, the idea of Peace, accompanied by her counterpart, a flesh and blood young woman who is the embodiment of fruitfulness. The point to be emphasized is that peace and fertility must be brought to earth from the abode of the gods; they are not a product of earth, but a gift to earth. The vision is purgatorial, with people represented less as vicious than as helpless. The chief structuralizing virtue of this middle stage of comedy is hope, just as its highest reach of attainment is the earthly paradise, an image of which is presented to us in the festivals celebrating the marriage of the old farmer with Opora.

Birds, however, is paradisal comedy, bizarre, strange, and otherworldly. It is generally considered Aristophanes' most puzzling play, though much admired for its exquisite lyricism and gorgeous spectacle. It has been interpreted as pure fantasy (that is, as having no meaning except wish-fulfillment), as a drama of escape, as a kind of Nietzschean act of impiety, a satire on a Utopian scheme, and even as the description of a plan for the military expansion of Athens.[24] To see it as apocalyptic, as a fantastic dramatization of man's assumption into a spiritual kingdom, is to resolve many of its difficulties.

Like the other two plays, *Birds* begins with a disenchantment with Athens. It is not a desire to save the city, however, that moves the two comrades to set out on their journey to the birds; rather, it is a longing to get away from the tedium and unpleasantness of a community that has lost its life-spirit. Like Dionysus and Xanthias in *Frogs*, Peisthetairos (Plausible) and Euelpides (Helpful) are a pair of good-natured rogues setting out on an ostensibly impossible and, in their case, utterly selfish mission. Guided by a jackdaw and a crow, they wander into wild and desolate country, seeking Tereus, the Hoopoe, who was once the unhappy Thracian king. When he does appear, in his terrifying bird regalia, they manage, despite their fear, to inquire of him where they might find a pleasant city—one where good will and pleasure prevail. Then, on sudden inspiration, they question the Hoopoe about what it's like to live among the birds. "Not much amiss," he tells them. "You don't need a purse here at all" (154-55).

This is of course an appealing thought for the two Athenians. Peisthetairos suddenly comes up with the "happy idea"; "join together and build a bird city" (170). The hoopoe is dubious about the birds' ability to rule a town, but Peisthetairos reminds him that the feathery creatures are accustomed to power: the whole air is their domain, the realm between the gods and men. The hoopoe calls to his wife, the nightingale; great crowds of birds come in response, and, regarding human beings as their worst enemies, fall upon the two travelers with savagery. They are turned back, however, by the hoopoe's advice: You should listen even to your enemies. The two men, quaking with terror, begin to outline their plan. Peisthetairos, taking the lead, reminds the birds of their ancient royalty.

By reference to Aesop's fables and other myths, legends, and proverbs, he engenders in them some pride in their ancestry. The primitive birds, he tells them preceded the deities, the earth, the heavens (475-85). Later, in the lovely lyric choral parabasis, the birds sing of their own origins: In the beginning, a mystical egg was formed out of darkness; out of the egg flew Love, the golden and glorious Eros. This mighty force brought about the engendering that took place between Tartarus and Chaos, the parents of the birds, before the gods had come into being. The birds, then, are more ancient than the gods and have Love alone as their author (689-722). Thus their ancient rights are based on love, not law. The birds are finally convinced that they must have their rightful kingship. Peisthetairos and Euelpides are given an herb that enables them to grow wings and so themselves become, in a sense, birds. They build a huge fortified city, Cloudcuckooland, cutting the gods off from earth, so that the smoke of the offerings made to them is intercepted. The fame of the city spreads on earth, and anything having to do with birds or flying has become highly modish. Mortals seek to reap the benefits of citizenship in the new metropolis. A poet, a prophet, a surveyor, an inspector, a statute salesman, and other opportunists beg with persuasive words to be part of the new city, only to be rejected; they have come after the fact, without sharing in the absurd daring of the mighty deed. Prometheus, still the enemy of Zeus, arrives as a spy to tell the birds that the gods are sending an envoy in an attempt to make peace. He advises Peisthetairos not to accept their terms unless the gods restore the scepter to the birds and offer as wife Basileia (Royalty),[25] the maiden who keeps Zeus's thunderbolts in order. When the embassy arrives, made up of Poseidon, Herakles, and Triballus (one of the primitive gods), Peisthetairos states his terms: the birds will be agents for the gods and will cooperate with them, but only if he is given the maiden Royalty to be his wife. Poseidon objects but is finally overruled. Peisthetairos sends for his wedding garment, and the play ends with the dazzling brilliance of the nuptial celebrations and his general acclamation as lord of all things.

The vision of the mistress of Zeus, Basileia, coming down from Olympus to wed the *poneros* Peisthetairos is deeply shocking. It is like the dream of Bottom, in which he is "translated"—lifted up in the arms of the Fairy Queen. But it is more like the vision in Revelation of the heavens opening and the bride, the heavenly city, the New Jerusalem coming down to wed her beloved. Before one can understand the implications of the Aristophanic apocalypse, however, one needs to look closely at the character of Peisthetairos. Like Dikaiopolis (*Acharnians*), Trygaios (*Peace*), and to some extent Strepsiades (*Clouds*), Philokleon (*Wasps*), and the sausage-seller (*Knights*)—and certainly like the character Dionysus (*Frogs*)—Peisthetairos is an image of the god Dionysus. He loves revelry and pleasure; he is quick-thinking and spirited, outrageous and creative; he hates pretentiousness and pomposity. Though he is childlike and open, his advice is always wise; he is a skillful practitioner of the divine art of persuasion. Words themselves, as he tells one of the supplicants, are winged, a kind of bird. He is, in short, a comic figure of divinity. The crowning of Peisthetairos lord of the cosmos and the celebration of the *hieros gamos* that takes place represent the apotheosis of Dionysus, and along with him, the human race.[26] The gods will be closer to man because of the agency of the birds, ancient remnants of divinity, abiding with human beings as visible symbols of transcendence.

The kingdom of the birds thus represents a liminal region of the soul, wherein resides an intuition of human destiny, the apocalyptic images. The birds themselves are creatures of a universe that can only be imagined, one to which the poet has primary access, a comic terrain concerned less with good and evil than with the qualities of things in themselves and with an overriding *eros* that embraces them. To build a city with the birds is to build an imaginary city, full of lyrical forms and garish, unearthly beauty. Something innate in man is divine, the play tells us, deserving to have its royalty recognized and to be wed to the godhead. *The Birds* is a triumphal vision of things to come and a vindication of the true order that exists unacknowledged and unseen in the present. It is one of the world's few examples of true paradisal comedy.

The kind of transformation Aristophanes accomplishes in his plays is always the result of fantasy: it can be exercised as we have seen, through language, through sexual ecstasy, drinking and feasting, through daring to fly to heaven, setting out to invade the bowels of the underworld, or constructing a city in the sky. But nearly always the basic pattern is the same: the comic hero, the *poneros*, is willing to climb, drag, or hoist himself into this other world by the strength of his hope and his yearning. Whitman says of Aristophanic fantasy that it is "a structure, an elaborate and powerful one"; and he continues, "as such it evokes response from the mind's most basic function, which is to transform the chaotic spate of sense experience into an order of intelligible classes."[27] A fantasy, then, he believes, is an imaginatively constructed reality similar to the mind's creation of intelligible order. In Aristophanes, I maintain, this fantastic structure is not only a way of coping with or evading the intractability of the world but of projecting on the plane of the imagination archetypal and apocalyptic images. These figures allow hidden realities to manifest themselves and so enable the soul to attain the freedom for which it is destined and the city to renew its life-spirit.

For the task undertaken by Aristophanes is nothing short of the regeneration of the earthly city. Several of his parabases—choral odes at midpoint in the plays—indicate overt moral concern for the city; and though these addresses to the audience cannot be taken as literal statements of the poet's aims, they nonetheless serve as a kind of fictional interpretation of the dramas of which they are a part. As breaks in the narrative flow of the plot they serve as openings into the encompassing cosmos in which the plays exist—the world of the comic imagination, which possesses its own intrinsic structures. In his *Commedia* Dante verified the authenticity of his imagined world by having speakers come forward to instruct the two pilgrims and thus become part of the action. But the Aristophanic parabasis reveals the comic terrain in itself, existing independently of the comic plot, as though the characters in the *Inferno* joined hands and came forward to comment on life in general, totally apart from the goings-on around them. Later on, Rabelais, Cervantes, Sterne, Gogol, and others would use this device of apparent address to the reader and for the same effect: not so much to reveal the authors' thoughts on a subject as to open a larger universe in which their comic vision could operate.

In several of the early plays the choral parabases not only praise Aristophanes himself and attack his enemies but go on to a defense of the comic poet in general. The writer of comedies is declared one of the best benefactors of the city, blessing it with his "righteous and true" art that offers protection from flattery and lies (*Acharnians*). In *Wasps*, the parabasis adds a further dimension to the poet's benefits: it is not mere men that he attacks, but a fierce monster. The beast he challenges is "jagged-fanged, red-eyed, dirty, malodorous as a seal, his head covered with hundreds of slavering flattering tongues" (1030-36). The chorus speaks in the same way of the fearsome monster in *Peace* and makes clear that Aristophanes' comic art is a war against this beast, one in which he engages for the good of the people, even if they are unappreciative. These passages establish that it is not individuals against whom the comic writer does battle, but spiritual powers, like Dante's Geryon; Spenser's dragon of Error; Ivan Karamazov's tawdry devil; Faulkner's Flem Snopes—all images of the beast of the Apocalypse, the ultimate source and target of dark comedy. This is the falsehood that can enslave a people, debasing their taste and judgment, devouring their purpose and strength, flattering them into complacency. This monster symbolizes all that is wrong with the earthly city—the powers of darkness which must be overcome if the human enterprise is to prevail. Only in comedy can the beast be seen for what he is, his hollowness revealed by the cathartic principle of laughter.

Hence the comic writer's work is to reveal this essential "banality of evil," to borrow Hannah Arendt's phrase.[28] And the way he performs this task is not only by ridiculing falsehood and vice, but by positing another world over and beyond this one, where the right order of things prevails and harmony and love are dominant. This invisible reality—the comic universe—may exist only as memory or hope for some writers of comedy; or it may lie in the standard domestic happy ending of romance. For the apocalyptic writer, such as Aristophanes, Dante, Dostoevsky, and Flannery O'Connor, this realm is gained by a fantasy, by scaling heaven, so to say, and then, through superimposing one image on another, seeing the ordinary world with a double vision. This duality allows the writer to be possessed by a spirit of nonsense, absurdity, and contradiction, so that he may undertake his supremely difficult task of raising earthly existence to a new plane of being.

Athens failed to heed Aristophanes' warnings, continued its moral decline and its war with Sparta, moving inexorably to its defeat in a parallel course with Aristophanes' comic writings. Did the poet fail? Was the city not aided by his writings? How do we go about answering these questions? We must first admit, I think, that the poet is never concerned primarily with restoring a particular political regime (one thinks of Shakespeare's England, Dostoevsky's Russia, Faulkner's South, Joyce's Dublin) but with giving form to—realizing—the city hidden within the earthly community where the right order of being resides. The city Aristophanes "saved" in these and his other plays makes up a permanent part of the *mundus imaginalis* available to all citizens everywhere through the comic imagination—an image of that one city we keep dreaming of building.

Notes

1. M. C. Bradbrook, *The Growth and Structure of Elizabethan Comedy* (Baltimore, 1963), 21.
2. Walter F. Otto, *Dionysus: Myth and Cult* (Bloomington, Ind., 1965), 79.
3. C. Kerenyi, *Dionysos: Archetypal Image of Indestructible Life* (Princeton, N.J.), 139.
4. Ibid., 179.
5. Otto, 202.
6. Kerenyi, p. 179. Kerenyi makes a distinction between *bios* and *zoe*, the two Greek words for life, the first meaning "characterized life" (xxxiii) and the second, "non-death" (xxxiv). The difference, he feels, is clear: *zoe* presupposes "the experience of *infinite life*" (xxxvi).
7. James Hillman, *The Myth of Analysis* (Evanston, Ill., 1972), 269.
8. Moses Hadas, Introduction, *The Complete Plays of Aristophanes*, ed. Moses Hadas (New York, Toronto, London, 1962), 11.
9. *Anthologia Graeca* IX 186 3-4 (Paton, ed., III, 96), as cited in Kerenyi, 333.
10. Alexis Solomos, *The Living Aristophanes* (Ann Arbor, Mich., 1974), 43.
11. Michail Bakhtin develops the idea of carnival as a popular festive medieval form in *Rabelais and His World*, trans. Helene Iswolsky (Cambridge, Mass., 1968) and *Problems of Dostoevsky' Poetics*, trans. R. W. Rotsel (Ann Arbor, Mich., 1973).

12. Mikhail Bakhtin, *The Dialogic Imagination*, trans. Michael Holquist (Austin, Tex., 1981), 219.

13. C. G. Jung, *Modern Man in Search of a Soul* (New York, 1959), 156–57.

14. For a discussion of the apocalyptic tradition, see Christopher Rowland, *The Open Heaven: A Study of Apocalyptic in Judaism and Early Christianity* (London, 1982); Klaus Koch, *The Rediscovery of Apocalyptic*, trans. Margaret Kohl (Naperville, Ill., 1972); H. H. Rowley, *The Relevance of Apocalyptic*, rev. ed. (New York, 1963); Rudolf Otto, *The Kingdom of God and the Son of Man*, trans. Floyd V. Filson and Bertram Lee-Wolf (London, 1943). The apocalyptic mode, according to Otto and others, was not "purely" Jewish, but eclectic, partaking of Oriental and Hellenistic elements as well. I mean to be treating it as a mode of vision universally available to the poetic imagination, totally apart from its special revelation in the Judaeo-Christian tradition.

15. Northrop Frye, *Anatomy of Criticism* (Princeton, N.J., 1957), 141.

16. It is no longer agreed among scholars, as it was until fairly recently, that a secret cult of "Orphism" existed among the Greeks, that it was from fragments of an Orphic apocalypse that Plato took his details of the Other World, or that Aristophanes' *Birds* is a parody of an Orphic "Theogony." See E. E. Dodds, *The Greeks and the Irrational* (Berkeley, Los Angeles, 1951), 147–56.

17. Rudolf Otto, *The Kingdom of God and the Son of Man*, 57.

18. Kerenyi, xxviii–xxix.

19. This is Jeffrey Henderson's phrase: *The Maculate Muse: Obscene Language in Attic Comedy* (New Haven, 1975).

20. Cedric Whitman, *Aristophanes and the Comic Hero* (Cambridge. Mass., 1964), 269.

21. See Whitman's brilliant analysis of this quality in the Aristophanic comic hero, 29–58.

22. Aristophanes, *Acharnians*, 195–98. The line numbers cited for all the plays refer to the Greek text of Aristophanes edited by F. W. Hall and W. M. Geldart (Clarendon: Oxford Press, 1906–07). I have consulted and compared the following translations: *Acharnians*: Patric Dickinson, vol. 1 (Oxford Univ. Press, 1970); Douglass Parker, The Mentor Greek Comedy Series (New American Library, 1961); B. B. Rogers, vol. 1 (William Heinemann Ltd., G. P. Putnam's Sons, 1927); Alan H. Sommerstein, *The Comedies of Aristophanes*, vol. 1 (Aris and Philips, Ltd.: Biddles Ltd., 1980); *Birds*: William Arrowsmith (Ann Arbor: Univ. of Michigan Press, 1961); Dickinson, vol. 2; Dudley Fitts, *Four Comedies* (Harcourt Brace, 1954); Gilbert Murray (London, 1908); Rogers, vol. 2; R. H. Webb, in Hades; *Lysistrata*: Dickinson, vol. 2; Fitts; Douglass Parker, in *Four Comedies by Aristophanes*, ed. William Arrowsmith (Univ. of Michigan Press, 1961); Rogers; R. H. Webb (Univ. of Virginia Press, 1963); *Peace*: Dickinson, vol. 1; Rogers, vol. 2.

23. Douglass Parker, Introduction, *Lysistrata*, in *Four Comedies by Aristophanes*.

24. For a comprehensive survey of critical opinion concerning *Birds*, see Arrowsmith's introduction to his brilliant translation.

25. K. J. Dover, in *Aristophanic Comedy* (Berkeley and Los Angeles, 1972),

argues convincingly from the scansion of the lines that the Greek word is *basileia*, queen, a title of goddesses, not *basileia*, monarchy (p. 31).

26. Gilbert Murray, in the introduction to his translation (London, 1966), refutes the apparent "impiety" of the ending of the play by referring to the familiarity of the Greeks with the vegetation cults, in which an old king is overthrown by a new. He cites a passage from the *Orphica*: "His father seats him on the royal throne, puts the sceptre in his hand, and makes him king of the Cosmic gods" (p. 7).

27. Whitman, p. 260.

28. Hannah Arendt, *Eichmann in Jerusalem: A Report on the Banality of Evil* (New York, 1963).

4

Dante, Hegel, and the Comedy of History

BAINARD COWAN

THE happy ending in comedy always comes under the sign of the impossible or the miraculous; it is that which cannot come about yet does. The comic solution can be seen retrospectively as having taken place, but it cannot be projected in advance as a workable solution inherent in the nature of things or in human capacities for progress. And yet an affirmative view of history, so far from being foreign to comedy, forms part of its very essence.

As a theory of history, comedy has to be a way of seeing events unfold by a logic not their own—perhaps, in some instances, by a nonlogic. The comic form is itself the way of seeing, a sudden shaping up of events into a recognizable figure, a concord or temporary truce. Interpretation is the catalyst in this sudden transformation, hinging as it does on the recognition of form and hence of meaning. Yet the interpretation required is often so strained or improbable that comedy frequently resorts to allegory, transmuting pain, suffering, and mindless destruction into their opposites. In so reversing the meaning of the action it portrays, comedy gives a form to events that is not implicit in any one of them. This reversal and imposition is so radical that in fact comedy may be said to be about the transmutation of events into form through interpretation. If this is so, therein would lie what comedy has to tell us about history, for designating any set of events a "history" implies that they have a story to tell, a lesson inherent in their sequence, a coherence, a form.

In thinking of pain, suffering, and destruction together with the term *comedy*, one begins to tread a worn path in literary history that eventually leads back to the strange coexistence of Dante's long poem of suffering and distress with the title he gave it—*Commedia*. Often viewed as a misnomer that little reflects the content or spirit of the poem, the term *commedia* was in fact chosen by Dante with deliberate logic. His comments on poetic genre in his letter to Can Grande reveal something of the broad cultural web his choice touches upon:

> A comedy is a certain kind of poetic narration different from all others. It differs then from tragedy in subject matter, for a tragedy at the beginning is admirable and quiet and at the end or outcome it is foul and horrible; . . . A comedy begins with some adversity but its subject ends prosperously, as is seen through Terence in his comedies. . . . Likewise they differ in their manner of speech: tragedy is elevated and sublime, comedy is careless and humble, as Horace says in his *Art of Poetry*, where he allows that sometimes comedians speak like tragedians and vice versa:
>
> > Yet sometimes comedy her voice will raise,
> > And angry Chremes scold with swelling phrase;
> > And prosy periods oft our ears assail
> > When Telephus and Peleus tell their tragic tale.
>
> And therefore it is evident why the present work is called a comedy, for if we look at the subject, at the beginning it is horrible and foul because it is Hell; at the end it is happy, desirable, and pleasing, because it is Paradise. If we look at the manner of speech, it is lowly and humble because it is vulgar speech which even simple women use. And thus it is evident why it is called a comedy.[1]

Robert Hollander has recently dealt with the problem of Dante's designating his poetic style as "low," because it is in the vernacular and uses the resources of all levels of diction. This strategy, Hollander shows, allows Dante to assert several points crucial to the stature of his undertaking. He can maintain his difference from "tragic" Virgil of the "high" style (being at once subservient to and spiritually more enlightened than his great mentor). He can demonstrate his own full participation in the Christian humble style, the *sermo humilis*

(Hollander's reference is to Erich Auerbach's definitive essay on early Christian style), and therefore his historic mission of working "humbly" with "low" material for a supremely high purpose.[2] These distinctions take quotation marks here because they are based on a codified equation now lost to us, the classical prescription of high style for epic and tragedy, middle style for history and oratory, and low style for lyric and comedy. Even in the part of his definition that adheres strictly to these distinctions, however, Dante leaves room to imply a theology of history impelling his choice of poetic medium, the theology derived from the Incarnation that defines the role for Christ's followers as a humbling of self in order to redeem the world.

Thus Dante's first definition, "a comedy begins with some adversity but its subject ends prosperously," is hidden within and dominates the second definition that hinges on the more strictly generic categorization of styles. The movement from adversity to solution enunciates a pattern that Nevill Coghill has shown to be the recurrent structure of comedy in the Middle Ages and in Shakespeare, in contrast to the classical view of comedy as ridicule of vice, which Ben Jonson's comedies adopt.[3] Clearly linking the comic plot to Christian doctrine, Medieval writers on genre such as Vincent of Beauvais often identified the adversity-to-prosperity structure explicitly with the progress of the soul to God. Dante himself makes this identification later in the same letter to Can Grande, when he illustrates the fourfold way of reading his poem by exegeticizing the Psalm verse "In exitu Israel de Aegypto," seeing the ultimate meaning of the Exodus as the flight of the soul from the bondage of sin to its salvation in Christ. Indeed, as Coghill's findings indicate, what makes stylistic features of Medieval comedy remarkable is not so much their mere use as the fact that in using them a writer was aware of their underlying connections to theology: comedy was viewed by poets and poetic theorists alike as a mimesis or interpretation of the Christian plot of history and the progress of the soul.

Auerbach's and Coghill's tracings of cultural lines indicate the deep and coherent system of thought out of which the *Divine Comedy* emerges. Admittedly, however, such indications may be no more than ideological if they are not fully motivated in the poetic text. And there remains the problem that to read Dante's poem is to be made excruciatingly aware of the extent of human depravity and misdirection, the stuff of real history and not of mere theory. In turning to the poem itself one must therefore face this critique and either discard the notion of Christian comedy as a pious misrepresentation of Dante's portrait of the confusion of his age or commit oneself to seeing more closely how comedy assimilates the pain, suffering, and destruction with which it must work.

Comic theorists are right in insisting that what makes actions laughable is their emotional distance from reader or audience; and Dante's principle of distantiation in the *Inferno* is massive and absolute, unmatched by lesser works of any age; it is the stern, unpitying scorn for the nothingness at the heart of all self-seeking human action. Hollander brings to our attention the comment by Dante's contemporaneous commentator Guido da Pisa that Christ has no compassion for the damned because "in this world there is time for mercy, in the other only time for justice."[4] The moment of judgment in comedy participates in the final character of the apocalypse; and the progress through the realms beyond death, in Dante's poem, is in part a process of coming to understand how the harshness of judgment can be part of the redemptive movement of comedy.

Dante does not soften the force of that crossroads between judgment and redemption; he is not concerned as Wordsworth was to gloss over this abyss apotropaically, nor like Milton to justify God's ways to man. What Dante does is to make "justice" uncanny. In the inscription over hell gate, in *Inferno* 3, the cruelty of the infernal regions is equated with love: "JUSTICE MOVED MY HIGH MAKER; THE DIVINE POWER MADE ME, THE SUPREME WISDOM, AND THE PRIMAL LOVE."[5] The words state baldly the absolute that governs the entire poem, but they are written in stone, both literally and in the biblical metaphorical sense. Dante the traveler is alienated from that pronouncement and cannot understand it: he turns to Virgil for some explanation, beseeching, "Maestro, il senso lor m'è duro ("Master, their meaning is hard for me," 12). Charles Singleton glosses *duro* as meaning "hard to understand," with a possible connotation of "harsh," juridically severe. Surely the primary meaning of *duro*—"hard" as in stone—must lie here as an undertone as well. It is impenetrable for Dante, and Virgil must "read" its meaning not by explicating it but by telling how to respond to it. In contrast to the last line of the inscription, "ABANDON EVERY HOPE, YOU WHO ENTER" (9), he counsels, "here must all fear be left behind; here let all cowardice be dead" (14-15).

Virgil virtually reverses the literal message of the inscription in giving Dante the meaning-for-their-journey. His response indicates the crucial function Virgil is to have for his companion on the pilgrimage. Virgil's activity in the *Divine Comedy* is hermeneutic, and not least because he stands in the role of Hermes, conductor between the living and the dead. His role of go-between is also that of interpreter, conductor between is and ought, between the actual and the ethical. But he is with Dante precisely because that bridge of understanding between the two poles is not actually there: it is not within Dante, and it is lost forever to the souls in hell. As long as he accompanies Dante he serves as a living stand-in for the comprehension Dante has not yet acquired.

It is not only Dante who is in the predicament of being unable to read. The notion of justice seems nowhere to intrude into the self-understanding of the damned. On the other hand, Virgil apparently thinks better of trying to explain how justice, wisdom, and love can found a place of infinite punishment. The message of the inscription, and hence the entire premise of the *Inferno*, is indeed unreadable. "LA SOMMA SAPIENZA," the supreme wisdom, is unattainable by human understanding: even to Nino de' Visconti, one of the redeemed, God is "He who so hides his primal purpose that there is no fording thereunto" (*Purg.* 8, 68-69).

From the beginning, then, the point of view represented by the concept "justice" is given as a seeming self-contradiction, an *aporia* that opens up an abyss for the progressing soul as well as for the reader of the account. This is precisely the gap between the letter of the law and its spirit, according to Saint Paul, between the iron bondage to the law in the old dispensation and the freedom from the law in the new. But at the same time it is announced as a goal that the reader and Dante must strive to comprehend the two as one. The sense of progress insofar as it happens within the journey of the *Comedy* is equated with a growth of understanding. Hence the journey must begin at a place where understanding is at an absolute loss, at the entry into hell, where Virgil informs Dante that here they will see "the wretched people who have lost the good of the intellect" (*Inf.* 3, 17-18).

While Virgil is pointing out the most prominent souls among those damned for lust, Dante the narrator paraphrases this demonstration by saying that Virgil named those whom love had parted from life, "ch'amor di nostra vita dipartille" (*Inf.* 5, 69). This statement, with its echo of "nostra vita" in the first line of the poem, is a clue to the disjunctive state in which the poem begins. Love and life are at opposite poles from each other, according to a literal reading of Dante's line; or, to put the matter more accurately, the *understanding* of these two essences places them here poles apart.

This is hardly a solely theoretical understanding: it carries the lived ineradicability of two fated lovers. When Dante first sees Francesca and Paolo and desires to speak with them, Virgil suggests he entreat them "per quello amor che i mena" (5, 78), by that (particular) love that guides *them*, a divisive love separating them from others and from eternal life. What characterizes this scene and the entire spirit of the *Inferno* is the multiplication of differences, divisive differences which serve to alienate and set at odds fellow from fellow and man from Creator. When Francesca speaks of Paolo's love for her she speaks of her "fair form that was *taken* from me (emphasis added, 5, 101-02). The only unification spoken of in this episode is one equated with death: "Amor condusse noi ad *una* morte" (emphasis added): love led us to *one* death (5, 106). Paolo is referred to as the one "who will never be parted [*diviso*] from me" (135); and Francesca's final monologue, telling of the scene of their first adultery, overcome as they were by passion while together reading of the kiss of Lancelot, concludes with the famous understatement: "that day we read no farther" (5, 138).

The entire episode depicts a stopping of reading. Francesca's is a consciousness that perceives only disjunction, with no way of "reading" or understanding the partitions. God is "il re de l'universo" (5, 91), a feudal king whose will is not only inscrutable but unintelligible—the question of its making sense or not never even arises. Such a consciousness develops its own erotic dynamics, to be sure, and it is one in which oneness is desired everywhere, is found nowhere, and is finally embraced in death.

No laughter sounds in the hell of Paolo and Francesca. The impact of their experience seems to threaten an extinction to understanding, the demise of a divine coalition between justice and love. Dante's reaction to the tale of the lovers is radically disjunctive: he swoons. This is rather the opposite of an act of understanding, and in the next canto he awakes literally in a lower, not a higher, place than before. Virgil must explain to Dante that he has fallen into the next circle of hell. Because Virgil's commenting presence is needed through so many episodes in hell, it becomes clear that the ability to reflect and interpret is absolutely necessary to redeem human experience of any sort. This point comes home all the more sharply the farther down into hell the two poets journey, as they move from the still-dignified shades such as Farinata, Pier delle Vigne, and Brunetto Latini, who possess elaborate but parodically limited interpretations of their lives, to the souls such as Maestro Adamo and Ugolino, who can scarcely be called individuals any more. The constant aggression of these latter shades toward an other—Adamo attacking Sinon and Ugolino eternally gnawing the nape of Ruggieri—typifies an existence of reaction, not reflection. In an unending closed circle that no longer permits hermeneutic activity at all, their action has degenerated to what Renè Girard calls "reciprocal violence."

To contrast this imprisonment within the vicious circle of unreflective revenge with the breaking out of the circle necessary for interpretation, one might take the scene in *Inferno* 30 in which Dante observes the grotesque quarrel between Maestro Adamo and Sinon as it gathers splenetic rage, each shade intent only on taunting the other with his own foulness. They become violent mirrors of each other, caught in a shrinking circle of imitation in which one's enemy becomes one's double. And when Virgil's words to Dante interrupt the narration of this battle—"Or pur mira," as Singleton translates it, "Now just you keep on looking!" (30, 131)—suddenly we realize that Dante has been drawn into this circle as well and that, standing there and taking it all in for his own enjoyment or curiosity, he has failed to distance himself from the morally collapsed world of the souls in hell. Dante here exhibits all the marks of the non-reader that characterize him throughout the crucial early scenes of the *Commedia*, marks of inattention and naiveté that are not too different from the habits we impute nowadays to our media-saturated youth: fascination, interest in spectacle, vicarious identification with erotic or violent scenes, idle question-posing, and disregard for logical consequences or larger implications. And once again it is Virgil who wrenches Dante out of this closed circle, in this instance through sarcasm so biting that Dante is still smarting in the next canto from the words that were "both poison and cure" to him.

This scene is far from being the only one in the *Inferno* that accomplishes a distancing from the actions of the damned. Most frequently such removal of the wayfarers from the world of the lost souls is accomplished simply by some act of judgment by Dante and Virgil that may be as crude as their shoving Filippo Argenti off the ferry and back into the Styx (a judgment in which, for the first time, Dante participates, so that Virgil exclaims with joy, "Indignant soul, blessed is she who bore you!" 8, 45).[6]

There is always more than a hint of farce in these scenes.[7] A more subtle, if less famous, example occurs in *Inferno* 19, where Pope Nicholas III lies plunged head down in filth among the simonists. Unable to see, he hears Dante's approach and supposes it to be the long-awaited arrival of his hated successor, Boniface VIII. To the comedy of mistaken identity is added the kind of stock-comic episode in which a character, placed in utterly besmirching circumstances, mocks himself further by ridiculous attempts to maintain his pretenses of dignity. Nicholas is the first of those many damned who await the coming of an other—always a mirror of themselves—whom they can abuse and torment eternally. Thus Nicholas addresses his supposed co-resident, reminding him of his simony as he ostensibly inquires, with rhetorical skill, concerning his appearance in hell before his appointed time: "Are you so quickly sated with those gains for which you did not fear to take by guile the beautiful Lady, and then to do her outrage?" (55–57). The Lady is the Church, and Nicholas is condemning himself unawares. Dante, fully his equal in rhetorical strategies, answers and identifies himself by way of condemning Nicholas and distancing himself from him—"therefore stay right there (*ti sta*), for you are justly punished" (97; again Dante uses the reflexive for distancing). Launching into a diatribe against simony that ends with a full denunciation of the Donation of Constantine, Dante so astounds Nicholas that he is unable to retort, but instead, as Dante observes, "whether anger or conscience stung him, he kicked hard with both his feet. And indeed I think it pleased my guide, with so satisfied a look did he keep listening to the sound of the true words uttered'' (119-23). One almost sees the comic "humors" of the Renaissance stage come alive here; but running in stern counterpoint to this business is the real barb of the joke, the truth ("the true words uttered"), expressed in an inexorable judgment that reveals the damned, by their chosen self-ignorance, to be eternally marked as bad and hence eternally laughable.

In short nearly all the episodes of the *Inferno* make clear that the moment of judgment is what gives form to Dante's experience of the shades he encounters. This moment announces the failure of interpretation in the lives, both past and present, of those unhappy souls from whom Dante separates himself by his judgment. Further, it constitutes the working of interpretation—albeit at its most brief and rudimentary—in Dante's life. We may recall from Coghill's important distinction between Jonsonian and Shakespearean comedy that the theory dominating the ancient rhetorical approach to comedy and culminating in Ben Jonson views the comic art as a tool of moral discernment and castigation of vices. Although Coghill is right in linking Dante to the other, salvific theory of comedy emerging in late antiquity and the Middle Ages, one must affirm that Dante's hell is governed by the grimly moral classical outlook. It is in the *Inferno* that character remains constant and unchangeable, as it was required to be on the ancient stage.

Purgatory presents a quite different theater; it is, as the title of Francis Fergusson's book aptly states it, Dante's drama of the mind. In this realm of transition and motion, it is not Dante's mind alone in which we observe the stirrings of interpretive activity: every soul present here has already undergone a drastic reinterpretation of his own life, a conversion that, like Augustine's in the *Confessions*, requires a radical re-envisioning of one's own past and aims. As if to emphasize the crucial character of his moment of reinterpretation, Buonconte da Montefeltro appears as one of the first souls Dante encounters in the Antepurgatorio. The son of one of the most grotesque damned souls described in the *Inferno*, Buonconte led a dissolute life, but as he lay dying, his throat slit, his eyes already blind, he whispered the name of the Blessed Virgin. This could be called an act of self-reinterpretation simply because it stands in such marked contrast to all that has gone before in his life. It is nonetheless a shockingly minimal pivot upon which to base a re-reading of Buonconte's character, and the angel of hell that comes for Buonconte feels cheated of his soul and takes his body as revenge, washing it into the Arno. Buonconte must wait for unspecified ages before he can actually enter purgatory, but clearly the crucial swerve has been accomplished.

Quite often the souls Dante meets in purgatory—for instance, Omberto Aldobrandesco, Oderisi, Sapia, Pope Adrian V—voluntarily castigate their own past life, naming the vice that they now see particularly characterized them on earth. Furthermore, the structure of Mount Purgatory can be said to be heuristic, designed to lead the sinner to new understanding of the wrongness of his sin and the necessity for consistent practice of virtue. The ingenious carved reliefs exhibited on all the levels of the mountain announce their own function, giving historic examples of particular vices and virtues and calling for the active responses of the viewer. When a group of souls makes their way up the First Terrace chanting the Our Father, they intersperse each verse of the prayer with two verses of exegetical comment.

Hence the whole of Dante's action portrayed in the *Commedia* demonstrates that it is comedy, among all the poetic genres, that is most consistently concerned with reflection and interpretation. As we know, however, few of Dante's interpreters in his own time and afterward successfully grasped his implicit point about comedy. It remained for the generation of the Romantics to intuit the interior action of mental awakening and self-renouncing progress in the *Commedia*. Of the theorists of comedy it is Hegel who most clearly explains the philosophical basis for the intellectuality of comedy, and hence, if we are to follow to its analytic deep structure this paradoxical conjunction of comedy and justice that informs Dante's poem—a paradox, as I have suggested, that is at the heart of the comic view of history—we must now turn to some exposition of the thought of another of the West's most complex and difficult writers. Hayden White, in his pioneering study of literary form in history writing, terms Hegel's work "comic on the macrocosmic" level and maintains that in it an entire philosophy of history is envisioned from the essential perspective of comedy. For Hegel, says White, "comedy is the form which reflection takes after it has assimilated the truths of tragedy to itself."[8]

The very action of reflection, then, according to White, takes on a comic coloration in Hegel's interpretation of history, and indeed one must be aware of this dimension in order to perceive the depth of Hegel's thought. For the *Philosophy of History* is far from the blithe optimism it is often charged with being: the moments of triumph and progress Hegel posits are won, in the last analysis, only at the cost of devastating destruction and loss. The words "triumph" and "progress," in his thought, shed their root Latin meaning of a public procession by the official regime; the victory of which Hegel speaks is one that only consciousness in its essential form, apart from all its cultural supports, finally attains and preserves.

Yet it is striking that Hegel's scene for this victory of consciousness is not the lonely study-room of the philosopher but the escaping wagon of the comic hero. Progress is won *in history*, according to Hegel, by the birth of that frame of mind to which only comedy can provide access. Hegel maintains in his *Lectures on Aesthetics* that the comic vision consists in an "infinite light-heartedness and confidence felt by someone raised altogether above his own inner contradiction and not bitter or miserable in it at all." The comic frame of mind is accordingly "a hale condition of soul which, fully aware of itself, can bear the dissolution of its aims and achievements."[9]

Whereas the hero or heroine in comedy is characterized either by the gradual growth into this hale condition of soul or the steady possession of it, the action depicted in comedy—and especially what may be called the enveloping action, the social-historical condition—does not necessarily, according to Hegel, demonstrate such growth or healthiness at all: "in the action of comedy the contradiction between what is absolutely (*an und für sich*) true and its specific realization is posed more profoundly" (1201). Thereby comedy is distinct from romance, which strives constantly to annihilate the difference between the real and the ideal essence of a situation. Equally, however, Hegel insists that comedy is not nihilistically satiric in negating the existence of an essentially true world, even though it exposes the contradictoriness and even despicability of the real. The character of comedy consists in its maintenance of difference between the two realms; for while it never renounces the real world, it nevertheless "assigns neither the victory nor, in the last resort, permanence, in the real world to folly and unreason, to false oppositions and contradictions'' (1202).

Hegel makes these comments apropos of Aristophanes, but they might be applied with even greater justice to Dante. In his remarks on the *Divine Comedy*, elsewhere in the *Aesthetics*, Hegel makes clear that he sees Dante's poem as engaged poetically in work very much like what he has hoped to accomplish in philosophy. Mark Taylor has brought out Hegel's acknowledged reliance on Saint Bonaventure's *Itinerary of the Soul toward God*, a twelfth-century spiritual tract that was also formative for Dante as the structure for his poem.[10] Hence Hegel's admiration for the *Divine Comedy* not only outstripped the prevailing Romantic appreciation of Dante but was, in terms he would approve, a form of self-admiration in admiration of the other.

Hegel focuses on the ability of comedy to transform potentially tragic events by subjecting them to interpretation. The death of Socrates at the hands of the Athenian government seemed to bring the irony and fatality of tragedy off the stage and into historical reality; but in Hegel's view, Aristophanes was able to redeem those events for comedy by portraying Socrates as a comic type, exaggerating his character to accord with the destructive side alone of his philosophical method. Dante, as we have seen, carried the transformative nature of comedy even further, using love as well as justice as a means of distancing his inferno and hence viewing with increasing detachment dozens of personal tragedies ending in destruction and eternal torment. In numerous instances Dante is portrayed as leaving with a sense of relief, even of narrow escape, the shades he has met. Following the motif of the journey, comic distantiation in the *Inferno* takes on a literal spatiality, a repetition of rites of passage, culminating in his crawling headfirst down Satan's body to exit from hell.

For both these authors it is not a subjectivity *within* the work that could be termed "triumphant": Socrates in the *Clouds* is smoked out of his think tank, and Dante's pilgrim leaving hell is a mere survivor who does not have the time, energy, or spiritual presence to reflect: "I did not die and I did not remain alive; now think for yourself [reader], if you have any wit, what I became, deprived alike of death and life!" (*Inf.* 34, 25-27). Dante's address to the reader at this point is telling: what triumph there is here consists not in the mind of the protagonist but in the *sense* of the comic action, the clear vision of what is left standing after the destructive judgment of the bad has been accomplished.

In an important exposition of Hegel on comedy, Anne Paolucci emphasizes the social and political aspects of his argument.[11] She notes that, according to his thought, comedy is the "universal dissolvent" that removes "the accumulated debris of *anciens regimes* or outworn conventions and standards" (92). Its function is "to clear away the one-sided insistence on prejudices of all kinds, formal beliefs, and misdirected actions" (93). Through its agency, society is made more tolerant of its own idiosyncrasies and comes to see its standards as capable of a great deal more variation than tragedy would allow. According to Paolucci's interpretation of Hegel, "Comedy is the exhaustion of an age and clears the stage for what follows; it is historically a *negative* force." On the other hand, continues Paolucci, comedy is "a positive force . . . in its own right, beyond history," as a form "in which the comic poet traces the refracted, multifaceted reflection of his age . . . in order to expose sham and restore through ridicule and laughter a proper balance." Thus Hegel, according to this author, maintains that the comic catharsis "prepares our own hearts, as well as the stage of history, for the restoration of essential values in a new social structure" (93).[12]

We may sum up these points by saying that for Hegel comedy functions as a clearinghouse at the end of a particular civilizational course. The triumph of the strong personality "over the ruin of serious things that are beyond salvation" (104), as Paolucci phrases it, at once unswervingly looks at the corruption of a civilization and affirms that somehow life, strength, and joy will survive. To Hegel this affirmation marks the highest achievement of all art. He concludes his *Aesthetics* on this note: "We end with the romantic art of emotion and deep feeling where absolute subjectivity moves free in itself and in the spiritual world. Satisfied in itself, it no longer unites itself with anything objective and particularized and it brings the negative side of this dissolution into consciousness in the humor of comedy" (1236).

Comedy is thus the form that most purely expresses Hegel's view of the movement of history—a progress only because life and consciousness survive, and thus in a measure redeem, the catastrophic falls of great civilizations. The most strikingly historical element in Hegel's analysis of comedy, then, is its identification with the *dissolution* of a civilization rather than with the formation of new social bonds, as Northrop Frye has maintained. This interpretation of history is a highly paradoxical one. However, the way to a thoroughgoing irony and satire is barred by Hegel, who, as we have seen, distinguishes strictly between comedy and satire. The bitterness of satire, the *collapse* of meaning brought about in irony, may be employed by comedy but cannot be its distinguishing note. But neither can the *completion* of meaning be proper to comedy: the progressive schemes of history, epic projects of civilization, are defeated by the comic consciousness, which arrives too late and has seen too much for such naiveté. The comic consciousness has learned to rise above the destruction of its own aims, not in the retreat of stoicism, however, but in laughter.

Hegel is aware, as he points out, of how many faces laughter can assume, by no means all of them producing the comic note. But a certain mode of laughter can be understood as explicating comedy. Like the breaking out of speech, laughter is a marking of the impossible passage into affirmation and redemption after the moment when it has come to appear as impossible. Hegel's view of laughter would accord in part with Baudelaire's comment in his essay "On the Essence of Laughter": "Joy is a unity; laughter is the expression of a double, or contradictory, feeling: and that is why a convulsion occurs."[13] The distinguishing mark of comic laughter then, one would say, is the crossing over—or crossing out—of the contradictory without doing away with it, indeed while still preserving it.

As a view of history the crossing of comic laughter is therefore one with the Judaeo-Christian belief that the pattern of history was first given in the crossing of the Red Sea, an impossible passage that should remind us, though it all too seldom does, that some passages are impossible *even if they are successful*. Similarly, crossing this passage in the opposite direction, Dante relies on the Augustinian view that even the worst catastrophes in history are not utter defeats because secular history is preeminently a track of vagaries, violent and regrettable, while the invisible City of God advances and grows in the same place as these disasters, but disjunct from them, escaping them.

The impossible or miraculous transition, as I am trying to develop it here, though it is not a point explicitly recognized by Hegel, is one to which his analysis implicitly leads, particularly in his insistence upon two equally preeminent features of comedy: catastrophe and triumph. The comic wisdom arising from the contemplation of these two moments affirms life, love, virtue, and intelligence, while sparing no illusions about their permanence in civilized institutions. This is precisely the consciousness into which Dante grows in the course of the *Commedia*. Encountering the exempla of all the virtues in Paradise one by one, he comes to understand them with increasing intimacy at the same time that he realizes with ever greater sharpness their absence in Florence and the warring neighbor-states of his day.

Before he makes his famous final affirmation of love in the last line of the *Paradiso*, Dante has had to come to accept as permanent his status as exile. Several prophecies made to him throughout his journey have given him an inkling of his destiny; it remains for his ancestor Cacciaguida to state it baldly and for Dante, in contemplation of its bitterness, to pledge to himself his obligation to write the truth. Even though it may lose him what little favor he still may have among his patrons, he realizes that he faces harsher judgment from future generations if he courts favor and betrays his calling: "I have learned that which, if I tell again, will have for many a savor of great bitterness; and if I am a timid friend to the truth, I fear to lose life among those who shall call this time ancient" (*Par.* 17, 116–20).

Cacciaguida's reply carries a triumphant note: "But none the less, all falsehood set aside, make manifest all that you have seen; and then let them scratch where the itch is. For if at first taste your voice be grievous, yet shall it leave thereafter vital nourishment when digested" (17, 127–32). His tone here is "comic" in the stylistic sense, using "low" words, as Singleton notes. This tone emerges precisely at the moment reached in comedy when the hero realizes his release from the limitations of his own historical moment: disregard the immediate, supposedly practical consequences—"let them scratch where the itch is." The action of comedy always moves toward liberation, and this is Dante's moment. Paradoxically, he has just learned of how tied to his own earthly fate he will be; but with the help of his ancestor and co-citizen he achieves the supernal point of view that has separated out the chaff of history and can laugh at it.

The affirmation of the substantive out of a portrayal of mostly nothing but the insubstantial—this is the essence of Hegel's characterization of comedy. It is also the kernel of allegory in all comedy. One might just as well call it the kernel of the impossible, for allegory is essentially a form of the impossible. It arises at times in history when bridges between the real and the commonly accepted vision of the ideal are manifestly absent in cultural forms. As a discourse that speaks of the bridge between real and ideal worlds, it cannot do so without leaving unmistakable traces everywhere of the failure of that bridge. To call comedy allegorical or impossible, however, is not to diminish or annul its note of triumph. Thus Hegel can assert, "And when the essentially unsubstantial has destroyed its show of existence by its own agency, the individual makes himself master of this dissolution too and remains undisturbed in himself and at ease" (*Aesthetics*, 1202).

Hegel strikes the note of allegory at the end of his *Aesthetics*, when explaining what he means by dissolution and the negative function of the absolute in comedy. There he points out that although comedy achieves the triumph of bringing the dissolution of the particular into full consciousness, "yet on this peak comedy leads at the same time to the dissolution of art altogether" (1236). Here is the moment of *Aufhebung*—the simultaneous culmination and dissolution of art in comedy. What does this "peak" (*Gipfel*) imply, however, but that consciousness is always other than its own form—that difference, and most centrally difference from itself, is the preeminent condition of consciousness? Had Hegel pursued this implication further he might have evolved a quite different aesthetic, one not so biased (although his comments acknowledge his bias) toward the necessity of a unity of inner and outer expression. An aesthetic of tensions rather than correspondences is what Hegel's aesthetics strives to be all along. Even the identity of substance and subject, eternal and ephemeral, is achieved "*only as its self-destruction*, because the Absolute, which wants to realize itself, sees its self-actualization destroyed by interests that have now become explicitly free in the real world and are directed only on what is accidental and subjective" (emphasis added). In the end—in history—culmination and destruction are indissolubly related. And if this paradox seems like a tragic insight, Hegel is asserting rather that it is precisely comic. To maintain that culmination is otherwise would be to monumentalize it in a way that finally denies life as well as the activity of interpretation, the very stuff of comedy and philosophy.

The two concepts that bring Dante and Hegel together in their view of comedy and of history, then, would be reconciliation and distantiation. The latter of these—equivalent to Hegel's "judgment" in his *Aesthetics*—is an improvement on Northrop Frye's term "displacement," which indexes the society a given comedy portrays along a line from the utterly bad to a paradisal kind of dream-fulfillment that is completely "undisplaced" and is self-admittedly no longer comedy but romance.[14] Distantiation, by contrast, would be a perpetual factor, an ineradicable difference which persists and casts everything in a light that does not ridicule, scorn, nor sentimentalize, but redeems. Moreover, this redemption comes without miraculously transforming reality into the wholly unreal, as in romance.

Usually comedy finds a way of expressing this paradoxical perspective by presenting in some way a coexistence of opposites. In *The Second Shepherd's Play*, for instance, the low-life shepherds suddenly are shifted to the setting of the Incarnation, the supreme moment of coexistence of the high and the low in all history. Dante's recurrent device is the juxtaposition of individual lives lived in ordinary human scale but cast against an eternal setting. And this strategy achieves more than to affirm all in a sentimental negation of reason, an all-forgiving amnestic gesture which could only be made in bad faith—"God bless us every one." In contrast to Dickens, Blake wrote, "A Last Judgment is Necessary because Fools flourish." Seen from Dante's perspective, which, again, is made explicit in Hegel's comments, comedy performs the action of winnowing out history, a function fulfilled in stage comedies by casting out the pharmakos. What is false, petty, or impermanent is finally driven out or away in comedy. And whereas Dante drives out these money-changers in the name of God the Father, he draws his power to do so from his poetic imagination. He thus stands to Hegel as a model for the self-sufficient spirit accounting to itself for all of history—the "triumph of subjectivity."

Where modern existentialist commentators on Hegel tend to find him especially unacceptable is in his recurring claims, throughout his system, for reconciliation. But the reconciliation Hegel sees in comedy is not the closing of the circle that the Hegelian Romantic (or the

Romantic Hegel) sometimes dreams of: it is more in the nature of a working compromise, an uneasy peace, or truce, between the spirit and the world as it is. The notion of "judgment" sticks like a sharp bone beneath the soft flesh of this "peace." Reconciliation in comedy demands hard choices: it is not a complete making-over of the world in the image of the heart's desire, but neither is it a resignation to a sadly imperfect world. And against the argument often taken in praise or blame of comedy (often seen in critical studies of comedy of manners), it must be said that comic reconciliation is not a return to the socially acceptable norm. It is the recognition of a norm, however—a norm that lies beyond any currently existing manifestation: a norm that exposes the paltriness of the purported norms. In some way, too, that incommensurable norm takes on life and vibrancy, coming to dominate the existing human scene and to stamp it with the insignia of irrational joy.

In the *Paradiso* Piccarda Donati makes her famous statement that she is content with her station in heaven because "in his will is our peace" (3, 85). That her life has an outcome of comic joy is a radical expression of the triumph of comedy over tragedy, one close to Dante's own life since he married into the Donati family and was a close friend of Piccarda's brother Forese. Her other brother, Corso, forced Piccarda into a hated marriage which she did not long survive; and it is significant that both Piccarda and Forese, whom Dante has encountered earlier in the *Purgatorio*, avoid mention of Corso's name. Corso seems to be a comic villain, a pharmakos who is so thoroughly chased off the stage that there is no trace left of him. Whereas on earth tragedy can turn into comedy through the slow workings of society against its own grain, through compromises and judgments, Dante shows in Piccarda's experience how in heaven it can be transmogrified instantly through the shift to a celestial *mise-en-scene*.

It is in the *Paradiso* that one sees the pertinence of some earlier remarks of Hegel's on comedy, those occurring in his first published treatise—an indication of the abiding importance of comedy in Hegel's thought, even if his comments are somewhat at odds with his triumphant praise of the genre in his *Aesthetics*. In the early essay "The Scientific Ways of Treating Natural Law," he characterizes the *Divine Comedy* as "without fate and without a genuine struggle, because absolute confidence and assurance of the reality of the Absolute exist in it without opposition, and whatever opposition brings movement into the perfect security and calm is merely opposition without seriousness or inner truth."15 In this scheme the serenity of "Divine" comedy gradually turns into the disillusioned "modern" comedy. Hegel then announces his difficulty with comedy in both its earlier and later forms:

> Comedy so separates the two zones of the ethical [i.e., the real and the ideal] that it allows each to proceed entirely on its own, so that in the one the conflicts and the finite are shadows without substance, while in the other the Absolute is an illusion. But the true and absolute relation is that the one really does illumine the other: each has a living bearing on the other, and each is the other's serious fate. The absolute relation, then, is set forth in tragedy.16

This is a younger, more earnest, less cautious text. It throws a different light on the *Aesthetics* to read a Hegel who is not at all comfortable with the straddling, manifestly incomplete nature of comedy and opts rather for tragedy, the genre of fate, finality, and absolute relation. But if, as he claims, the real and the ideal, the finite and the absolute, are each other's "serious fate," then each is what the other has ignored or left out: each is the other's blindness. This would imply a relation within comedy between the finite modern "individualistic" comedy and the Absolute "Divine" comedy wherein neither can be read completely on its own terms. Would this call for a new *ordre du jour* for reading Dante ironically? Probably rather it would posit as the "end" of the *Commedia* not the vision of the Incarnation in the final canto, but that return Dante must make to earth, Italy, and exile. But it also suggests that the *Commedia* lies as a palimpsest beneath the text of the most modern, alienated, dark comedy, as the continual reminder of what always might come about, of what vision is the motive of all the frustrated, limping actions (Aristotle's "the ludicrous") that play themselves out on our stage. Following the trace of Dante in the ludicrous leads to the serious and necessary endeavor of our time—reading history as comedy.

Notes

1. Dante Alighieri, "Dante's Letter to Can Grande," trans. Nancy Howe, in Mark Musa, ed., *Essays on Dante* (Bloomington, 1964), 38-39.

2. Robert Hollander, "Tragedy in Dante's Comedy," *Sewanee Review* 91 (1983): 240-60; Erich Auerbach, "Sermo Humilis," in his *Literary Language and Its Public in Late Latin Antiquity and in the Middle Ages* (New York, 1965), 25-66.

3. Nevill Coghill, "The Basis of Shakespearean Comedy," *English Association Essays and Studies* 3 (1950): 1-28.

4. Hollander, 245.

5. Quotations from the *Divine Comedy* are taken from the Petrocchi text as given in Charles S. Singleton's bilingual edition, 6 vols. (Princeton, 1970-75). I am using Singleton's translation with some alterations for literal accuracy. This passage is *Inferno* 3, 4-6; further references to this text will be given parenthetically.

6. Singleton points out in a note to *Inf.* 8, 38 that Dante's reply to Filippo employs a reflexive construction, *ti rimani*, "stay right where you are," used for what Singleton calls a "distancing effect." In a note to *Inf.* 7, 94 he further explains that "the reflexive pronoun in this usage . . . serves to set apart or 'distance' the subject" from its surrounding. Hence the comic judgment is performed on Filippo, and later on other figures (as I shall mention) even at the grammatical stratum of Dante's text.

7. Leo Spitzer's brief article "The Farcical Elements in 'Inferno,' Cantos XXI-XXIII," in Musa, 172-76, is fundamental to a consideration of the relation of farce, and the tradition on which it draws, to the *Commedia*.

8. Hayden White, *Metahistory: The Historical Imagination in Nineteenth Century Europe* (Baltimore, 1973), 30, 94.

9. G. W. F. Hegel, *Aesthetics: Lectures on Fine Art*, trans. T. M. Knox, 2 vols. (Oxford, 1975): 1200. Further references to this text will be given parenthetically. The few citations of the original are taken from the text of the second edition, ed. D. H. G. Hotho, 3 vols. (Berlin, 1842).

10. Mark Taylor, *Journeys to Selfhood: Hegel and Kierkegaard* (Berkeley, 1980), 217.

11. Anne Paolucci, "Hegel's Theory of Comedy," *New York Literary Forum* 1 (1978): 89-108. Page references to this article will be given parenthetically.

12. Karl Marx shows his thoroughgoing debt to Hegel's aesthetics, as well as a distinctive emphasis of his own, in a remark from his "Toward the Critique of Hegel's Philosophy of Law": "The last phase of a world-historical form is its comedy.... Why does history take this path? So that mankind may divorce itself from its past *with hilarity*." In Lloyd D. Easton and Kurt H. Guddat, trans. and eds., *Writings of the Young Marx on Philosophy and Society* (Garden City, N. Y., 1967), 254.

13. Charles Baudelaire, "On the Essence of Laughter," quoted by Howard H. Schless in "Dante: Comedy and Conversion," *Genre* 9 (1976/77): 415. Schless adds that Baudelaire's distinction "fails only at the critical moment, that is, when we must move from one plane of understanding to another."

To assay the distance between nineteenth-century and medieval systems of tropes, one might hold up Dante's definition of laughter in the *Convivio* for comparison to Baudelaire's: "And what is laughter but a flashing forth of the delight of the soul, that is, a light appearing outwardly according as it exists within?" (quoted in Singleton's note to *Purg.* 21, 114).

14. Northrop Frye, *Anatomy of Criticism: Four Essays* (Princeton, 1957), 185.

15. G. W. F. Hegel, *On the Scientific Ways of Treating Natural Law*, trans. T. M. Knox (Philadelphia, 1975), 106.

16. Ibid., 108.

5

Commedia dell'Arte: The Image of Comedy

MARY LOU HOYLE

TRAGEDY may offer an experience of the heights and depths of human feeling, but comedy gives form to a realm where most of us, in fact, live out our lives. In so doing, the comic outlook offers a more subtle wisdom than the cataclysmic and ultimate vision of tragedy. Yet over the years literary criticism has directed a far more searching and extended scrutiny toward the tragic genre than toward the comic. This imbalance is due in part to an unexamined assumption that the nature of the comic catharsis is fairly generally understood, since it is a part of human life in which all commonly share. And though it is no doubt true that everyone has participated in the kind of event on which "comedy" is based, its very familiarity has, ironically, prevented the *action* at the heart of comedy from receiving real attention.

It is not only that familiarity has rendered the action of comedy largely invisible to critics, but that its language has so consumed their interest as to screen the comic event from analysis. One way to penetrate this veil of language and look directly into the center of the comic action is to turn to a kind of comedy which, by its nature, has left no written record. *Commedia dell'arte* thus offers a unique point of departure for the investigation of comedy. *Commedia* was a popular Italian comedy performed in the sixteenth to eighteenth centuries by companies of actors trained to improvise dialogue and stage business around standardized situations and certain stock characters. Although scenarios of these comedies exist today, they are only outlines of the action performed. The absence of dialogue in these records has prevented most critics from exploring *commedia* as an art form, since dramatic criticism usually depends heavily on interpretation of dialogue, which, unlike stage directions, is expected to remain consistent among various productions. Pierre Louis Duchartre, for example, despairs of the possibility of determining what *commedia* was really like from the "handful of dry and brittle scenarios" which he likens to "a little heap of ashes left from a great and spectacular fire."[1] By reversing this traditional position, however, and focusing on the presence of action rather than on the absence of words, we may not only understand *commedia* more clearly, but also penetrate some of the secrets of the comic genre.

In order to begin such a consideration, it is necessary to understand something about the true nature of *commedia dell'arte*. *Commedia* has been generally regarded as pure show in its most mindless form. Those who study this form of drama often think of *commedia dell'arte* as an actor's theater, blissfully free from the troublesome poet's insistence on hearing actors speak the words he wrote, in precisely the way that he wrote them. If, as we are told, the actors frequently wrote their own plays—while they performed them—then we are led to believe that the resulting performance was as impromptu as were the "happenings" of our own recent theatrical past.

It is a pretty fantasy—and in some cases it may even have been true, for certainly, the entire ensemble was involved in the construction of the work and no single author can take full credit for a work to which so many contributed. The nature of the actor's improvisation, however, must be understood with caution, for these were professional actors working as an ensemble under the guidance of a director. Indeed, the designation, *commedia dell'arte*, is most frequently translated as "professional comedians." Its practitioners were not high-spirited amateurs indulging the impulse of the moment. The scenarios which we have, then, are not mere recordings of transitory comic effusions, but outlines of events created by specialists in the arts of comedy.

Thus, even though they are not "written," in the sense that a drama usually is, they merit equally careful study.

Two kinds of scenarios are available to us today. The first is actually an outline used by the players during the play itself. Carlo Gozzi gives an example of this type of format from a play, *Contrats Rompus*, in which he appeared:

> *Brighella* enters, looks about the stage, and seeing no one, calls.
> *Pantaloon*, frightened, comes on.
> *Brighella* wishes to leave his service, etc.
> *Pantaloon* recommends himself to him.
> *Brighella* relents and promises to aid him.
> *Pantaloon* says (in a stage whisper) that his creditors, especially Truffaldino, insist on being paid; that the extension of credit expires that day, etc.[2]

In contrast, Flaminio Scala's scenarios, written after he had retired from his career as Flavio—one of the lovers—and as stage manager of *I Gelosi* company, are not so concise as those used during performance. The opening scene of a play called *Isabella's Fortune* follows a cast list and a list of properties to be used in the play:

> Pantalone enters and learns from the two brothers that Gratiano, their own father, is in love with Franceschino and that he is making no effort to find them wives as he should. Suggesting, as a friend, that it is better to marry when old than when young, Pantalone tries to console them. But Flavio complains that his father has kept him in school, not to get a degree, but to prevent him from getting a wife. Then Flavio informs Oratio that they are rivals for the love of Flaminia. Finally they ask Pantalone, as a friend of their father, to divert him from his foolish behavior, and off they go, leaving Pantalone to confess that he is also in love with Franceschina.[3]

Because this type of scenario contains descriptions of what was done, it may be of more assistance to the scholar than those briefer scenarios which were actually used by the performers.

The brevity of *commedia* scenarios is tantalizing. Despite their incompleteness, however, the similarity to the ancient plays they resemble and the later ones they influenced is obvious. Kenneth McKee details many familiar devices in his foreword to Flaminio Scala's collection of scenarios:

The innumerable plot devices—mistaken identities; disguises of one or more characters; young people of unknown origin who turn out to be brother and sister of high birth; a friend torn between love and loyalty to his comrade; a lover posing as a servant to be near the girl he adores and hopes to save from marriage to a rich old man; a girl dressed as a man; the use of twins, sometimes two sets of twins *(Zanni Incredible)* and even three *(Li sei Simili)*; combinations of the fanciful with reality—all these and a host of other farcical inventions which flooded the stage of Europe in the seventeenth and eighteenth centuries had been exploited ad infinitum by the *commedia dell'arte*.[4]

The devices, as well as the entire plots, deserve our study not only for the influence on later writers which McKee mentions, but also as the inspiration for and the subject matter of many pieces of music, ballets, paintings, and other works of art.

The appeal of *commedia*, however, does not depend on its history. On the contrary, it is not what we do know, but what we do not, which makes an irrepressible demand for our attention still, long after the companies themselves were either disbanded or absorbed into the theatrical styles of France, Germany, England, Poland, Russia, and the Orient. What does it mean, we wonder, that it was only the sequence of events that was tacked up backstage for the actor's reference each night? And why was the sequence different at each performance? Of course the actors spoke dialogue; the more fully developed scenarios mention it, and some record speeches, or give the dialogue's intent. But it is clear from the emphasis given to what was *done*, as opposed to what was said, that plot was paramount in this kind of drama. I suggest that it was not a historical accident that it is chiefly the action of *commedia* performances, not the language, that the actors remembered in their old age and that gives us our impression of the performances. Rather, this tradition is an indicator of the true nature of *commedia*.

Action is the material of comedy in the same way that words, or the ideas which they express, are the material of tragedy. Although comedy is frequently garrulous, the intent of its words is often to delay the progress of events with wit until action can be taken. Seldom does a comic character reveal himself to the audience in the abstract transmission of ideas that we so often see in tragedy, especially in soliloquies. The comic actor talks to his audience about what he is going to do, not who he is. In fact, as *commedia* demonstrates, a comic character can be perfectly well understood even if his conversations are carried out entirely in pantomime; this diagrammatic economy could never be true of the tragic characters.

The opening moments of a *commedia* scenario can be seen to place the audience in a distinctly comic relationship to the work, a relationship which is different from that obtaining in any other genre. A serious study of *commedia* reveals a way of seeing that audiences have naively practiced for centuries but that critics have neglected.

Audiences have instinctively understood the perspective of comedy. *Commedia* audiences, for example, knew that when the servant Arlecchino began a performance by conspiring with his friend Brighella—in full view of his audience—to play a trick on his master, the old miser Pantalone, that the audience would be included in the action. The opening moments of a play are especially important to its success in engaging the audience, for it is here that the real world is breached, and the work begins to create a world of its own. The first events in this dramatic reality tell the viewer what kind of world he is going to see, what sorts of things can—and cannot—happen there. As the audience watches the conspiracy between the two servants, the *commedia* audience senses that although secrets may be kept from Pantalone, none will be kept from the spectators. The openness of plotting, which *commedia* practiced, is the first signal that *commedia* represents the comic tradition in a structural way as well as by simply making people laugh.

In this openness, the convention of comedy, Albert Cook asserts, is essentially different from that of tragedy:

> the basic convention of the stage is objective perspective, the audience and the actors stand in a third-personal, not the normal second-personal relationship to one another. In tragedy the players are as objective to the spectators as if they were in a book. But comedy always violates this convention; the actor reaches out of the frame of objectivity, and addresses the audience second-personally.[5]

Indeed, we might think of the comic actor as having entered into a contract with his audience and that the comic contract depends on this face-to-face relationship with its audience established at the beginning of the performance. As Baudelaire has pointed out, "in order to enable a comic emanation . . . there must be two beings face-to-face with one another ... the special abode of the comic is ... the spectator."⁶ Whether or not Arlecchino actually makes eye contact with the members of the audience by winking or placing his finger to his lips to indicate that they must not give him away, he does perform from an open position, his body inclined toward his audience in order to make it clear that they are co-conspirators. Actors in comedy rarely turn their backs on their audiences. The openness of the comic actor's very body position echoes the comic attitude Stephan Haggard characterizes as that of talking to a friend "over the port."⁷ Form follows function in comedy as it does in all art.

The opening moments of any comedy are also critical to the audience's understanding of who will be the protagonist. Rarely does that problem arise in the other genres. Plays like *The Merchant of Venice*, however, continue to baffle critics who ignore the title character, Antonio, and try to force the character of Shylock into service as protagonist. Antonio appears in the opening moments of the play and becomes engaged in the action which results in his kinsman's successful suit of Portia long before Shylock comes onto the scene to complicate matters. At other times comic heroes are difficult for critics to identify because they lack both virtues and stations that those trained in the analysis of tragedy associate with a hero. This disparity is especially evident in *commedia*, where only the lovers conform to usual morality. And they are so absorbed in themselves and each other that they are not as attractive as the mischievous servants the audiences find enchanting. *Commedia* scenarios mislead the critics into thinking of the lovers as the protagonists because the plots are almost always constructed as love intrigues.

The servants, or *zannis*, however, are attuned to their world and represent it to their audiences. The audience trusts them to know what is going on. Their masters, the three old men of the *commedia*, are only economically better off than their servants; they are neither of noble birth nor sensibility. Pantalone, for example, is a tradesman. Duchartre explains that "he has become so sensitive to the value of money that he is an abject slave to it."⁸ His passions overwhelm him and he is always someone's dupe. The pedantic Doctor, another of the old men who bear the brunt of the *zannis*' pranks, is as obsessive as is the miserly Pantalone. Upon his birth, Duchartre says, instead of wailing like an ordinary infant, "his first utterance was a fine Latin quotation, slightly mutilated."[9] The doctor may appear in the same scenario as a combination philosopher, astronomer, man of letters, barrister, grammarian, diplomat, and physician. The swaggering Capitano, the third old man, is best described by a popular verse from the seventeenth century:

> This captain makes a splendid show
> And his valour is so great
> That he is the last to join the combat
> And the first to beat a retreat.[10]

Although he always boasts of the graveyards he has filled, the captain's victims have a way of turning up alive and well. These merchants, soldiers, or pedantic professors are just wealthy enough to lord it over their servants, but the servants are not fooled by them. The audience, which traditionally elevated the servant characters to greatest popularity, knew instinctively that a superiority in wit marked the protagonists.

In order to determine who the comic protagonist is, it is usually possible simply to notice who initiates the action. In comedy, unlike tragedy, it is the deed, not the doer of the deed, that tells us what the play is about. *Hamlet*, it might be noted, is a study of a man who swears revenge. But it is the testing of that man that forms the action of the play, not the successful achievement of his avowed purpose. Not so for comedy. And it is because of the importance of the action to the meaning of the play that *commedia* is a useful entrance into the study of the comic genre. Most critics who have studied the nature of comedy have pointed out that it has an instructive function. Arlecchino's pranks are not entirely mean-spirited, for in most scenarios Pantalone, his master, is obsessed with money. Occasionally he is obsessed with money and young women. Sometimes he is obsessed with money, young women, and food. Comedy always warns against obsessive behavior because it disturbs the balance of the community. By defining the physical and spiritual limits beyond which man may not go, *commedia* accomplishes the teaching function that critics have observed in comedy as a whole. Even though comedy celebrates man's flaws, it rewards the ability of people to transcend them for the good of the community. In *commedia*, the protagonist is flawed, as are all the other characters. The wily servants—Arlecchino, the sly Brighella, the sensual Pulcinella, the naive Pedrolino—however, must modify the anti-social behavior of their masters simply in order to stay alive. They expose the greed, pretentions, and excessive seriousness of their employers in such a laugh-provoking way that the master is brought into harmony with his community.

Comedy does not imply that one person corrects the behavior of another simply because it is wrong. Comedy exists among groups of people and takes up the proper relationship among human beings. As early as the twelfth century, one authority wrote, in a modification of the classical moralist's outlook:

> Laughing at thief or villain or seducer,
> Thereafter brings him back to good behavior
> So tragedy dissolves our human life
> But comedy confirms and strengthens it.[11]

However difficult it is to admire the tricky servants' methods for bringing their masters back to good behavior (in one scenario these include pulling out all his teeth), their stratagems do lead to an understanding of the implicit meaning of all comedy: to "confirm and strengthen life."

Even the setting for a *commedia* scenario makes it clear that it is to be more than a story of a single person. Not only is the locale a city, but it is normally placed in the midst of a crowded street. Usually the action occurs in front of the house in which the servants perform their labors. What goes on within the houses is only alluded to; it is the public life of the characters that makes up the comic plot.

Tragedy, by contrast, shows us one man alienated from his community by his noble choice to follow a particular course of action. This choice puts him outside the community which, in comedy, is the focus of the protagonist's attention and an important source of help when he is in trouble. Although he is flawed, the comic protagonist is not as besotted by his mania as are those he strives to correct. He is worldly wise. He lives by his wits, using information gathered by his five senses, and works toward a better time to come. Comedy's concern, or its meaning, is the formation and preservation of the harmonious community within society. Victor Turner defines *communitas* as a group united by a sense of common purpose. In *communitas*, Turner says, people confront each other as persons, and as such they are basically equal.[12] Servants can defy social codes and correct their masters if they see that their master's deeds threaten the health of the community.

Comedy moves to unite its characters against the seven deadly sins—pride, envy, wrath, sloth, avarice, gluttony, and lechery—which hover over the *commedia* as they do all of comedy. Unlike the pantheon of gods which guide tragedy, these deadly gods are models of what must be avoided if one is to live within a group.

In *commedia*, stereotypical characters embody these sins. Usually they are particularly apparent in the old men, those who have authority. The braggart Capitano is foolish pride personified. The miser, Pantalone, represents greed, sometimes combined with lechery. The pedantic Dottore, envious and slothful, renders those sins unpalatable. Although it is the use of the stereotype which is largely responsible for the critical neglect which comedy, as a whole suffers, the one-dimensional character is meaningful precisely because he is not a real person. The *commedia* audience knew what was expected of each type and this expectation acted as a restraint upon the actor/playwright. Such an exaggerated character has no hidden depths to impede the action. Susanne Langer notes that the protagonist of comedy, unlike that of tragedy, changes little in the course of the play. In tragedy, she says, "there is development." In comedy, "there are developments."[13] The comic protagonist functions; he does not live, for he is the agent of the action.

In *commedia* this depersonalization stands forth with particular clarity. The actors themselves were completely submerged in their roles. An actor was an Arlecchino, a Capitano, or a Pantalone throughout his career. Even his name disappeared or was combined with the name of his mask, as in the case of the Scapino Gabrielli. The audience knew the character's personality; it was just not sure what he might do on a particular night. Not only was the actor hidden behind the stereotypical character, but he was further depersonalized by the wearing of a mask. In a sense, the mask was an action. It was the action of greed, or lechery, or gluttony. The half-mask abstracted the personality of each character into a few representative features. Arlecchino's mask was black with a bird-like beak of a nose. Pulcinella, the sensual bumpkin, had a large parrot nose. The flesh-colored mask of the Capitano had a great menacing nose and bristling moustaches designed to emphasize the contrast between a brave appearance and a craven nature. Only the lovers played without masks.

Frequently the lovers were the cause of the conflict between the servants and their masters. Most plots concerned the inappropriate meddling by the older characters in the love affairs of the young. Sometimes the Pantalone or Dottore wanted to marry a young woman who already loved someone her own age. The Arlecchino or Pulchinella was enlisted to cover her escape with some of his trickery—that extended stage business which was called *lazzi*. While he distracted the old man with his famous "eating the fly" *lazzi*, for example, she and her lover were safely married and out of danger.

Most who describe the unmasked "hero and heroine" believe that these actors refused to cover their faces because they were vain. And many must have been so, of course. But when the unmasked character is seen as having a thematic function, it is appropriate that the lovers, who represent natural love in the midst of mania and obsession, be presented as real people. Although they did not occupy the important position assigned to the servants and the old men, they served as emblems of order. Theirs is the love which must be preserved if the community is to continue. The scenarios ended, like most comedy, with a marriage ceremony or celebration of everyone's reconciliation to natural order. At the end of the *commedia* scenarios it can be seen that their action was far from random, for these professional comedians simply knew the rule that Dante articulated about comedy: It begins in adversity and ends in prosperity.[14] They had no real need for detailed scripts to direct their progress to the final celebration, which is the comic conclusion.

In the pageantry of *commedia*'s concluding events, its audience sees its meaning embodied in an image. All the characters are together on the stage, happily eating and drinking as a community, enjoying that collective life which Auden says "exists neither by chance like a crowd, nor actually, like society, but potentially."[15] The new sense of life which the audience feels as it grasps the image of comedy at a performance is the realization of that potential community.

Drama itself is communal, and it is for this reason that we go to the theater. The comic and tragic genres of drama provide different experiences of the communal; in tragedy we see the dissolution of an established community, whereas in comedy we witness the founding and nurturing of a new one. The response of the theater audience as a communal group is likewise different. The audience of a comedy smiles, laughs, wonders, as a whole; and in the end the spectators breathe a collective sigh of relief. But the tragic experience is ultimately individual, and the members of the audience are, like the tragic hero, isolated from the community of spectators.

If we attempt to identify the image of comedy according to the same criteria we use for tragedy, it may appear that comedy falls short of the philosophical importance of the somber genre. Comedy is the image of mortal experience, touching only obliquely on the ultimate questions which tragedy may confront. The emphasis on action that characterizes comedy may obscure its larger import. We see that comedy, much like life itself, is presented as a series of adventures. Its episodic nature allows its audience to enjoy the present scene; thus, the image of comedy works in a subliminal fashion to integrate its viewers into life.

The integrational character of comedy shows itself as the inclusiveness of love. If it is true, as Terence said, that nothing human is alien to comedy, it is also true, as Thoreau observed, that "all that a man has to say and do that can possibly concern mankind is in some shape or another to tell the story of his love.[16] Everything pertinent to the human condition touches in some way on the phenomenon of love and may find its place in comedy. In the image of comedy in which the *commedia* participates, the lovers establish the proper norm as governing the whole.

The central achievement of the servants is to delay their masters' rush to catastrophe. Perhaps the design of comedy centers on the moment when the course of avoidance is chosen, and the seemingly pointless *lazzi* which suspends action while events right themselves is the servants' major claim to their role as protagonists. They literally stop time. And by so doing, assure that *commedia* ends in prosperity.

In an attempt to understand more fully the hold that *commedia* has long exerted on the imagination, we have looked to its structure, identifying the openness of plotting which characterizes all comedy, realizing that the mischievous servants who are its protagonists do not merely amuse their audience, but truly entertain, a word which means "to hold between." As they provide the tension which comedy extends to its audience, they direct the satisfactory outcome of the traditional comic plot, and ensure the preservation of the characters whose love includes the community, and hold out hope for a future which is better than its past. Through an examination of comic structure, we may earn the right to say that comedy, or the comic vision, must not be reduced to mere amusement or abstracted into moral instruction—though it is a little of both—but rather must be preserved and respected as an illumination of the human enterprise.

Commedia dell'arte serves as *locus* for the study of comedy because it can be seen stripped of all but the essential purpose of comedy: to celebrate and to admonish. Through a celebration of the worst that man can be, it admonishes him against excessive behavior. Words are secondary to its action because language *is* civilized behavior. In the stage of man's progress which *commedia* represents, the characters have not yet achieved true civilization. But, at the end of the scenario the audience is left with the hope that the man/beast has risen off his paws and can begin to utter rudimentary sounds, at least. And they have seen him begin the process of living in a community. And that is more than most civilizations can do.

Notes

1. Pierre Louis Duchartre, *The Italian Comedy*, trans. Randolph T. Weaver (New York, 1966), 50.
2. Ibid., 51.
3. Henry F. Salerno, trans., *Scenarios of the Commedia dell'Arte: Flaminio Scala's Il Theatro delle favole rappresentative*, Foreword by Kenneth McKee (New York, 1967), 23.
4. Ibid., xvii–xviii.
5. Albert Cook, *The Dark Voyage and the Golden Mean* (Cambridge, Mass., 1949), 144.
6. Charles Baudelaire, "On the Essence of Laughter," *The Mirror of Art*, trans. and ed. Jonathan Mayne (London, 1935), 153.
7. Athene Sayler and Stephan Haggard, *The Craft of Comedy* (New York, 1946), 9.
8. Duchartre, 181.
9. Ibid., 196.

10. Ibid., 227.

11. Tzetzes, as cited in Northop Frye, *A Natural Perspective* (New York, 1965), 97.

12. Victor Turner, "Passages, Margins, and Poverty: Religious Symbols of Communitas," *Worship* 46 (August–September 1972): 390–412.

13. Susanne K. Langer, *Feeling and Form* (New York, 1953), 335.

14. Dante Alighieri, "Letter to the Lord Can Grande della Scala," in *A Translation of Dante's Eleven Letters*, trans. Charles Sterrett Latham (Boston: Houghton Mifflin Co., 1891), pp. 22–24.

15. W. H. Auden, "The Virgin and the Dynamno," *The Dyer's Hand and Other Essays* (New York: Random House, 1948), p. 64.

16. As cited in Northrup Frye, "The Argument of Comedy," *English Institute Essays, 1948*, ed. D. A. Robertson (New York: Columbia Univ. Press, 1949), p. 165.

17. Henry David Thoreau, "Selections from the Journal," *The Works of Thoreau*, ed. Henry S. Canby (New York: Houghton Mifflin, 1937), p. 23.

6

The Communal Action of
The Winter's Tale

KATHLEEN LATIMER

T*HE Winter's Tale*, with its distinctly tragic first half and exceptionally joyous second half, has often proved a problem for critics. It has not always, or even often, been studied as a comedy. It is traditionally classified as a romance, is sometimes called a tragi-comedy, and E. M. W. Tillyard, in his seminal study of the last plays, considers it a tragedy.[1] The question on which its generic classification usually hinges—how the tragic first half of the play resolves into the joyous conclusion—is often approached by a consideration of the transitional scenes at the end of the third and beginning of the fourth acts.[2] Although such treatment has provided valuable insight into the shift of tone in these passages, it has offered little help in tracing the basic action of the play which makes the shift in tone necessary. To trace that action points us toward not only the import of *The Winter's Tale*, but also the heart of comedy. If we can understand how this play can be a comedy—this play, with its lack of social criticism, its troubled hero, its generally somber tone, and its actual, not merely threatened deaths, all these traits counter to our ideas about comedy—we shall have grasped something essential to the action of the genre.

A clue to the nature of that underlying action is suggested by F. M. Cornford's study of the origins of comedy.[3] Cornford traces the origins of tragedy and comedy to different parts of the same ritual, one which involves the death of a fertility figure through which the health and strength of the community is renewed. The first half of the ritual, the death of the scapegoat figure, suggests the tragic pattern; the second half, which includes the figure's rebirth or replacement, reveals the comic pattern. This close relationship between tragedy and comedy is seen in many Shakespearean comedies, where heroes and heroines often undergo a kind of symbolic death and rebirth. But in most comedies the tragic part of the ritual is either nonexistent or merely suggested. *The Winter's Tale*, in contrast, enacts the entire pattern of the ancient ritual from which tragedy and comedy derive. Through it we can see not only the ultimately comic shape of the total action, but also the means by which the comic pattern is obtained.

The character of Leontes and the action which issues from his mistaken conviction of Hermione's unfaithfulness have always been the greatest stumbling blocks for any consideration of *The Winter's Tale* as comedy. And critics have been right in seeing that character and action as more tragic than comic. In comedy the resolution of the action is generally effected by the conduct of the protagonist. The comic hero responds in a flexible, imaginative manner to the problems which confront him. Whether he chooses evasion, delay, or deceit, he manages somehow to avoid the kind of destructive confrontation that the tragic hero seems to seek. Leontes, however, displays none of the comic characteristics. Instead he is tyrannical, single-minded, and rash, exhibiting qualities we associate with the tragic protagonist. Like the tragic hero, he is isolated from friends and loved ones and, eventually, from the gods themselves by his refusal to accept the truth of Apollo's oracle. As a king, Leontes' decisions affect the health of Sicilia, and his conduct leads, as tragic action often does, to the deaths of seemingly innocent persons—Mamillius, Antigonus, the mariners, and, apparently, Hermione. If this were all we were given in the first half of the play, we could justifiably conclude that the happy ending is forced and remain hesitant to accept the play as a comedy.

This movement of isolation, pride, and death is not, however, all that the first three acts provide. There are moments which open onto a wider view of the action and place it in a comic perspective.[4] One such moment is the brief scene (3.1) in which the visit to Apollo's oracle is described. The image of harmony which the travellers report hints at the possibility of a pattern different from the tragic action which Leontes enacts. This scene is not the first of such moments of hope in the play; the end of act 1, scene 2 with Camillo and Polixenes and act 2, scene 2 are also times in which those surrounding Leontes come together and not only hope but also take action to steer Leontes from his disastrous course.

It is in these moments when Leontes is off-stage that the existence of another kind of response to the problem which faces Sicilia can be clearly seen. That response, shared by all the members of the Sicilian court, but centered in Camillo, Paulina, Antigonus, and Hermione, is predominantly a comic one. These characters work to deflect Leontes' rage as much as possible from his intended victims and to prevent his potentially tragic action from becoming fully developed. They form a community which surrounds Leontes and protects him from his own worst deeds and which works continually to restore him to the communal group. This comic action, moreover, is not isolated in the scenes mentioned, but begins the moment Leontes' suspicions are first aired and forms a continuous line of action that unifies the entire play, containing and modifying our view of the tragic action.

The response of Camillo is typical of the entire community. Camillo's first reaction to Leontes' accusation of Hermione is simple disbelief. Leontes can offer no proof which can sway him from his centainty that the Queen is incapable of the conduct with which Leontes charges her. His response is one of anger and desire for revenge, not unlike Leontes' attitude, though in Hermione's defense:

> I would not be a stander-by, to hear,
> My sovereign mistress clouded so, without
> My present vengeance taken.
>
> (1.2.279–81)[5]

This is not, however, the course he actually follows. Convinced quickly that Leontes is of a "diseas'd opinion" (1.2.296), Camillo embarks on a course which will ultimately make possible the King's cure. The disease metaphor is important here. Throughout the play, Leontes is considered by those around him as ill rather than evil, and they treat him accordingly, with concern and tenderness. It is important to note that the image of disease, contrary to its use in *Hamlet*, for example, is applied to no one except Leontes. There is no suggestion that the Sicilian court is sick or disordered in any way; it is affected by Leontes' actions, but does not share his disoriented view of reality.

Camillo is asked by Leontes to murder Polixenes, and he seemingly consents. Whether or not he actually forms his plan at this time is not clear. What is clear, however, is that the language with which he swears does not actually commit him to do the murder. He first agrees "to fetch off Bohemia for't" (1.2.334), on the condition that Leontes will take no action against Hermione and will "take again your queen, as yours at first" (1.2.336). With this bargain he prevents Leontes from seeking elsewhere for someone to kill Polixenes and, he hopes, protects Hermione. His second promise is similarly ambiguous and suggests his future course. Of Polixenes he says,

> I am his cupbearer:
> If from me he have wholesome beverage,
> Account me not your servant.
>
> (1.2.345-47)

Even if he has no clear plan in mind, Camillo is here clearly "buying time" in which to form one.

Left alone, Camillo ponders his dilemma:

> O miserable lady! But, for me,
> What case stand I in? I must be poisoner
> Of good Polixenes, and my ground to do't
> Is the obedience to a master; one
> Who in rebellion with himself, will have
> All that are his, so too.
>
> (1.2.350-6)

He cannot poison Polixenes, but if he does not, and remains at court, he eventually will be called into account. Like Viola in *Twelfth Night*, he finds it too hard a knot to untie. He chooses, with considerable pain, to leave the court, to avoid the issue and let time resolve it. By refusing to obey Leontes while he is in rebellion with himself, Camillo averts immediate disaster and leaves open the possibility of future happiness.

Before he can flee, Camillo encounters Polixenes who, despite

Leontes' promise to hide his disturbance, has sensed the change in his friend's attitude toward him. Pressed by Polixenes, Camillo discloses Leontes' suspicions and the plot against his guest's life. Camillo's description of Leontes stresses the intractable nature of the King's passion:

> you may as well
> Forbid the sea for to obey the moon,
> As or by oath remove or counsel shake
> The fabric of his folly, whose foundation
> Is pil'd upon his faith, and will continue
> The standing of his body.
>
> (1.2.426–31)

Leontes' belief is as unchangeable as the laws of nature, but that, in itself, is a sign of hope. The moon, as we have been reminded, is a "watery star" (1.2.1) which changes with the progress of time. The laws of nature allow for change and progress in the fullness of time. By fleeing, Camillo and Polixenes not only protect themselves; they prevent Leontes from being responsible for their deaths. Camillo must also know, as is soon evident, that there are others in the court who will attempt to dissuade Leontes and protect Hermione. His basic strategy, clearly a comic one, is summed up in Polixenes' last line in the scene: "Let us avoid" (1.2.462).

The task of saving Leontes is taken up by various other members of his court, although at first they seem to have little effect. Hermione, like Camillo, does not attempt to confront Leontes. She does not respond with anger, bitterness, or vengefulness. Leontes has been shown to be immune to counsel; we now see, as Camillo predicted, that he is immune to oaths. When Hermione's avowals of her innocence are brushed aside, her only course is patience. Unable to remove herself from court, she must retire and wait. Accepting imprisonment, she explains her own conduct:

> There's some ill planet reigns:
> I must be patient till the heavens look
> With an aspect more favourable . . .
> . . . .
> . . . beseech you all my lords,
> With thoughts so qualified as your charities
> Shall best instruct you, measure me: and so
> The king's will be perform'd.
>
> (2.2.105–15)

In this scene Hermione sets the tone for the court's subsequent treatment of her husband. By so doing she acts as a positive force in his regeneration. Like Camillo, she levels no charge of evil against Leontes, but simply insists he is misguided. Hermione does not hope, but assumes, that the falseness of his accusation will be revealed in time. Meanwhile, she, and Leontes, are to be judged through charity.

With those closest to Leontes separated from him, the burden of protecting the King falls to the lesser members of his court. Again, counsels of reason and prudence are lost on him, but the King has not lost all contact with his better self. Out of his "natural goodness" (2.1.164) he continues to listen to their advice even as he denies it. He also recognizes the necessity for some prudence and sends for confirmation from the oracle of Apollo.

The final attempt of a member of the court to change Leontes' opinion comes from Paulina. Paulina's appeal, which is planned in part by Hermione, "Who but to-day hammer'd of this design"(2.2.48), is substantially different from those made by Camillo and the other lords. By placing before Leontes the innocent child, whose features are said to resemble his, they hope to sway his heart rather than his mind:

> We do not know
> How he may soften at the sight o' th' child:
> The silence often of pure innocence
> Persuades, when speaking fails.
>
> (2.2.39-42)

Leontes is called upon to make actual, by publicly accepting the child, the truth of her lineage which her features image forth. This is one of several instances in the play, culminating in the statue scene, where an image of reality is expected to persuade when words fail. This superiority of images to words is expressed in the final scene: "That she is living,/Were it but told you, would be hooted at/Like an old tale" (5.3.115-7).

But Leontes' self-deception is so thorough that he is as unable to see the image as he is to accept the statements of truth. His disease is not, in fact, jealousy, but a total loss of belief in anything outside himself, so that he is subject to his own whims and fantasies. His jealousy is but a symptom of his deep estrangement from the human community itself. He has lost the faith by which we credit the actions and words of those with whom we live, the basic trust in human goodness on which human communal life depends. Without this faith even Leontes' own actions have for him no reality, but become a role, a disgraced part, which he must play. His actions stand, as Hermione precisely observes, on the level of dreams.

The members of the surrounding community do not share Leontes' loss of faith. Moreover, they step forward willingly, person after person, to act upon their faith, even to the point of pledging their own lives:

> For her, my lord
> I dare my life lay down, and will do't, sir,
> Please you t'accept it, that the queen is spotless
> I' th' eyes of heaven, and to you—I mean
> In this which you accuse her.
> (1.1.129-33)

The preciseness of the gentlemen's oath is typical of the comic response, which avoids the passionate and often extravagant oaths which so often contribute to the ruin of the tragic hero,

In addition to their staunch defense of Hermione's honesty, the members of the community also act with continuing faith in Leonte's basic goodness. Their attitude throughout is not that accorded a tyrant whom they have learned to fear and distrust. Leontes is right when he responds to Paulina:

> Were I a tyrant
> Where were her life? She durst not call me so,
> If she did know me one.
> (2.3.121-23)

If Leontes behaves tyrannically now, it is clear from the court's open and free attitude toward him that this is not his accustomed attitude. The court addresses Leontes as if it normally expects common sense and justice from him. It is as if by continually insisting upon a certain image of the King, it can lead him to reestablish that image as a reality. As with the child, however, Leontes is blind to the significance of the image, and it remains unrealized.

Paulina's presentation of the baby to Leontes does not have the desired effect, and Leontes, contradicting his announced intention to await the word of Apollo, condemns the child to death. At this point

Antigonus intervenes to prevent Leontes from committing a horrible crime. Like the lord before him, he offers his own life as a substitute:

> Anything, my lord,
> That my ability may undergo,
> And nobleness impose: at least thus much—
> I'll pawn the little blood which I have left
> To save the innocent: anything possible.
>
> (2.3.162–66)

Unlike Camillo, who was able to phrase his bargain with Leontes in language which allowed him to break it without dishonor, Antigonus swears, as the King demands: "on thy soul's peril and thy body's torture" (2.3.180), to expose the child. At first it may seem that Antigonus has made a poor bargain; he himself comments that "a present death/Had been more merciful" (2.1.183–84). Still, the child is given life, and, in comedy at least, life on its barest terms is better than no life at all, as the opening scene reminds us. Like the flight of Camillo and Polixenes, the exposure of the child saves Leontes from the responsibility for a more terrible crime and leaves hope for his, as well as the child's, eventual recovery.

The potentially tragic action of *The Winter's Tale* is thus continually countered by small but important efforts on the part of members of the Sicilian court which deflect and soften the effects of the King's rage. Although their individual actions may seem ineffectual, their sum effect is to lessen the damage for which Leontes is responsible and thereby make possible his eventual regeneration. Their actions constitute a pattern of comic action which balances and controls the tragic action of Leontes. It cannot, however, overcome that tragic action as long as Leontes remains isolated from the community. The law of Sicilia, which Leontes controls with tragic obstinacy, must be tempered with the spirit of love embodied in Hermione before the comic action can proceed. This blending begins in the trial scene, although not before Leontes' blindness has cost him the life of his son.

The trial is ostensibly the trial of Hermione, but it is clear from the beginning that Leontes considers it his own trial as well:

> Let us be clear'd
> Of being tyrannous, since we so openly
> Proceed in justice, which shall have due course,
> Even to the guilt or the purgation.
>
> (3.2.4–7)

The issue of the trial is not Hermione's but Leontes' guilt and purgation. Much of the scene is taken up with Hermione's dignified and eloquent defense, which ends with an appeal to her father:

> The Emperor of Russia was my father,
> O that he were alive, and here beholding
> His daughter's trial! that he did but see
> The flatness of my misery, yet with eyes
> Of pity, not revenge!
>
> (3.2.119–23)

Through the appeal of her father Hermione calls on all, including the audience, to share her attitude toward Leontes. Just before his most terrible mistake we are urged, once again, to judge Leontes with charity.

The oracle is read and, as we knew it would do, clears Hermione, Polixenes, and Camillo of all crime and proclaims that "the king shall live without an heir, if that which is lost be not found" (3.2.134–36). The oracle offers Leontes one more chance to seize his lost faith, but he is immune to these words as he has been to all others. His denial of the oracle is followed immediately by the death of Mamillius, in what seems to be perfect justice. Leontes' reversal is immediate. The death of his son is a reality he cannot deny; it is also an image of the consequences of the dominance of justice over mercy on which Leontes himself has insisted. In recognizing and accepting the appropriateness of the punishment and the god's hand in it, Leontes also recognizes the injustice of his own insistence on law: "Apollo's angry, and the heavens themselves/do strike at my injustice" (3.2.146–47).

Leontes stops his headstrong course before it leads to his own destruction. The actions of those around him have saved the lives of at least four others—Camillo, Polixenes, Hermione (although the audience does not know it yet), and Perdita—for whose deaths he might well have been responsible. The tragic action of the play, however, seems to require a victim. *The Winter's Tale*, we have noted, embodies the entire pattern of the ancient ritual, which begins with tragedy but whose form is ultimately comic. Unlike most comedies, where the tragic half of the ritual is missing or only suggested (as in Hero's mock death in *Much Ado About Nothing* or Viola and Sebastian's supposed drownings in *Twelfth Night*), in *The Winter's Tale* it is given full value, involving actual as well as threatened deaths.

Leontes stops short of causing his own destruction, as the tragic hero often does; the child takes the role of sacrificial victim whose death renews the society.[6] Mamillius's death is, however, only the midpoint of the ritual and of the play, whose end, the regeneration of king and community, is the end of comedy.

Antigonus, in another sense, also takes on the role of scapegoat. Antigonus (along with he mariners who, we assume, could have refused to be a party to the deed) dies because, by his own act of swearing to carry out Leontes' command, he is locked into the tragic action and cannot escape from it. Antigonus interprets his dream as an indication of Hermione's guilt; like Leontes, he loses faith. Antigonus's and Mamillius's deaths complete the tragic action of the play, clearing the stage for the development of the comic action.

Antigonus dies as Perdita is found, and the shepherd says to his son: "Now bless thyself: thou met'st with things dying, I with things new born" (3.3.112-13). What dies with Antigonus is "all the instruments which aided to expose the child" (5.2.70-71), and, as noted above, the whole tragic action of the play. What is newborn is Leontes and the society from which he has been estranged and which is given renewed strength and vigor by his return. The community which protected Leontes in the first half of the play continues to work to complete his healing and to effect the restoration to him of the family he believes he has lost.

The working out of Leontes' regeneration requires him to enter into a period of mourning and penance during which the memory of Hermione serves as a major means by which Leontes regains his faith in the harmony and goodness of the world. During this period the image of Hermione is presented to the audience through her daughter, Perdita, who mirrors her mother's open and generous nature as well as her physical appearance. Leontes' struggle is presented dramatically through the story of Polixenes, whose similarity to Leontes is stressed in the first act. The affinity between the two kings makes it possible to see Polixenes' visit to the pastoral feast as part of Leontes' regeneration.[7]

The sheep-shearing scene, with its rich blend of pastoral setting and festive occasion, is central to the meaning of *The Winter's Tale*. It is an image of the power and beauty of the communal bond which has protected Leontes throughout the first half of the play. The sense of love and harmony imaged in the sheep-shearing scene is one which many critics have noted as a crucial element in comedy. It is closely related to the feeling of harmony with men and nature which C. L. Barber identified in *Shakespeare's Festive Comedy* as the clarification gained in the saturnalian experience which he saw as a key element in the comic action.[8] The experience in the pastoral festival is very close to that described by the anthropologist Victor Turner, to which he gives the name *communitas*.[c]

Turner makes a clear distinction between *societas* and *communitas*, a distinction which is significant to the interpretation of *The Winter's Tale* and to our understanding of the comic action. *Societas*, or society, includes both social structures and *communitas*. Social structures are those patterns and organizations through which men live peacefully together. They include not only laws, but also customs and manners. *Communitas* is the communal bond which unites human life by a recognition of man's common humanity and place in the natural order. It is a state of inclusive harmony in which natural fellowship and a stress on nature rather than culture are dominant. Because it cuts across the boundaries of social structures, this liberating union is often looked upon by authority as a threat to structure, thus its association with carnival and similarly unrestricted festive occasions. *Communitas* is also frequently identified with an Edenic state, such as that celebrated in the pastoral tradition. The communal experience is, however, post-Edenic. It arises, in fact, in times of crisis, such as that created by Leontes' loss of faith, caused by the imperfect nature of man and the world in which he actually lives.

The central feelings associated with *communitas*—love, trust, good fellowship, harmony with nature, enjoyment of sensual pleasure—are all present in the great sheep-shearing scene. Though poor, the shepherds are rich in all these values. They enjoy a degree of closeness to nature which is indicated by the occasion itself and by its place in the cycle of the seasons and natural life. They also possess a spontaneous enthusiasm and a healthy enjoyment of sexuality which is normally restricted by social mores. They are fully accepting of their place in the natural cycle of life and death. All these qualities are beautifully summed up in the character of Perdita, whose identity with nature, buoyant energy, and innocent sexuality have often been noted. Perdita's careful distribution of appropriate flowers to her guests reflects her awareness of the cycles of nature. Her innate shyness does not fully hide a vital and passionate love, as is seen when she responds to Florizel's suggestion that she would cover him with flowers like a corpse:

> What, like a corpse?
> No, like a bank, for love to lie and play on:
> Not like a corpse; or if—not to be buried,
> But quick, and in my arms. Come, take your flowers:
> Methinks I play as I have seen them do
> In Whitsun pastorals: sure this robe of mine
> Does change my disposition.
>
> (4.4.129-34)

Perdita's costume reveals more than changes her nature. As the hostess of the celebration, she invites all to join in the natural fellowship of the communal feast whose qualities she embodies.

Although in some ways an outsider, an intruder in the community festival, Autolycus also symbolizes many of the qualities associated with *communitas*. Amoral, antistructural, and totally engaging, he reduces all he meets—shepherds or princes—to a single level. To the extent that the level is one of a gull, Autolycus emphasizes that saturnalian aspect of community which seems to be a threat to social structures. He is a carnival figure, a trickster. As a "snapper-up of unconsidered trifles" (4.3.26), however, he embodies, like the old shepherd and Florizel, the ability to see value in the most lowly things around him. Further, his humor is not without humility:

> How blessed are we that we are not simple men!
> Yet nature might have made me as these are;
> Therefore I will not disdain.
>
> (4.4.747-79)

Autolycus is, equally with Perdita though in another way, a walking embodiment of *communitas*.

It is this sense of community, based on a belief in the fundamental goodness of the world and on the full acceptance of all aspects of human nature, that Leontes and Polixenes must regain. From the beginning of the play Leontes lacks this feeling of inclusive harmony which binds the other characters. This is the essence of his loss of faith. Polixenes exhibits a similar lack of faith in his refusal to accept the love of Florizel and Perdita.[10] When called upon to witness their pledge, he seems to be willing to agree to it, with one reservation:

> The father (all whose joy is nothing else
> But fair posterity) should hold some counsel
> In such a business.
>
> (4.4.409-11)

The shepherd responds: "Let him my son: he shall not need to grieve/ At knowing of thy choice" (4.4.416-17). Polixenes can accept the breaking down of social structures, which matches the prince with a shepherdess, for he, like everyone else, responds to Perdita's innate beauty of spirit. He cannot accept the denial of the family structure upon which Florizel insists. He is unwilling to relinquish the sense of immortality which comes through one's posterity for the greater sense achieved through the oneness with the cycles of nature found in *communitas*.

The understanding required of Leontes and Polixenes can be seen in Florizel. It is he who finds, in the pastoral world, the sense of a communal bond beyond that of his family ties. But it is not possible to remain forever in the pastoral world without the danger of "dropping out" of society altogether. The good society consists of both *communitas* and social structures. Florizel's plan would commit him and Perdita to an uncharted course, to chance, as Camillo recognizes. He offers them an alternative:

> A course more promising
> Than a wild dedication of yourselves
> To unpath'd waters, undream'd shores; most certain
> To miseries enough....
>
> (4.4.566-69)

It is Camillo and, later, Paulina who accept the task of conveying the principal figures back from the Bohemian world to the established society which is invigorated by their new-found sense of harmony.

The art through which Camillo and Paulina accomplish this task is essentially a dramatic one.[11] They each establish situations in which the principal figures can demonstrate they have absorbed the spirit of *communitas*. Camillo arranges Florizel and Perdita in an artificial scene which reflects their real situation. Leontes, who was unable to recognize the truth of the images presented to him in the first half of the play, now must demonstrate his faith by recognizing the validity of the image before him and turning it into a reality. The arrival of Polixenes forces Leontes to accept the responsibility of turning the order and harmony of Camillo's created image into actuality. By taking up the task of mediation between Florizel and Polixenes, Leontes shows that he has joined the comic community. As it once protected him, he now joins it in protecting others from their own folly.

Leontes' open and generous act is echoed in the following scene by the Clown in his acceptance of Autolycus's professed conversion. In their newly bestowed gentility, in itself evidence of the egalitarian spirit of *communitas*, the rustics remain simple and gracious. By validating the image Autolycus presents, the Clown, like Leontes, would make it a reality:

> If it be ne'er so false, a true gentleman may swear
> it in behalf of a friend: and I'll swear to the
> prince thou art a tall fellow of thy hands and that
> thou will not be drunk; but I know thou art no
> tall fellow of thy hands and that thou wilt be
> drunk: but I'll swear it, and I would thou would'st
> be a tall fellow of thy hands.
>
> (5.2.175-82)

The clown is not being gullible; he is being "gentle, now we are gentlemen" (5.2.152-53). With or without their titles, the old shepherd and his son are indeed "gentlemen born" (5.2.128). This brief scene is a perfect example of the trust on which the comic community depends.

The final scene of *The Winter's Tale* involves another, more complex use of art to convey the spirit of community into the world of social structures. Paulina's staged scene approaches, in its almost liturgical questions and responses, another means by which the sense of totality is imaged forth in society. In the final scene Leontes and the court are not only audience to a drama, but participants in a ritual. This event, at which the entire court, including its newest members, is present, is, like the sheep-shearing festival, an occasion in which social classes are leveled by equal participation in the event at hand. All take part in Leontes' act of faith which, like his previous loss of faith, is beyond logic. It is an act of love through which, in his acceptance of Hermione in whatever terms she has returned, Leontes demonstrates his total acceptance of the human condition. The faith he gains does not negate the tragic experience, but places it in a larger context. The stressed identity of the two kings with each other and with their children and countries, established from the beginning of the play, allows us to see in Leontes' active involvement in the completion of the comic action evidence of the infusion of the communal bond throughout the entire society of the play. The reunion of Leontes and Hermione, the regeneration of the marriage of the King and Queen of Sicilia, completes the fusion of social structures and *communitas*, of law and love, into a renewed society. It is the creation of this harmonious society which is the aim of the comic community of *The Winter's Tale*.

The Winter's Tale, then, can be seen to be unified by a single action which encloses the protagonist's potentially tragic action within an ultimately comic pattern. Moreover, it reveals the importance of the comic community to the development of this comic action. The resolution of the play is achieved through the response of this community. Its various members, especially Camillo and Paulina, use the comic strategies of evasion, delay, deceit, and, in the last acts, disguise and sheer luck, to move the action toward a happy ending. They seek through their involvement not their personal preservation, but the preservation and growth of the communal spirit. The community they serve is united by a common belief in the basic order and goodness of the world, by a closeness to the natural order, and by generous love for their fellowmen. It is characterized by its unflagging efforts to create a harmonious society through the blending of *communitas* with social structures. This fusion creates a society which has strong laws, but which enforces them with leniency. Its tolerance of human failing stems not from an inability to recognize and condemn evil, but from an impulse toward mercy and forgiveness rather than strict justice. It has authority without tyranny, freedom without license.

This communal action which unifies *The Winter's Tale* is the central action of the comic genre. The formation of a harmonious society is the outcome toward which the comic action moves. Like the ritual from which it grew, comedy has as its aim the preservation of society, but comedy makes it clear that that society must be one which is grounded in the spirit of *communitas*. In *The Winter's Tale* the securing of such a community can be seen to have several phases, including the upsurge of *communitas* in a moment of crisis, the formation of a loosely organized community on the fringes of society, and the growth and spread of that comic community until its values permeate the social structure. Only a few comedies contain the entire communal action as it is revealed in *The Winter's Tale*, and fewer still present the full achievement of the good society which is found at the end of this play; but all comedies present some phase of this total comic action.[12]

The community, then, can be seen as the central agent of the communal action of comedy. But the final scene of *The Winter's Tale*, perhaps echoing comedy's ritual origins, seeks to involve the spectators on a far deeper level than that of witnesses to this growing community of love. Because the preservation of Hermione has been hidden from the audience as well as from the characters in the play, it stands in precisely the same relationship to her unveiling as do the persons on stage. Along with the court, the spectators are given a moment of choice:

> It is requir'd
> You do awake your faith. Then all stand still:
> Or—those that think it is unlawful business
> I am about, let them depart.
>
> (5.3.94-97)

All who choose to remain in the theater ritually join the human community imaged on stage and its endeavor to inform and invigorate human social structures. The theater itself becomes, like the sheep-shearing festival and the ritual of Hermione's awakening, a means by which man incorporates the sense of the communal bond into his society.

The comic art, *The Winter's Tale* suggests, not only presents to us the image of a harmonious society; by stirring in us feelings of *communitas*; it urges us to join in the pursuit of that society. Like the dramas arranged by Camillo and Paulina, comedy serves as a ritual through which the image of the communal action is conveyed to the society of its audience. As in *The Winter's Tale*, comedy asks its audience to respond, to take up the task of making the harmonious society a reality in its own world. Thus the comic tradition holds forth the hope of man's happiness on earth, not only through its imitation of the communal action, but also by its capacity to awaken that action in its succeeding audiences.

Notes

1. See E. M. W. Tillyard, *Shakespeare's Last Plays* (London, 1958). D. T. Childers discusses the problems with the term romance in "Are Shakespeare's Late Plays Really Romances?" in *Shakespeare's Late Plays: Essays in Honor of Charles Crow*, ed. Richard C. Tobias and Paul G. Tobland (Athens, 1974), 44-54. For a consideration of the play as tragi-comedy, see Caesarea Abartis, *The Tragicomic Construction of* Cymbeline *and* The Winter's Tale, Salzburg Studies in English Literature, Jacobean Drama Series, 73 (Salzburg, Austria, 1977).

2. For excellent discussions of this transition, see Dennis Biggens, "'Exit pursued by a Beare': A Problem in *The Winter's Tale*," *Shakespeare Quarterly* 13 (Winter 1962,): 3-13; Nevill Coghill, "Six Points of Stage-craft in *The Winter's Tale*," *Shakespeare Survey* 11 (1958): 31-41; and William Blissett, "This Wide Gap of Time: *The Winter's Tale*," *English Literary Renaissance* 1 (1971): 52-70.

3. Francis McDonald Cornford, *The Origin of Attic Comedy* (Cambridge, England, 1934).

4. Charles Frey points out this structure in "The Tragic Structure of *The Winter's Tale*: The Affective Dimension," in *Shakespeare's Romances Reconsidered*, ed. Carol McGinnis Kay and Henry E. Jacobs (Lincoln, Nebr., 1978), 113-24.

5. All quotations from Shakespeare's *The Winter's Tale* are from The Arden Shakespeare, ed. J. H. P. Pafford (London, 1963), and are indicated by act, scene, and line(s) in the text.

6. For an interpretation of Mamillius as scapegoat see F. C. Tinkler, "*The Winter's Tale*," *Scrutiny* 5, no. 4 (March 1937): 343-64.

7. This interpretation is made by Peter Lindenbaum in "Time, Sexual Love, and the Uses of Pastoral in *The Winter's Tale*," *Modern Language Quarterly* 33 (1972): 3-22. John Vyvyan sees the whole scene as a projection of Leontes' internal state in which he, mentally at least, now woos his queen; see *The Shakespearean Ethic* (New York, n.d.), 127-32.

8. C. L. Barber, *Shakespeare's Festive Comedy* (Princeton, N.J., 1939).

9. Victor Turner, "Passages, Margins and Poverty: Religious Symbols of *Communitas*," *Worship* 46 (August-September 1972): 340-412.

10. See Peter Berek's excellent essay "'As We Are Mock'd with Art': From Scorn to Transfiguration," *Studies in English Literature* 8 (1978): 289-305, for a discussion of the role of social structures in *The Winter's Tale*.

11. See Robert Egan, *Drama Within Drama: Shakespeare's Sense of his Art in* King Lear, The Winter's Tale, *and* The Tempest (New York, 1975).

12. Shakespeare's *As You Like It*, for example, concentrates on the second phase, the gathering of the community, but ends prior to that community's return to the social structures of the court. Molière's *The Misanthrope* illustrates the first phase, where the community responds to the impending crisis caused by Alceste's threat to leave society.

7
Carnival and *Don Quixote*: The Folk Tradition of Comedy

MARILYN STEWART

WHEN the reality of modern existence seems to have degenerated into another Iron Age, comedy can teach the imagination how to fight despair. But contemporary comedies alone will not suffice; the centuries-long tradition of European comic art, which includes the novel, is the most effective teacher. For example, when *Don Quixote* is understood in light of the long tradition of the comic folk ritual of carnival, Cervantes' poetic achievement holds a particular relevance for audiences of our present Iron Age, whose idea of comedy has been formed exclusively by modern literature. As a communal, preliterate patterning of imagination, carnival can be traced to antiquity, to Dionysian and Saturnalian rites in ancient Greece and Rome. In medieval folk ceremonies commemorating Mardi Gras, Midsummer's Eve, and Halloween, and even today at occasional celebrations of weddings and funerals, the attitude of carnival may be apprehended as a link between the actual world of human existence and the imaginative world of artistic creation.

Ever since the philological and anthropological movements of the late nineteenth century, scholars have striven to establish connections between folk rites and literary forms. The Cambridge Anthropologists called attention to the relationship of primitive fertility rites to the development of drama.¹ More specifically, recent works by such literary scholars as C. L. Barber and Anthony Caputi connect the more sophisticated folk customs of ancient, medieval, and Renaissance Europe with the dramatic tradition of comedy.²

It is hardly controversial to call *Don Quixote* a comic novel.³ But what contemporary readers of *Don Quixote* may miss is that it is not simply the incongruous figure of Quixote the knight-errant nor even the pairing of Quixote and Sancho that constitutes the novel's comic orientation. We are too ready to assume that comedy merely pokes fun at vulnerable targets. The example of carnival, on the other hand, shows us that comedy at its most profound level of meaning emerges from an imaginative world in which the human community functions in a particular way. The Russian critic Mikhail Bakhtin, working independently of Barber and Caputi, has argued that the attitude prevalent in carnival ritual, with its communal task of seeing and shaping reality, is fundamental to the development of the modern novel.⁴ Though he never analyzed Cervantes' masterpiece in any detail, Bakhtin designates *Don Quixote* "the classic and purest model of novel as genre."⁵ and in his thoughtful study of *Gargantua and Pantagruel* frequently calls attention to the fact that Cervantes, as well as Rabelais, was writing in a Renaissance culture still permeated by carnival folklore. Where Barber confines his study of Shakespeare to the Renaissance culture of England, both Bakhtin and Caputi make clear the depth and breadth of the phenomenon of carnival in European culture as a whole.

Four elements of carnival celebration seem especially relevant to a comic paradigm: disguises or masks which suggest some kind of metamorphosis (for example, men dressed as women or clowns in painted faces), a reign of confusion where boisterous anarchy appears to prevail, contests or attacks, and ritual execution (of *pharmakoi* or of King Carnival). The world of carnival is thus a peculiar construction which loosens the conventional boundaries between fantasy and reality and mocks ordinary ways of perceiving time and space. During carnival time, riotous behavior, obscene gestures, and abusive language singularly inappropriate in daily life are not only tolerated but seen as "normal." Conventional groupings of people—for example, in terms of sex, age, social rank, or ethnic group—temporarily lose their significance, and unexpected alliances of people who seem to have little in common are typical. Bakhtin calls attention to carnival's deliberate and systematic degradation of status: "Carnival brings together, unites, weds, and combines the sacred with the profane, the lofty with the lowly, the great with the insignificant, the wise with the stupid, etc."[6] But though Caputi rightly observes that one may apprehend in carnival festivity "a world seething with potential for disaster,"[7] the carnival attitude does *not* encourage a frivolous abandonment to nature or a nihilistic deconstruction of social norms.

As a critical metaphor, carnival may be said to identify a style of artistic consciousness, a heuristic principle that is fundamentally comic in its orientation to reality. An artist need not be conscious of the historical tradition of carnival within such an orientation; rather, he must apprehend what Bakhtin calls the "peculiar logic" of this way of artistically comprehending life.[8] Caputi locates the impulse to carnival in "an instinctive, uncritical, frenetic species of fun" which he has termed 'buffo'"[9] and which he connects both with primitive notions of the earth's fertility and with the more complex ground of a fertile imagination. The effect of carnival, he says, is "to startle the beholder, to upset his expectations, and by this process to suggest fresh possibilities in the world, an unexpected potential for creativeness."[10] Bakhtin would probably agree with Caputi that what the metaphor of carnival points to is a basic human capacity to "find joy whether the facts of life justify it or not."[11] However, where Caputi believes that the "pleasure of comedy consists in its power to affirm the sufficiency of the individual in the world,"[12] Bakhtin argues more convincingly that the carnival attitude depends upon a peculiar consciousness of human community, a recognition that the world becomes meaningful only in dialogue: "the truth is not born and does not reside in the head of an individual person; it is born of the dialogical intercourse *between people* in the collective search for truth."[13]

The studies of both Caputi and Bakhtin call attention to the religious significance of the carnival's preoccupation with the "vulgar" reality of an Iron Age: whatever is mocked or seemingly destroyed is simultaneously being prepared for renewal and rebirth. Caputi's concise scheme for the full pattern of carnival action is "death, resurrection, and a wedding."[14] But Bakhtin goes on to say that where a culture loses sight of the bonds of community, the external gestures of carnival move toward the banality of a mere holiday or the desperate hilarity of alienated individuals.[15]

Barber asserts that the carnival festival of England "provides the clearer paradigm" for Shakespeare's comic art and connects such celebrations with the ancient festivals of urban Romans (the Saturnalia), the Freudian concept of release from inhibition, and the basic human pleasure in harmonious relations:

> A saturnalian attitude, assumed by a clear-cut gesture toward liberty, brings mirth, an accession of wanton vitality. In the terms of Freud's analysis of wit, the energy normally occupied in maintaining inhibition is freed for celebration. The holidays in actual observance were built around the enjoyment of the vital pleasure of moments when nature and society are hospitable to life.[16]

But Bakhtin is surely correct in insisting that despite the atmosphere of jolly festivity, which appeared to Puritan eyes as pagan indulgence, the medieval carnival was deeply permeated by, and ironically dependent upon, "the spiritual and ideological dimension" of "official" (social, political, religious) existence. As it is a ritualized mocking of customary or official existence, the eccentric behavior of carnival also requires a kind of inhibition, despite what Barber appropriately terms its "clear-cut gesture toward liberty." Moreover, Bakhtin's detailed analysis of the masquerading and buffoonery of carnival suggests that such celebrating is related specifically to crisis and not simply to those "moments when nature and society are hospitable to life."

Although the eccentricity that predominates in carnival revelry appears to be spontaneous, it is actually ritualistic and as such temporarily inhibits individuality. More precisely, carnival eccentricity frees the individual from the practical or everyday view of life from which a sense of crisis may be hidden, but the energy so "released" is directed toward deeper, public concerns, not toward private desires or physical drives. Within the attitude of carnival, the resources of the individual bear fruit only in community; but because this attitude runs counter to the post-Renaissance exaltation of the ego, carnival festivities, like mythological tales, began by the second half of the seventeenth century to seem quaint and outmoded and to be associated by literate people with primitive consciousness. In the last 200 years, the gap between popular culture and high culture has widened even further. We have difficulty perceiving the carnival attitude, which persists in life as well as in literature, because we have lost confidence in the spiritual values of the folk, and consequently have lost any sense of the profound significance of folk humor.

Bakhtin observes that the laughter of the folk conveys "a specific ethical attitude toward reality [which] . . . is untranslatable into logical language; it is a specific means of seeing and capturing reality."[17] Laughter makes something material, visible, and concrete. Carnival laughter is *impersonal*, directed to the highest ideals of a community, rather than to the comical event itself. Thus, we laugh not so much at a man who tilts with windmills as at the heroic ideal of chivalry in the presence of an unexpectedly concrete and ordinary reality. The laughter of carnival celebrations counteracts, though it does not negate, that human seriousness which perceives reality not as it reveals itself, but as it conforms to predetermined ideals. The ironic laughter of carnival dissolves the distance between the ideal and the real; it "brings the world close to man and man close to his fellow man."[18]

At the time of the composition of *Don Quixote*, European culture, especially in Spain, was on the threshold of change. An old order, the medieval culture, which manifested its ideals in the figure of the knight, was breaking up, forced to encounter conflicting images from science, from the classical civilizations of Greece and Rome, from the New World across the Atlantic, from the newly emerging aspirations of a middle class. The highest ideals of the old, medieval world are parodied throughout the pages of *Don Quixote*. But Cervantes' laughter is ambivalent and not derisive; whatever is ridiculed is simultaneously being praised and called upon to regenerate itself. Don Quixote's ideals are the ideals of Christian Europe, which the laughter of carnival humor degrades in order to renew. The spirit of this laughter must be understood in a public, communal context:

> The satirist whose laughter is negative places himself above the object of his mockery, he is opposed to it. The wholeness of the world's comic aspect is destroyed, and that which appears comic becomes a private reaction. The people's ambivalent laughter, on the other hand, expresses the point of view of the whole world; he who is laughing also belongs to it.[19]

Thus when we laugh at Don Quixote, we laugh freely at human foolishness; if we set ourselves above such foolishness, we lose the attitude of carnival and the possibility of vitality its world holds out to us.

Peculiar to carnival ritual is the unexpected discovery of multiple planes of coexisting realities typically brought about by the use of masks or disguises. It is a communal activity. In the novel, reader and narrator must work together to form this carnival community. For example, when the narrator of *Don Quixote* reveals the decision of a certain ingenious gentleman to become a knight-errant, a dialogue of perspectives impossible in everyday life may be set in motion with the cooperation of the reader's imagination:

> At last, when his wits were gone beyond repair, he came to conceive the strangest idea that ever occurred to any madman in this world. It now appeared to him fitting and necessary . . . to become a knight-errant and roam the world on horseback, in a suit of armor; he would go in quest of adventures, by way of putting into practice all that he had read in his books. . . .[20]

To accept the fiction of such a masquerade as that of Don Quixote is to cross over the boundary of everyday consciousness and to allow the possibility of carnival. A knight-errant is an imaginary person from an idealized past who suddenly becomes embodied in the more real but still imaginary character of Don Quixote. When a reader participates as he reads in the world that comes to life in Cervantes' novel, whatever might be practical, and even necessary and functional from an everyday attitude, is turned upside-down and inside-out.

The image of Don Quixote stands between two temporal dimensions. La Mancha resembles the ordinary present, whereas chivalric romances embody an image of an ideal past. La Mancha is, in the beginning of the novel, recognizably mundane. The narrator carefully details the "facts" of a typical gentleman's day-to-day existence: what he eats on what day of the week, how he dresses, with whom he lives, what his favorite pastimes are; none of these details belongs to the feudal world of romance, a realm (recognizably poetic) which exists from the point of view of La Mancha *only* as a memory of an idealized past.

Of course, any fiction makes a complex of meaning from another time appear to unfold in the presence of the reader, and Cervantes continually—and explicitly—refers to this fact. For example, the story of the great duel between Don Quixote and the Biscayne stops abruptly because, we are told, the original manuscript stops. The narrator then relates his search for the conclusion of the narrative, his discovery of the documents written by Cid Hamete Benegeli, the translations of these documents—all of which make possible, finally, the resumption of the action. This interruption of the action breaks the magic spell of narration, reminding readers that in the act of writing and in the act of reading, an idealized past becomes present and visible—and at least temporarily relevant.

The fact that any reader can move beyond the boundaries of "clock time" sheds light on what happens to the protagonist of *Don Quixote*. The old gentleman becomes so caught up in a poetic world which he encounters in the pages of his books of chivalry that the practical boundaries culture has erected between this realm and the more prosaic one in which his household lives begin to blur. As Ortega y Gasset tells us, Don Quixote seems to live on the "beveled edge" where two worlds meet.²¹ What is even more remarkable is that Don Quixote comes alive through an interweaving of several perspectives or points of view. The narrator tells the reader that Don Quixote is an imaginary character, invented by a mad old man; the reader easily forgets that the mad old man is also an imaginary character. The parodic rhythm of the action of the novel leads the reader to perceive the value of the "real" Alonso Quijano (or Quejana, Quijada or Quesada) as that value is embedded in the "imaginary" Don Quixote. The narrator comments in the concluding chapter of the novel:

> ... as has been stated more than once, whether Don Quixote was plain Alonso Quijano the Good or Don Quixote de la Mancha, he was always of a kindly and pleasant disposition and for this reason was beloved not only by the members of his household but by all who knew him. (985)

The celebratory, ironic interweaving of many perspectives of meaning by the narration of the action makes this character familiar and "beloved": not merely a target of satire and not simply a romantic hero.

Of crucial importance to the understanding of *Don Quixote* is the recognition, so familiar as to be taken for granted, that this novel as a whole is a parody of what continues to be a popular narrative form: the romance. Of course, a literary parody (something "beside the song") presupposes a lyrical, idealized image of man and world. The significance of Cervantes' parody is that it is festive and ambivalent; in *Don Quixote*, the heroic image is both admirable and laughable because it is permeated with the ironic attitude of the carnival spirit. In this first "modern" novel, the centuries-long tradition of medieval folk humor merges, as Bakhtin suggests, with the Renaissance philosophy of laughter:

> The Renaissance conception of laughter can be roughly described as follows: Laughter has a deep philosophical meaning, it is one of the essential forms of the truth concerning the world as a whole, concerning history and man; it is a peculiar point of view relative to the world; the world is seen anew, no less (and perhaps more) profoundly than when seen from the serious standpoint. Therefore, laughter is just as admissible to great literature, posing serious problems, as seriousness. Certain essential aspects of the world are accessible only to laughter.[22]

This understanding of humor, expressed in the plays of Shakespeare and in the fiction of Cervantes, appears to have been lost in the epochs following the Renaissance; laughter becomes a weapon in the hands of satirists like Swift and Voltaire, rather than a means of reconciling the innate desire for romance with the extrinsic demands of artistic realism.

The central event of medieval carnival ceremony was the crowning and "discrowning" of a carnival king. The Christian paradigm for this ceremony is the crowning of the King of the Jews, a historic event which has ambivalent, ironic meaning for the present. The mock crowning, the abuse, and the "discrowning" of Christ on the cross constitute an event in which all humanity participates; in recognizing and in sharing the guilt and horror of this event, however, mankind also discovers the possibility of its redemption. Similarly, the spirit of medieval parody is neither destructive nor frivolous; according to Bakhtin, carnival parody is "the creation of a double which discrowns its counterpart. Everything has its parody, i.e., its comical aspect, because everything is reborn and renewed through death."[23] Cervantes' parody of chivalric romances may be compared to the medieval parodies of sacred literature, which were imaginative attempts to comprehend its depth of meaning, not to deny its seriousness. Thus, a profoundly Christian irony generates the parodic humor of *Don Quixote*.

Don Quixote is truly comic only when the image of the knight-errant and the ideals of chivalry retain a symbolic value; unless the reader accepts the values which the chivalric tradition attempts to articulate, *Don Quixote* becomes a literary monument, much like one of the books the curate and the barber were willing to save from the fire, a work with historic and aesthetic merit but little emotional appeal. The parodic humor of *Don Quixote* emerges from the *interplay* between the poetic ideal of chivalry and its "other side," the prosaic reality of La Mancha. We miss the point of Cervantes' artistic achievement if we fail to accept either one of these spheres of meaning. The chivalric ideal is enhanced, not destroyed by the ironic duplicity of *Don Quixote*; moreover, the busy, familiar reality of La Mancha also reveals surprising values of its own not to be scorned.

We are told in the opening pages of *Don Quixote* that the ingenious gentleman's fondness for chivalric romances was indulged to such an extent that the poetic world of chivalry became not simply an entertaining diversion or an interesting reminder of a heroic past, but "more real to him than anything else in the world." What is noteworthy about the transformation of an ordinary middle-class gentleman, who belongs to the present reality of La Mancha, into Don Quixote is that two contradictory perspectives of meaning are brought together in a single image; neither is denied or rejected. Don Quixote's quest is both poetic and scientific; he dedicates himself to the high ideals of chivalry: honor and loyalty and courage and justice; however, he will go in quest of *already completed* adventures: "by way of putting into practice all that he had read in his books...." (27). Like a scientist in a laboratory, he will put formulas to the test, applying what he knows to be true (or at least "more real"); all his adventures will be consciously patterned, in advance, after the adventures of real (that is, fictional) knights-errant. His service will be "unofficial"; he is not (like the heroes he imitates) responding to the official call of bishop or king but to the call of his imagination, filled as it is with the romantic exploits of ideal heroes.

W. H. Auden, who assumes that *Don Quixote* offers a believable portrait of the Christian saint, comments on the ironic contrast, carefully underlined by Cervantes, between Don Quixote and the heroes he imitates:

When we first meet Don Quixote he is (a) poor, (b) not a knight, (c) fifty, (d) has nothing to do except hunt and read romances about Knight-Errantry. Manifestly, he is the opposite of the heroes he admires, i.e., he is lacking in the epic *arete* of birth, looks, strength, etc.[24]

Thus, the image of Don Quixote *dismembers* the conventional or "official" image of the hero. Don Quixote and Amadis de Gaule, in Bakhtin's terms, can be understood as the careful pairing of opposites which characterizes the ritual pattern of carnival. When the ingenious Don Quixote takes a rusty morion for a helmet, turns a broken-down nag into Rosinante "the first and foremost of all the hacks in the world," and transforms a good-looking peasant wench into the peerless Dulcinea del Toboso, a dialogue of these opposing perspectives of meaning is set in unexpectedly dynamic motion.

The district of La Mancha represents the "official" world in *Don Quixote*; its citizens include Don Quixote's household, his neighbors the curate and the barber, his friend the Bachelor Sanson Carrasco, as well as innkeepers, muledrivers, farmers, peasant wenches, and respectable ladies. The images of Don Quixote and Sancho Panza become eccentric in the context of this busy, prosaic world of action; like carnival clowns, they live on the boundaries of communal life without being estranged from it. Don Quixote's voice speaks of a "higher" ideal world than the official community, where essentially the same values are given lip service but not lived; Sancho's voice descends beneath the official world to the "lower" material realm of bodily concerns. In the dialogues of the knight and his squire, obviously focal points in the novel as a whole, romantic idealism encounters stubborn literalism; neither perspective cancels the other.

Throughout the novel, the image of Sancho Panza complements the image of his master in complex and unexpected ways. After the capture of Mambrino's helmet, Sancho asks "what are we to do with this dappled gray steed that looks like a gray-colored ass, that this fellow Martino whom your Grace just routed left here?" Don Quixote rails against depriving his enemy of his mount, but Sancho persists, inquiring what will happen to the beast's trappings. Here, Sancho demands attention, as he does time and time again, to *details* of chivalric life not included in the world of romance; Don Quixote is forced to make concessions: "being in doubt and until I am better informed, I should say that you might exchange them [the trappings] in case of extreme necessity'' (160–61).

Having exchanged his own meager trappings for those of the luckless barber, Sancho begins to wonder aloud about further improving their lot. Why must they seek adventure "in these wasteland and crossroad places," Sancho observes, when serving "some emperor or other great prince who has some war on his hands" would be more likely to earn the knight the fame he seeks (161). In answer, Don Quixote spins a fantasy beginning with the period of "probation" served by all knights and ending with the assurance that when the knight's virtue is rewarded with a kingdom, as it must be, his squire will surely be made a count. This romance momentarily sweeps Sancho, too, into the dream of a world where things are what we would like them to be: "That's what I want, and no mistake about it," said Sancho. "That is what I'm waiting for" (164). Throughout the novel, dreams of heroic ideals are questioned, tested, pulled into battle with prosaic realities. While it is Sancho's function to bring Don Quixote down to earth, to the level of prosaic reality, Sancho never negates the value of the dream.

The playfully ambiguous spirit of carnival explicitly moves the action of many scenes in *Don Quixote*, but the rhythm of action—the systematic shifting from one extreme to the other that reveals the carnival's ironic orientation—may be seen most clearly in the famous scenes at the enchanted inn in *Don Quixote*, part 1. In both these scenes we see the pattern of carnival festivities: ceremonial entrance, disguises, contests and combats, the temporary reign of confusion or disorder (where the world is turned "upside down"), and the precarious re-establishment of order concluded by a ceremonious leave-taking. These scenes, along with their counterpart in part 2, the adventures at the castle of the Duke and the Duchess, are pivotal; in them are gathered the major themes of *Don Quixote*: the meaning of play, the mysterious complexity of reality, and the operation of love in human lives.

The inn which Don Quixote and Sancho Panza approach in part 1, chapter 15, is a communal space, like a public market or a town square: travelers stop at an inn to eat, to rest, and to meet on official or unofficial business. The inn is an image of enclosed space, symbolizing such communal values as hospitality and political order; it draws together in a temporary world of action and meaning people whose everyday lives appear unrelated. Don Quixote, "greatly to Sancho's disgust," perceives the inn as a castle, his fancy taking the tavern's official reality as a communal symbol to its highest earthly form. As with the basin-helmet, there is admittedly a certain logic involved: if he is a knight engaged in chivalrous adventures, then the homely inn must be a castle to accommodate him.

Actually, the narrator comments, the innkeeper's wife, while not exactly a chatelaine, "was naturally of a charitable disposition and inclined to sympathize with those of her neighbors who were in trouble" (115). Thus, the knight, who has been cudgeled by ignoble horse-traders, is accorded the ceremonies of hospitality; he is carried to the attic of the inn, "which gave every evidence of having formerly been a hayloft" (115). Ordinary transformation from hayloft to resting place for travelers gives way to a more extraordinary metamorphosis as Don Quixote begins to fantasize that Maritornes, the innkeeper's servant, has fallen in love with him. That Don Quixote sees the hayloft-attic as a romantic trysting-place is already suggested by the fact that a muledriver lies within, waiting for a visit from the same Maritornes. Prosaic reality carries within it the possibility of poetic ideals. Maritornes too becomes a double-image: a lusty servant girl who attracts a muledriver and a lady worthy of a knight's devotion.

When Maritornes crosses the threshold of the "starry stable" to keep a rendezvous with the muledriver, the ritual action of carnival is set in motion; what is hilarious confusion on one level of response also teases the reader into reflection. As Cervantes shows his readers from the opening pages of the novel, giving recognition to the multiple dimensions of reality has a surprising effect: the earthy details that might seem to negate the poetic world of chivalry reveal both the limits and the value of the dream. The reader is pulled into this scene through Cervantes' vivid animation of objects and characters coming together at a giddy pace. Perceiving how each character is partially correct in his interpretation of objects and people, the reader begins to comprehend that each point of view is also partially invalid, or at least incapable of defining the meaning of the action as a whole. Thus, the ironic double-imagery of the carnival tests—and finally enlarges—the limited perspective of the individual.

Carnival and Don Quixote: The Folk Tradition of Comedy

Bakhtin calls attention to the effect of carnival upon the community of participants: "people appear for a moment outside the normal situations of life. . . . and a different, more genuine, sense of themselves and of their relationships one to another is revealed."[25] The ideal of love is tested by the carnival confusion in the starry stable; the relationship between Maritornes and the muledriver is thrown against the relationship of Don Quixote and Dulcinea—and of Maritornes and Don Quixote. Simple lust at its lowest is interwoven with platonic love and with a gentleman's tender affection for a fair damsel-wench. When the muledriver observes Maritornes struggling with Sancho, she becomes for him a lady in distress; thus, the muledriver leaps to her defense, as if *he* were a gallant knight: when the muleteer "perceived by the light of the lamp what was happening to his lady, he left Don Quixote and went to her assistance" (120). The angry innkeeper arrives to investigate the commotion; from his point of view, Maritornes is a slut who has invited the violence he observes. The innkeeper, whose official role is to keep order in this community, enters the fray to punish the girl: "The best part of it was, the lamp went out, leaving them in darkness, whereupon there ensued a general and merciless melee. . . ." (120). Into the darkness comes another image of official authority: a patrolman of the Holy Brotherhood. Glancing at the sorely wounded Don Quixote, the officer believes a murder has been committed and cries out, "Close the gateway of the inn!" The cry startles the participants into ending the battle. Sancho, struck with amazement, decides this new arrival can be none other than the enchanted Moor his master has warned him about. As order begins to be restored, Don Quixote draws the most reasonable conclusion from the "merciless melee": "no notice is to be taken of such things where enchantments are concerned, nor should anyone be angry or annoyed by them" (124).

A comic world of enchantment, or carnival, finds personal blame or guilt inappropriate. Conversely, the tragic representation of the world insists upon the recognition and acceptance of blame and guilt; the pattern of tragic action would sweep us into perceiving the value of the heroic ideal by feeling its loss. In the comic action of carnival, the heroic ideal is discovered unexpectedly as the heart of the community itself. But the discovery is typically preceded by contests or struggles and death.

The reign of confusion or "merciless melee" ends as day breaks, and each participant returns to the day's labors. Don Quixote and his squire both drink of "Fierabras' balm," concocted by the knight to relieve bodily suffering. The squire "began to discharge at both ends and with such force that neither the cattail mat on which he had dropped down nor the coarse linen coverlet that had been tossed over him was of much use afterward" (125). Again, the image of Sancho brings the action down to a physical, bodily level of meaning. Don Quixote, on the other hand, begins to feel "quite himself again" and "was all for setting out at once in search of adventures." He prepares to leave with appropriate ceremonies before a crowd of onlookers. When he expresses his gratitude to the innkeeper, promising to avenge all his host's enemies, the innkeeper, "equally tranquil," replies that a guest need only pay for his lodging. Don Quixote admits he must have mistaken the inn for a castle but refuses to pay because he has never read of knights-errant paying for hospitality. The innkeeper persists, but Don Quixote brooks no compromise with the laws of chivalry recorded in his romances; he arrogantly calls his host a "stupid, evil-minded tavernkeeper," and sails forth from the inn, lance (a pike retrieved from a corner of the inn) in hand (127).

Sancho, left behind in weakened bodily condition, is treated to a ceremonious blanket-tossing, as if the community, having failed to bring the master to earth, would elevate the squire. Safely outside the inn, Don Quixote observes his squire "... going up and down in the air with such grace and dexterity that, had the knight's mounting wrath permitted him to do so, it is my opinion that he would have laughed at the sight" (128). According to Bakhtin, it is Sancho's function as clown to bring the rhythm of action "down to a strongly emphasized bodily level of food, drink, digestion and sexual life."[26] Bakhtin goes on to call attention to the ironic or double-edged significance of the image of Sancho: Sancho's concreteness, his earthiness, is festive,

> the bodily grave (belly, bowels, earth) which has been dug for Don Quixote's abstract and deadened idealism.... This is a bodily and popular corrective to individual idealistic and spiritual pretense. Moreover, it is the popular corrective of laughter applied to the narrow-minded seriousness of the spiritual pretense (the absolute lower stratum is always laughing): it is a regenerating and laughing death.[27]

What Bakhtin is pointing out is that the images of Don Quixote and Sancho Panza enter into active dialogue in the narration of the novel: Sancho is a "corrective" for Don Quixote, but as is typical of carnival parody, the *reverse* is also true. Thus, Sancho is "elevated" by the blanket-tossing, witnessed by the silent laughter of his master. The parodic humor of carnival is at its most profound level of meaning a response to a communal crisis and a call for change, for a new outlook on life. The festive laughter of carnival, however, is ironic; it is part of a ritualistic interweaving of praise and abuse. Thus, the fantastic chivalry of Don Quixote enters into dialogue with the "bodily grave" of Sancho's concreteness to be "degraded"; but the dialogue moves toward regeneration and renewal of the essential bonds which link human beings to their earthly existence and their spiritual destiny, not toward death or negation as a final end.

The ambivalent laughter so essential to the carnival attitude comes even more explicitly into play in the second scene at the enchanted inn, where we witness an elaborate scheme of disguise planned to rescue Don Quixote from his mad obsession with chivalry. Don Quixote's neighbors the curate and the barber, the mad lover Cardenio, and Dorotea, the farmer's daughter disguised as Princess Micomicona—a community of people who might appear to have little in common—join the innkeeper and his family at a meal. When human beings join others in a feast, barriers of significance in the practical world of affairs seem to be loosened. Don Quixote and Sancho Panza are temporarily absent from this community, having retired to the attic-hayloft, yet the ingenious gentleman continues to command attention. The conversation at the dinner table turns on Don Quixote's strange behavior and the defects and merits of chivalric romances. When the innkeeper shows off his collection of chivalric books (which he cannot read), we are shown how intimately Don Quixote belongs to this community; he carries to extreme, or he literalizes, poetic fantasies that already live in communal imagination. Ironically, the company at table is listening attentively to the curate read the romance of "El Curioso Impertinente" (One Who Was Too Curious for His Own Good) when Sancho Panza —as if he were crossing a threshold—bursts in to tell of Don Quixote's heroic battle with a giant. This unexpected interruption signals the arrival of carnival disorder.

Everyone rushes to see for himself the truth of Sancho's tale; the image which greets them is clearly parodic. The inclusion of the concrete, bodily details of Don Quixote's appearance "dismembers" the conventional heroic image just encountered in the tale being read at table:

> He was clad in his shirt, which was not long enough in front to cover his thighs completely and was about six fingers shorter behind. His legs were very long, lean, and hairy and anything but clean. On his head he had a little greasy red cap that belonged to the innkeeper, and around his left arm he had rolled a red blanket.... (315)

This image of Don Quixote with his eyes shut, "for he was still asleep and dreaming," flaying the wineskins hanging near his bed, ridicules as well as celebrates knightly valor. As if we were seeing through a system of trick mirrors, we clearly see the oddly-clad old gentleman vying with wineskins, but we also see with Sancho a valiant knight battling an enchanted giant to keep a promise to the Princess Micomicona. With the innkeeper and his wife, we see a fool wasting wine and overturning the order of the household. With the assembled company and the author, we laugh: not only at the image of Don Quixote in battle but at the human inability to meet romantic expectations of heroic appearance. If the heroic image is limited to young, handsome males who never make fools of themselves, the ideal of heroism is itself limited and in danger of losing its essential vitality.

When the laughter which permeates *Don Quixote* is related to the humor of carnival festivities, we begin to see the affirmation engendered by such parodies as this dream-battle, which

> debase the hero and bring him down to earth; they familiarize and humanize and bring him up close; the ambivalent laughter of carnival turns to ashes all that is stilted and stiff, but in no way harms the genuinely heroic core of the image.[28]

Whereas satire attempts to make a distinction between the ideal and the real, carnival challenges our confidence in such distinctions.

The movement of carnival time, its "continual shifting from top to bottom, from front to rear," suggests that unless man's poetic dreams of an ideal or heroic world can touch base with the concrete and critical presence of everyday reality, human imagination can become merely a tool of escape, and humor can degenerate into a bitter mode of exposing evil. Carnival humor counteracts, though it does not negate, that human seriousness which, in the interests of practical order, makes absolute claims on reality and institutes an established way of seeing people and things. When the gap between the ideal and the real threatens to erupt—and, of course, the threat is fairly constant in human affairs—a carnival revelry of disorder serves to enlarge human perspective, "to bring the world close to man and man close to his fellow man."[29] The true hero of carnival action is not an individual, not even the clown, but the resourcefulness of the human community acting as a body.

The appearance of the barber from whom Mambrino's helmet was retrieved, like Maritornes' entrance to the attic-hayloft and Sancho's interruption of the storytelling, provokes a carnival resolution. Masquerading has thrown the inn into "hubbub and labyrinthine chaos," a state of confusion which signifies the human condition in an Iron Age of change and crisis. Don Quixote emerges once again as the focal point of celebration, the fool or mock-King who symbolizes the destiny of communal ideals. In this marvelous scene, a swelling crowd of people from almost every conceivable segment of society becomes involved in a dispute over an "official" reality, the barber's packsaddle. Sancho has assumed that if the barber's basin is Mambrino's helmet, retrieved in an honorable encounter, then the barber's packsaddle must also belong to the victor. Naturally, the barber can make no sense of Sancho's logic. Don Quixote, vouching for his squire's honor, takes it upon himself to act as peacemaker in the dispute: "picking up the packsaddle, he placed it upon the ground where all could see that it might lie there until truth was established" (403).

Don Quixote calmly explains that the trappings won in "honorable warfare" seem to have been transformed into a packsaddle. On the other hand, Mambrino's helmet, he proclaims, is clearly a helmet and not a mere basin. Don Quixote's friends, the curate and the barber, decide with Cardenio, Don Fernando, the Judge and the Captain, "to carry the joke a little further so that they might all have a good laugh" (404). They agree with Don Quixote, much to the surprise of the others assembled at the inn. The servants of Don Luis and the three patrolmen of the Holy Brotherhood who have just arrived can make no sense of the argument because they do not know Don Quixote: "To those acquainted with Don Quixote's mad whims, all this was very amusing indeed, but to the rest it seemed utter nonsense" (406). When the majority of the assembled community officially votes to establish the basin and the packsaddle as chivalric accoutrements, one of Don Luis's servants voices his misgivings: "I cannot but believe that there is some mystery behind their insistence upon something that is so contrary to what truth and experience teaches" (406–07). The mystery is the invocation of the carnival spirit.

When one of the patrolmen angrily protests the decision of the jokers, Don Quixote physically assaults him and the disorder of carnival prevails. What began as a deliberate deception turns in upon its perpetrators: "In short, the entire hostelry was filled with shouts, cries, screams, with tumult, terror, and confusion, with sword slashes, fisticuffs, cudgelings, kickings, bloodshed, and mishaps of every sort" (407). This time, the voice which suddenly interrupts the reign of confusion is that of Don Quixote: "Hold, all of you! Sheathe your swords, be calm, and hear me as you value your lives!" (808). The fool arrives at a resolution both playful and wise:

> Come, then, your Lordship the judge and your Reverence the curate; let one of you take the part of King Agramente and the other that of King Sobrino, and make peace between us. For it is a very great shame for so many persons of high rank as are gathered here to be killing one another over causes so trifling. (408)

Bakhtin points out that whenever the buffoon is crowned King of a carnival festivity, the mock-crowning acknowledges the reality of moral authority as a communal ideal.[30] Here Don Quixote assumes his place as the carnival king who must be executed by the community.

His position is challenged by "official" authority: the patrolmen of the Holy Brotherhood. But "official" authority is in turn subverted by Don Quixote's friends, who plead that he is mad and cannot be held accountable for the theft of the barber's equipment. A compromise with various claims about the reality of the barber's equipment is reached. The friends disguise themselves once again, capture Don Quixote while he is sleeping peacefully, and shut him in a cage. The barber makes a quixotic speech, to which the caged knight eloquently replies. The cage is carried out and placed upon an oxcart to be ceremoniously borne from the enchanted inn. This mock procession reinforces the structure of carnival and its function of renewal through death.

The rhythm of action in *Don Quixote* as a whole is circular, encompassing three journeys; each sally begins and ends at home in La Mancha. When the bachelor Sanson Carrasco disguises himself as a knight and defeats Don Quixote in battle, the ingenious gentleman returns to La Mancha for the last time. Having renounced the books of chivalric adventures and recovered his reason, he receives the sacraments and dies. But Carrasco cries out, "Long live Dulcinea!" at the death of his friend. The narrator also observes that "the notary who was present remarked that in none of those books had he read of any knight-errant dying in his own bed so peacefully in so Christian a manner" (987). The curate demands official recognition of the death, and the chronicler Cid Hamete Benegeli makes an eloquent address to his pen, warning other writers not to resurrect his "valiant knight."

Understood in the light of carnival, the death of the ingenious gentleman strongly suggests the possibility of imaginative regeneration not of chivalry as a literal mode of life but of cultural values chivalry taught us, among them courage, honor, and love. The entire community has participated in a kind of ritual execution which serves to stimulate imaginative possibilities for life. The usefulness of carnival as a critical metaphor, a topic for conversation with literary texts, is that it identifies the historical roots of a comic orientation toward life itself which the tastes and standards of a rationalistic society tend to suppress. The attitude of carnival, through its festive ironic dialogue of perspectives, tests deeply felt communal values by pushing them to extremes and finding them in unexpected contexts, where the highest truth is not the negation of evil but the most inclusive good. Bakhtin's seminal suggestion that the form of the modern novel, whose defiance of traditional poetic canons signifies its commitment to vulgar reality, has its roots in carnival demands further attention. The carnival attitude which permeates *Don Quixote* is, in any case, worth reclaiming in the present era as an important legacy of the comic imagination: an affirmation of the unexpected plenitude of human existence, of the real and ever-present possibilities for change and renewal of the human community, even in an Iron Age.

Notes

1. Sir Edward Tylor, *Primitive Culture*, 1871; Sir James George Frazer, *The Golden Bough*, 1890; see especially F. M. Cornford, *The Origin of Attic Comedy* (New York, 1934).

2. C. L. Barber, *Shakespeare's Festive Comedy: A Study of Dramatic Form and its Relation to Social Custom* (Princeton, 1959); Anthony Caputi, *Buffo: The Genius of Vulgar Comedy* (Detroit, 1978).

3. See, however, A. J. Close, *The Romantic Approach to "Don Quixote"* (Cambridge, 1978).

4. Mikhail Bakhtin, *Problems of Dostoevsky's Poetics*, trans. R. W. Rotsel (Ann Arbor, 1973); *Rabelais and His World*, trans. Helene Iswolsky (Cambridge, Mass., 1968). See also *The Dialogic Imagination*, trans. Michael Holquist (Austin, 1981), a posthumously published collection of Bakhtin's essays on the form of the novel.

5. Bakhtin, *The Dialogic Imagination*, 324.
6. Bakhtin, *Problems of Dostoevsky's Poetics*, 101.
7. Caputi, 200.
8. Bakhtin, *Rabelais and His World*, 11.
9. Caputi, 20.
10. Ibid, 196.
11. Ibid., 233.
12. Ibid., 203.
13. Bakhtin, *Problems of Dostoevsky's Poetics*, 90.
14. Caputi, 32.
15. See *Rabelais and His World*, 36-39.
16. Barber, 7.
17. Bakhtin, *Problems of Dostoevsky's Poetics*, 137.
18. Ibid., 133.
19. Bakhtin, *Rabelais and His World*, 12.

20. Miguel de Cervantes, *The Ingenious Gentleman: Don Quixote de la Mancha*, trans. Samuel Putman (New York, 1949), 27. All further references will be cited parenthetically in the text.

21. Jose Ortega y Gasset, *Meditations on Quixote*, trans. Evelyn Rugg and Diego Marin (New York, 1963), 136.

22. Bakhtin, *Rabelais and His World*, 66.
23. Bakhtin, *Problems of Dostoevsky's Poetics*, 105.

24. W. H. Auden, "The Ironic Hero: Some Reflections on *Don Quixote*," *Horizon* 20 (1949): 86-94; rpt. in *Cervantes: A Collection of Critical Essays*, ed. Lowry Nelson (Englewood Cliffs, N. J., 1969), 76.

25. Bakhtin, *Problems in Dostoevsky's Poetics*, 120. See also Victor Turner, *Dramas, Fields, and Metaphors: Symbolic Action in Human Society* (Ithaca, 1974), 231-71, for an anthropologist's exploration of this phenomenon as an element of *communitas*.

26. Bakhtin, *Rabelais and His World*, 20.
27. Ibid., 22.
28. Bakhtin, *Problems of Dostoevsky's Poetics*, 109.
29. Ibid., 133.
30. Ibid., 102-03.

8

The Copious Inventory of Comedy

ROBERT S. DUPREE

IF there were a rhetoric of comedy—and surely there should be—its main figure would have to be copia, the theme of plenitude and abundance. Even a work like Beckett's *Waiting for Godot*, which is ostensibly about absence and nothingness, is filled with long speeches, great pompous lists of abstractions, and endless paradings of trivial or inconsequential language, as though patience itself were a form of abundance. Yet critics seem to write of comedy as though it were concerned with constraint—with manners, categories, structures, and organization—formal impedimenta rather than an inexhaustible array of words and things. In an essay on Rabelais and Gogol, Mikhail Bakhtin complains that

> literary criticism and aesthetics, in general, take their point of departure from the skimpy and impoverished manifestations of comic literature during the last three centuries. They also attempt to force Renaissance laughter into this pigeonhole. Such a procedure is not even adequate for an understanding of Molière.[1]

The shrunken world presented by many modern theorists of comedy is the result of a focus on manners and morals rather than on the amazing sense of inexhaustible possibility that the comic vision implies. Comic writers manifest a universe that is laden, despite rules and regulations, with more matter and spirit than any individual or society can contain. Speaking of Beckett, Guenther Anders remarks that "nothing is funnier than totally unjustified total confidence."[2] For comedy is seldom concerned with the quality of the abundance it displays. It finds sufficient interest in the mere fact that so much goes on, begins, ends, and yet begins again in the dazzling spectacle of life as a circus of a thousand clowns and clones.

The approach to comedy that Bahktin criticizes for its narrowness is often characterized by a stimulus-response theory of laughter and a systematic search for the causes of levity. The comedy of manners is the primary model for this investigation, hence the well-known essays of Bergson and Meredith tend to have a mechanistic cast, even though their authors are by no means proponents of a mechanistic psychology. Despite the undeniably valuable insights contained in these essays, the result is a bit like a definition of tragedy that is founded on the medical sources of depression. As Thomas McFarland has pointed out, "Laughter is merely a comic tool; it has no necessary relationship to the comic essence, which is the criticism of individuality by the standard of the group." The group, which represents that very plenitude which is opposed to the narrowness of individual existence, is the standard by which laughter is defined. In support of his contention, McFarland cites Ben Jonson ("Nor is the moving of laughter alwaies the end of Comedy") and L. C. Knight ("Once an invariable connexion between comedy and laughter is assumed we are not likely to make any observations that will be useful as criticism").[3] What Bakhtin calls "Renaissance laughter" is a manifestation of the group in carnivals, crowds, and festivals, not a physiological phenomenon that can be traced to a mechanism. The inadequacy of modern laughter-centered theories of comedy has been recognized by others, of course, among whom C. L. Barber and Northrop Frye have had a considerable influence on English and American criticism since the fifties. Yet Bakhtin's attack suggests that more than a failure of critics is responsible for these unsatisfactory theories. He also implies that something has happened to comedy itself since the Renaissance.

There has long been a general agreement among scholars that tragedy in the classical sense has not truly flourished since the seventeenth century, at least on the stage. Yet most of us are inclined to see comedy as continuing in full force from Aristophanes to the present. The comic spirit, we are inclined to admit, has a universality that seems to suffer no abatement from era to era. However, could it not be maintained that the same tendency to turn the word "tragedy" into a synonym for "misfortune" has shrunken the infinite variety of comedy into mere humor? Granted that we have lost the impressive depths of stage tragedy, is it not possible that we have lost the profundity of comedy as well?

In his essay "Goethe and the Avoidance of Tragedy," Erich Heller speaks of the way that the great German author failed to provide consolation for war-torn Europeans in the mid-twentieth century:

> What was the nature of the experience in the face of which Goethe offered no help? It was the very kind of experience before which Goethe himself always proved helpless: the exposure to the manifestations of evil and sin. "The mere attempt to write tragedy might be my undoing," he once said, and it was the truth—at least for the greatest part of his life.... Iphigenie, Tasso, Faust ... are potential tragedies, indeed so much so that one may feel that the tragic conclusion could only be avoided at the price of complete artistic conclusiveness. They show a moving and yet unsatisfactory reluctance of mind and imagination to accept the role of the road leading to the very center of human destiny.[4]

Later in the same essay, Heller concludes that, in Goethe,

> the meaning of creative genius as well as the meaning of doing the sober work of the day, inwardness as well as action, had to remain puzzles to each other, anonymous, undefined strangers. They never met in a common dedication and could not be at peace with each other because they knew no will other than their own. And at such a distance from "la sua voluntade è nostra pace" neither divine comedy nor human tragedy can be written.[5]

It is this "divine comedy" that has been lost from the literary imagination in modern times; without it, the dimensions of the comic genre shrink from the vision of the mystic rose to the view of a peeping tom. Even the bedroom farce, which derives, after all, from a hearty and joyful celebration of plenitude, has suffered. Farce itself, derived from a word that means "stuffing" and implies fullness, has been assigned to a vocabulary of frivolity and meaninglessness. For evil is taken seriously in comedy; and in works like Ben Jonson's *Volpone*, the unspeakable ingeniousness of the wicked is a matter that, transformed by mimesis, becomes delightful. The optimism of comedy is not a denial of the existence of evil but a recognition that evil cannot, finally, prevail, even though the wicked characters may deploy and exploit as great a variety of devices and opportunities as the virtuous ones.

The dilemma of modern comedy has its foundation in a world that predates Goethe, of course, and the critic returns inevitably to the favorite whipping boy of twentieth-century intellectual history, Renè Descartes. According to Donald Phillip Verene, it was Descartes's mathematical comedy to which Giambattista Vico reacted in *The New Science*. In Vico's understanding tragic awareness alone provides an intelligibility that allows man to know himself. Self-knowledge cannot be reached by "the standpoint of a problem-solving or pragmatic logic."[6] The problem with Cartesian comedy is that it recognizes no evil and thus severs the tragic and the comic in as absolute a fashion as Cartesian psychology severs soul and body: "There is no tragedy in the logical comprehension of an event, because it has no plot. Logic is comic. The logical concept never faces the aspect of events that makes them tragic because it never participates in memory." The memoryless comedy of Descartes is attacked repeatedly in *The New Science* because, Verene says, the

> four-fold method of understanding in the *Discourse of Method* is comic rather than tragic. It begins with something already true, divides difficulties into parts, moves in due order from simple to complex, and ends in a review and enumeration to assure the clarity achieved. There is no sense of beginning and no sense of end that can be connected with the human event as lived.[7]

The resulting understanding, which Verene calls "a perfect happiness or comedy of reason," is certainly not tragic, but one could argue that it is not fully comic either, that it has transformed Dante's four-fold method into discourse that has nothing to say about human event. Nevertheless, this description of Cartesian method does have many points in common with modern theories of comedy and fits rather neatly into the supposed schema of comedy of manners.

Such an analytic comedy is the expression of the same spirit as the one that informs Cartesian geometry. But a recent work in the history of mathematics suggests that the geometrical analysis of the *Discourse of Method* is very different from the mode of analysis that characterized geometry in the ancient world. In their book *The Method of Analysis*, Jaako Hintikka and Unto Remes claim that what the Greeks "anatomized in an analysis was not a proof (deductive connection), but a configuration ('figure')."[8] The usual way of conducting an analysis in the modern world is precisely the one described by Verene. An indubitable truth is the starting point, and from it is deduced a series of propositions that lead to a clear conclusion. But Hintikka and Remes show that before Descartes and Newton, the mode of analysis was quite different. The achieved relationship—that is, the proof as intuited or guessed at—was where one began. From the relationships in that "figure" (such as two parallel lines), one worked back to some axiomatic truth. Thus, they ask, "Does analysis consist of a series of conclusions or does one proceed in an analysis from a hoped-for conclusion to its more and more distant premises?"[9] Ancient Greek method was, they conclude, a search for premises rather than "a sequence of conclusions."

The meaning of hope in comedy becomes clear if this latter paradigm is examined closely. The conclusion to the comic search is a confirmation of an image that has been in the memory or in the hopes of the protagonists from the beginning. They must unravel the complexities that allow this figure to emerge in all its ontological certainty. The figure is, of course, plenitude, as I have already suggested at the beginning of this essay. But plenitude can never be participated in directly. It must be reached, paradoxically, through a scheme that is applied over the simple image and works back to the clarity not of the conclusion, which is always a "complexity" (a weaving together), but of the origins of things. This version of comic action is precisely the opposite of the one described by Verene. It moves from the complex to the simple, from the uncertain to the certain, from parts to whole.

Ancient geometrical analysis depended heavily on what Hintikka and Remes call "auxiliary constructions." The figure itself is incapable of being analyzed until "new geometrical objects" are introduced into the figure. "They are needed," the authors claim, "because the desired proof or construction cannot be carried out without their mediation." The unpredictable part of analysis, as Aristotle recognized, lies in the discovery of the best constructions to use in analyzing a configuration. "They are therefore the heuristically crucial but at the same time heuristically recalcitrant element of the methodological situation."[10]

In Aristophanic comedy this auxiliary construction is often what critics have termed the "happy idea"; it does not contribute to the clarity of the figure but to the fulfillment of its nature. The discovery of the happy idea, like the finding of the best auxiliary construction, is as unpredictable as it is admirable or ingenious. With it the goal of fulfilling the promise of intuition can be reached in a satisfying, elegant manner.

It does not matter whether the auxiliary construction that brings about the comic resolution is invented by a rascal or a hero. It remains as morally neutral as an extra line added to a triangle. The construction is not a permanent part of the conclusion, only a means for fulfilling the hope that what one intuits is real. In Machiavelli's *Mandragola*, for instance, the "immoral" trick that allows Callimaco to bed the chaste Lucrezia simply reveals the narrowness and sterility of those who are taken in by it. In a world as shrunken as Lucrezia's household, the communal continuities of birth and trust are impossible. The happy idea that unites the lovers shows less that the end justifies the means than that the true wickedness is a refusal to see what life is all about.

The critics' search for a mechanism that will explain comedy is not unlike the Cartesian geometrical method. It is, as Bakhtin warns, the consequence of a variety of the comic for which given circumstances and predispositions lead inevitably to a certain conclusion, where no surprises, auxiliary constructions, or happy ideas are taken into account. This attitude toward comedy is like the belief, criticized by C. S. Lewis in *An Experiment in Criticism*, that tragedy somehow offers "the typical or unusual, or ultimate, form of human misery." Tragedy, Lewis argues, is a selection from reality of the exceptional. "The real story does not end: it proceeds to ringing up undertakers, paying bills, getting death certificates, finding and proving a will, answering letters of condolence. There is no grandeur and no finality. Real sorrow ends neither with a bang nor a whimper." Tragedy taken as a philosophy of life, he claims, "is the most obstinate and best camouflaged of all wish-fulfillments."[11] This attitude toward the tragic art is like the Cartesian geometrical comedy attacked by Vico; it betrays, paradoxically, an unthinking optimism about the dignity of suffering that may be true in fictions but is not so defensible in life.

What Lewis is saying is that one must not literalize art and assume that, because tragedy imitates the worst things of life, it is devoid of illusions. In this sense comedy is closer to reality, since it does not pretend to offer a realistic picture of human joy or suffering. Comedy is less likely to attract a reader into the trap of literalism. Roger Henkle, writing in *Comedy and Culture: England 1820–1900*, notes that if

> the objective of almost all comic works in the last two centuries has been to make us understand that most of our habitual and self-defensive behavior is made up of fictions in Kermode's sense, then we can see why comedy incorporates both the random chanciness of human existence and all manner of elaborate constructs and devices....[12]

During the nineteenth century, he attempts to show, comedy begins to move to an emphasis on "the elaborative rather than the reductive."[13] Indeed, tragedy is reductive; its theme is the indisputable, the inevitable, the geometrically certain. Oedipus's fate closes in on him with the precision of a theoretical demonstration. At the core of tragedy lies an axiom so terrifying and yet so certain that one's reaction to the sufferings of the tragic protagonist is more likely to be "I told you so" than "There, for the grace of God, go I." Yet that avoidance of tragedy, as Goethe exemplifies it, or the misreading of it that C. S. Lewis describes does not lead automatically to comedy. Comedy is about uncertainty and the willingness of the mind to dwell in it imaginatively. Comedy is the realm of faith, hope, and love—those things that are essential in a world without mathematical or logical certainties. Oedipus begins in one certainty and ends in another. Tragedy reveals a "true," if dark, certainty that replaces a deluded "human" certainty. It brings home the knowledge that we dwell in a cruel and unchanging universe. The avoidance of tragedy is the substitution of a few hoped-for certainties of the mind's invention for the terrifying certainties of the cosmos. Tragedy provides some kind of answer, and it is reassuring because it leaves one in no doubt. For that reason, nineteenth-century philosophers like Schopenhauer and Nietzsche espouse a tragic philosophy or view of life in the very sense that Lewis defines. Theirs is not an avoidance of tragedy—or suffering—but an exaltation of it. What they are truly avoiding is comedy.

Aristotle calls the unchanging the ground of knowledge. For the great pessimistic nineteenth-century thinkers, tragedy is attractive as a philosophy because its theme is knowledge of the unchanging, as devastating as that knowledge may be. It gives the impression that one has faced the worst. It is about knowledge, not simply or even primarily of oneself (for comedy is about that as well) but of the minimal certainties that man possesses concerning his place in the cosmos. Thus in the nineteenth century, from the *Sturm und Drang* generation to Nietzsche, tragedy was the occasion for some brilliant critical and philosophical reflection. Yet tragedy as an imaginative act was no longer available to European culture as a whole. It could be argued that the comedy of plenitude was equally unavailable. For comedy is not about knowledge but about change. It is about the uncertainty and strange directionless world that so capriciously satisfies or thwarts our expectations. Comedy is the dwelling in a teleological vacuum that can only be filled by human presence and human labors. The gods do not truly belong in it, except as witnesses to this presence. In tragedy they exist as emblems of the unchanging. In comedy they are attendants or hosts of celebration but little more than that. Comedy is about man's ability to survive within uncertainty. Up until the time of the Renaissance, comedy and tragedy were inseparably linked as complementary insights into human reality. Since then, the two genres have been rendered absolutely and mutually exclusive. Human life must be one or the other; it cannot be, as it was for the Greeks and for Shakespeare, both tragic and comic. The creation of melodrama and tragicomedy did not resolve this opposition; it only substituted a false compromise for it. Modern comic theory and practice do not simply reflect one another; they are generated by the limitations of a vision—whether comic or tragic—that is mechanical and narrow.

Yet, as Roger Henkle rightly insists, there is a tendency during the nineteenth century for comedy to become more engaged in the elaborative than in the reductive. By the turn of the century, a comedy of the absurd emerges that is closer to Renaissance laughter than the restraining cautions of comedy of manners. Moreover, though most of the nineteenth-century theorists of comedy are deeply ingrained in the Cartesian tradition, there are notable exceptions. Hegel, for instance, is one of the outstanding theorists of comedy in the modern world. In his

Aesthetics he ranks the different genres of poetry and concludes, "Nevertheless we find that in this very consummation it is Comedy which opens the way to a dissolution of all that human art implies."[13] Kierkegaard, who was a close reader of Hegel's comments on drama, agrees with him that comedy is the final aesthetic stage and consummation of human art. For the early Kierkegaard, comedy "moves in the direction of the metaphysical," according to Gregor Malantschuk. It does not need the anchoring in history that tragedy seems to require; it brings about "a metaphysical reconciliation" and, by dint of its universality, "points beyond itself to *actuality* and to the metaphysical ideality."[14] Kierkegaard understood clearly the indeterminacy of the comic. In *Stages on Life's Way* he says, "The more any given occasion accentuates the freedom of a rational being, the more comic the involuntary becomes."[15] And though it is a character who speaks here and not the author himself, the connections between love and the comic made in this dialogue represent an insight of clearly Kierkegaardian dimensions. The same is true of a later passage, in "Quidam's Diary":

> The more one suffers, the more, I believe, has one a sense for the comic. It is only by the deepest suffering that one acquires true authority in the use of the comic, an authority which by one word transforms as by magic the reasonable creature one calls man into a caricature.... [T]his authority over the comic must be so painfully acquired that one cannot exactly desire to have it. But this comic forces itself upon me especially when my sufferings bring me into relation with another person.[16]

Likewise, Quidam later shows his understanding of comic uncertainty when commenting on the plays of Scribe: "In his work one reads or hears lines which bring to confusion the whole of existence, as if comedy were not played before men, even before madmen, but before 'distracted June-bugs,' and yet these lines are so trippingly composed in a conversational tone that it all seems a matter of course."[17] Finally, Quidam is concerned with the unity of the tragic and the comic, and he points out that "in the existence of spirit the important thing is to hold out and to endure the contradictions, but at the same time to hold them off from oneself in freedom. Hence the narrow-minded seriousness is always afraid of the comic, and rightly so; but the true seriousness itself invents the comic."[18] The great comic theme for Kierkegaard is freedom, that meaningful indeterminacy that is the moral equivalent of plenitude.

Kierkegaard has much more to say about the comic, and his interpretation, obviously a major one, deserves an examination at full length that it has not yet received. What is clear, in any case, from this brief sketch is that his is one of the rare anticipations in the nineteenth century of that return to "Renaissance laughter" that Bahktin and others in our time have called for. But laughter, the signal and manifestation of freedom and indeterminacy, has a more readily analyzable verbal parallel in comedy. It is the inventory or list. Since there has been literature, there have been lists in literature. We unthinkingly consider this phenomenon modern—typical of Joyce, Nabokov, Beckett, Borges, or Barth—but it is pervasive. We cannot imagine *The Iliad* or the Bible without their lists, which contain no small part of their energy and reflect so much of their meaning. Lists are, by definition, a plural phenomenon. Yet, though they include many things and seem to have almost inexhaustible extensions, they all exemplify a definite pattern. Homer, for instance, provides one of our earliest lists, the famous catalogue of ships which, the poet says, he could not tell over the multitude of nor name, not if he had ten tongues and ten mouths, not if he had a voice never to be broken and a heart of bronze. The numbers of those who came beneath the walls of Troy are so vast that heroic strength and endurance are required merely for the naming of them. The poet emulates the heroes he enumerates by making the recalling of their names and places of origin a monumental task. Whatever it may have evoked in a contemporary audience, Homer's list acts on us principally as a melodious, rhythmic introduction to an age of lost grandeur. These men come from places that, in the mere recital of their names, resound with greatness. Homer's catalogue suggests the superhuman abundance of magnificent men who populated the remote world of his muse.

Likewise, the Bible, with its rhythmic and awe-inspiring expanse of human history suggests the authority of a divine covenant simply through the recital of long processions of the generations of men:

> Shem was a hundred years old when he begot Arphaxad, two years after the flood. After the birth of Arphaxad he lived five hundred years,

and had other sons and daughters. Arphaxad was thirty-five years old when he begot Shelah. After the birth of Shelah he lived four hundred and three years, and had other sons and daughters. Shelah was thirty years old when he begot Eber....[19]

And on it goes, impressing the reader with the enormous lifespans and incredible fertility of the earliest men. But the biblical list does not have the same effect as the Homeric. Homer's catalogue is spatial, taking its characteristic rhythm from an alternation of name and place of origin. The biblical genealogies balance names with the length of their temporal existences. Homer's evokes past names and recalls known places, but the heroes are beyond our experience. The biblical litany of begetter and begotten resounds with a different sense of history that speaks of the fulfillment of a people's destiny. We are part of that destiny in time. The Bible emphasizes continuity more than the remoteness of a mythical past.

Though they are among the most familiar elements in literature, lists and catalogues have seldom received much attention from critics.[20] The reason for this neglect is not difficult to find. The list is a verbal phenomenon so structurally simple as to defy useful analysis or commentary. Because enumeration appears to be very primitive—perhaps the first truly "literary" device—we tend to view the sharply intrusive and disruptive Homeric catalogue of ships or the biblical genealogy or the medieval inventory as naive survivals of an oral age, even when we know better. Certainly medieval audiences seem to have had an enormous predilection for lists, saturated as their lives were with roll calls of the past and litanies of the always-present angels and saints. Yet we continue to delight in the absurd concatenations of enumeration that spill from the agile singers in a Gilbert and Sullivan operetta or tumble forth in a satiric revue. Far from being a relic of some ancient social practice, the list pervades all of literature. One thinks of Sterne's hobby-horsical inventories, Melville's etymological and cetological fantasies, Gogol's census of dead souls, Joyce's directory listings of a whole city, Nabokov's tour of North American place names, Beckett's compulsive cataloguers, or, earlier, the baroque ramblings of a Marino, a Crashaw, a Gongora, or a Quevedo.

A list may seem almost to lack a definable structure, but it is far from being odorless and colorless. In fact, the inventory has a distinctive relationship to the genre in which it occurs. Besides the earliest literary enumerations, which enhance their narratives by expanding spatial or temporal limits, there are lyric lists that extend the atemporal vision of the poet as he gazes at the urn or hears the nightingale with Keats or catalogues the sins of mankind with Petrarch and Baudelaire or the names of trees with Chaucer. Furthermore, there are even tragic lists—though they are infrequent and barely recognizable—which render the horror of downfall more intense by multiplying its meaningless certainties in a wilderness of mirrors. One thinks of the sight Macbeth views when the witches evoke their apparitions of the eight kings:

> Thou art too like the spirit of Banquo. Down!
> Thy crown doth sear mine eyelids. And thy hair,
> Thou other gold-bound brow, is like the first.
> A third is like the former. Filthy hags!
> Why do you show me this? A fourth! Start eyes!
> What, will the line stretch out to th' crack of doom?[21]

In this tragic genealogy the successive figures are indistinguishable from one another, and it is this suggestion of meaningless repetition that produces their special horror. The tragic list offers not abundance but monotony in a world that has become nameless, faceless, and hopeless. Unlike the enumerations that in lyric poetry suggest celebrative openness, the tragic list reduces the variety of the universe to an endless, dreary sameness, an eternal return of the identical. It reflects tragic certitude. In *The Canterbury Tales* the Monk threatens to send his audience into depression (or at least slumber) with his morose recital of the fall of great men, and the Knight, as is proper in a work predominately comic, interrupts these tales of woe because they may well stretch out to doomsday: "That ye han seyd is right ynough, ywis/And muchel moore: for litel hevynesse/Is right ynough to muche folke, I guesse."[22]

The Knight's complaint is all the more significant because medieval writers are so prone to cataloguing, not excepting "The Knight's Tale" itself. *The Romance of the Rose* is a farrago of extended evocations including nearly every topos known to man. The encyclopedia is endemic to the spirit of the Middle Ages. It is part of that "Renaissance laughter" that begins to move from boisterousness to silence in the seventeenth and eighteenth centuries. The kind of list that appears in comedy has its own peculiarities, however, and it serves as a useful gauge for determining the dramatic changes that separate Ben Jonson from Samuel Johnson.

Inventory is particularly appropriate to the comic spirit, with its comic banquets where all are included and none excluded, stretching on, course after course, to an infinity of *ollas podridas*. Comedy, with its carnivalesque jumble and variety, is the true showcase for the literary list, and the spirit of inexhaustible comic invention appears to be irrepressible, even in the darker moments of contemplation. Chaucer's "Knight's Tale," again, may veer toward a sober uncertainty and grim acceptance at its conclusion, but the shadow of gloom that hangs over the lives of its noble pagans is constantly challenged by such passages as this one, in which the narrator promises not to produce a list and then proceeds to give, for over forty lines, a catalogue of the things he will not enumerate:

> the names that the trees highte,
> as ook, firre, birch, aspe, alder, holm, popler,
> Wyluch, elm, plane, assh, box, chastey, lynde, laurer;
> Mapul, thorn, bech, hasel, ew, whippeltree—
> How they were feld, shal not be toold for me;
> Ne hou the goddes ronnen up and doun,
> Disherited of their habitacioun....[23]

and so on in an ironic version of that familiar rhetorical ploy of asserting something by denying it. But unlike Homer's claim that the number of heroes is so great as to require superhuman powers in the bard who would name them all, Chaucer suggests not so much his limitations as a maker of lists as his restraint for the sake of the audience.

Nevertheless, the greatest comic inventories are found in Renaissance narrative, particularly in Rabelais. There *copia verborum* becomes more than simple comic exuberance. Words begin to pile up into dense realities that have existence in and of themselves. With Rabelais there is no longer a catalogue that merely invokes the weight of the past. Inventory is merged with discovery and invention; it suggests the power of the written language to create other worlds and other seas. In *Pantagruel*, the first of Rabelais's books, a new rhythm emerges from the encyclopedic litanies of medievel literature. Chapter 1, "Of the Origin and Antiquity of the Great Pantagruel," lists the hero's ancestors from among the race of giants:

> The first was Chalbroth, who begat Sarabroth, who begat Faribroth, who begat Hurtali—who was a great consumer of soups and reigned in the time of the Flood—who begat Nimrod, who begat Atlas—who with his shoulders kept the heavens from falling—who begat Goliath, who begat Eryx—who was the inventor of the game of thimble-rigging—who begat Titus, who begat Eryon, who begat Polyphemus....[24]

As we read through this hilarious genealogy, half learned, half bogus, we see that the giants who stand out in the list are notable either for inventing something or consuming something. They are the two aspects of the comic transaction between author and reader. The list is, like the book itself, a cornucopia of words meant to be swallowed whole by the reader. The multiple identities and disguises of Pantagruel and his friends; the many languages of Panurge; the claim made in the prologue to *Gargantua* that creating the text took place at the same time as the author ate and drank—implying an endless round of production and consumption—the praise of debts and debtors in *The Third Book*; the description of the Abbey of Theleme and of Pantagruelion; the long lists of games, arse-wipes, and educational activities; the tripe festival conversations; the Library of Saint Victor, with its absurd jumble of titles; and Diogenes' tub-thumping are only a selection from a work which, on the title page of its third book, requests the reader kindly to withhold his laughter until the seventy-eighth. The comic poet has the absolute right to go on forever, since life does; he may create as many things, new or old, normal or monstrous, as he pleases. The audience must respond by believing in their existence, as Rabelais warns with dire threats:

> may St. Anthony's fire burn you, the epilepsy throw you, the thunder-stroke and leg-ulcers rack you, dysentery seize you, and may the erysipelas, with its tiny cowhair rash, and quicksilver's pain on top, through your arse-hole enter up, and like Sodom and Gomorrah may you dissolve into sulphur, fire, and the bottomless pit in case you do not firmly believe everything that I tell you in this present Chronicle![25]

A chronicle is an unadorned catalogue of actual events; a curse is an inventory of desired effects. (Plenitude, it seems, can include ills as well as goods.) The list can be informed by the uncreating as well as the creating word. A list can recount the undoing as well as the doings of mankind if his world is not informed by a sense of human limits and the need for faith in the given order of things.

The first meeting of Pantagruel with Panurge introduces another kind of inventory with actual samples of most of the languages spoken in Europe, including German, Italian, Basque, Dutch, Spanish, Danish, Scots, Hebrew, Greek, Latin, and, at last, French, along with several totally imaginary languages. The Library of Saint Victor's adds, through parody, a catalogue of new titles to the world of books, consisting mostly of parodic versions of those already existing and certain volumes that should be but have not been written. But it is Panurge's desire to fill in the gaps in existence through the cuckolding of husbands and his praise of the cosmos as a totality of debts that takes the comic interchange of invention and consumption to its proper cosmic dimensions. For Rabelais the comic poet is a writer of menus—a list of things to be prepared and consumed. He improves the world by borrowing from the creative powers of nature and cooking up new combinations of what reality has given him. Nature, in turn, is soon in the poet's debt. Most of *The Third Book* is concerned with modes of prophecy—Virgilian lots, dying men's utterances, fools' babble, judges' decisions (settled by a throw of the dice), dumb men's signs, and dream visions. This impressive repertory of predictive devices leads inevitably to the fatal message in every case: if Panurge marries, he will be cuckolded, beaten, and robbed, and his wife will run away. It is almost the story of Menelaos—the oldest rule in the book, so to speak. But Panurge always interprets the omens in his favor. He refuses to accept the given, is always prepared to believe—however ill-advisedly—that events will conclude in his favor.

Panurge's dilemma takes up the rest of Rabelais's narrative—indeed, it is never resolved. His story, like the catalogues, will never be complete. His hope, like Vladimir and Estragon's waiting for Godot, is comic because it is so out of proportion to what is obviously going or not going to happen. Yet who is to say that the oracles are to be trusted? If Panurge's world were tragic, they would be certain. Since it is not, they are as indeterminate as his own trust in his own security. It is the quest for certainty that makes Panurge a comic figure, but it is

Pantagruel's refusal to think that knowledge of the future can ever be certain that makes him the book's real comic hero. For like Pantagruelion, the mysterious plant named after him whose encyclopedic array of properties is described at length toward the end of *The Third Book*, he is the comic spirit itself. By *The Fourth Book* the list and the quest are indistinguishable. The inventory is the key to comic narrative, with its episodic structure, its accumulation of details, data, and events, and its play on the crosspurposes that emerge when desire, confronted by opportunity, is consumed in its own inventions. The central figure in *The Fourth Book* is Messer Gaster, the stomach, who is the god and master of all arts. He is opposed by King Lent, who rules over self-privation, narrowness, restriction. They are, as Pantagruel points out in an allegory, Nature and Anti-nature, Harmony and Disorder. Lent spins fantastic images, but they do not fill the void they inhabit. The lack of order in the list of Lent's attributes points to the main force of Rabelais's inventorial argument: the list is a menu, an occasion for consumption through choice. Rabelais's inventories are not simply stylistic elaborations of the theme of plenitude; they are his testament of faith in a world that is full of good things but which requires man to consume and transform them. It is through words that man absorbs the world and yet adds to it. The world in Pantagruel's mouth is created by the tongue and buccal cavity. It is astonishingly full of things—cities and peasants, cabbages and garlic-plagues—but the world outside also has a sun and a moon and all sorts of good things as well. The mouth into which the morsel enters is the egress from which emerge the most profound and satisfying of human inventions.

Such images are absent from the drawing-room and court society of the comedy of manners; yet even the plays of Ben Jonson or Molière, which are often said to have been major influences on later English comedy, are still in the medieval-Renaissance tradition. Jonson's *Epicoene*, a play much admired during the Restoration but not at all a comedy of manners, is a rejection of the unproductive, a celebration of noise, inheritance, and procreativity. It is Morose, the extravagantly negative figure who is turned into the generous benefactor of his nephew through a devious disguise:

> Come, nephew, give me the pen. I will subscribe to anything, and seal to what thou wilt, for my deliverance. Thou art my restorer. Here I

deliver it thee as my deed. If there be a word in it lacking, or writ with false orthography, I protest before God I will not take the advantage.[26]

Yet though it is the nephew who appears to be the benefactor, Truewit's deception cannot detract from the fact that he truly is his uncle's deliverer. It is Morose's constricted imagination and his narrow relationship with the world that has trapped him, and this strategem has allowed him to escape those limits. All he really wants is the luxury of peace, and he leaves the stage without protest, having found his plenty in his privacy. The play ends with a promise of release from a restrictive—therefore false—imagination and proclamation of a transformation of eros as it emerges from its cocoon-like disguise:

> Madams, you are mute upon this new metamorphosis! But here stands she that has vindicated your fames. Take heed of such insectae hereafter. And let it not trouble you that you have discovered any mysteries to this young gentleman. He is almost of years, and will make a good visitant within this twelvemonth. In the meantime, we'll all undertake for his secrecy, that can speak so well of his silence.—[Coming forward.] Spectators, if you like this comedy, rise cheerfully, and now Morose is gone in, clap your hands. It may be that noise will cure him, at least please him.[27]

It is the fullness of participation that transforms silence and secrecy into erotic festivity, into comic play. Even Morose could be healed if the role he plays is acknowledged for what it is, an opportunity to bring the riches of laughter to this and future audiences.

Other plays of Jonson manifest the same pattern. The world of social privacy—whether it be Volpone's deathbed or the secrets of the alchemist's laboratory—yields to public forces—justice in *Volpone*, the neighbors in *The Alchemist*. In *Volpone* the avaricious choke on their own desires and, at play's end, are locked out of the public world from which they attempted to hide their appetites. Typical of this appetite that seeks satisfaction in privacy is Dapper, in *The Alchemist*, whose desire to win at gambling through the kind offices of the Queen of Fairy lands him in a privy, gagged with gingerbread. But it is above all in *Bartholomew Fair* that Jonson's comic genius for inventory achieves its climax. The Fair is a public place where men go to fulfill certain desires. Its center is fat Ursula's pig stand, which the obsessive, self-congratulating constable Adam Overdo calls "the very womb of enormity." John Littlewit and his wife, who is pregnant, go to the Fair to satisfy a longing for roast pig—forbidden by his Puritan mother-in-law. But he is also proud of his way with words and has written a puppet play to be performed there. The Puritans persuade themselves that the eating of pig at the Fair is lawful because, as Zeal-of-the-Land Busy says, the eating of pig

> hath a face of offence with the weak, a great face, a foul face, but that face may have a veil put over it, and be shadowed, as it were. It may be eaten, and in the Fair, I take it, in a booth, the tents of the wicked. The place is not much, not very much; we may be religious in the midst of the profane, so it be eaten with a reformed mouth, with sobriety, and humbleness; not gorged in with gluttony or greediness; there's the fear: for, should she go there, as taking pride in the place, or delight in the unclean dressing, to feed the vanity of the eye or the lust of the palate, it were not well. . . .[28]

It is all right to eat pig at the Fair because it is done "in a booth," which is a very small and private place. Busy's attitude is the very antithesis of the Fair, as he intends it to be, but not because he is opposed to "the tents of the wicked." He is uncarnival-like because he thinks that the Fair can be entered into in a private spirit without any real participation. Littlewit's play is equally offensive because it utilizes idols, that is public imitations of private actions. Busy's domain is the realm of secrecy and hiddenness, where hypocrisy may flourish.

Adam Overdo, the inept constable who seeks out "enormities" (that is, petty crimes), also leaves his public position and attends the Fair disguised as a madman. Like Busy, he too hopes to justify a dual perspective by hiding from the public eye, but he only succeeds in providing still more occasions for further enormities. Both the disguised constable and the hypocritical Puritan end up in public confinement, in the stocks. Both have a hunger for justice, though Overdo, by far the more sympathetic figure, is the more detached and theoretical of the two. Busy is said to hunger for the destruction of the theater like an oyster gaping for the tide, and his claim of zealousness for the cause is described by Lanthorn Leatherhead as being like a dog's for the bone. He has a prodigious physical appetite, in fact, and satisfies it fully before denouncing the Fair and the play. It is Dionysus himself—or rather the puppet playing that role—who bests him in argument and converts him into a beholder of plays by convincing Busy that his zealousness is all puppetry.

The absurd puppet play, a ridiculous parody of the Hero and Leander and Damon and Pythias stories, is the occasion for revealing, in public, all the disguises, foibles, crimes, and secrets that circulate in the Fair. It also reveals the essentially histrionic nature of Busy, who enters just as the puppet (called Dionysius) is denouncing an insult to one of the dramatis personae:

> *Busy.* Down with Dagon, down with dagon! 'Tis I will no longer endure your profanations.
> *Leatherhead.* What do you mean, sir?
> *Busy.* I will remove Dagon there, I say, that idol, that heathenish idol, that remains, as I may say, a beam, a very beam, not a beam of the sun, nor a beam of the moon, not a beam of a balance, neither a house-beam nor a weaver's beam, but a beam in the eye, in the eye of the brethern; a very great beam, an exceeding great beam; such as are your stage-players, rhymers, and morris-dancers, who have walked hand in hand in contempt of the brethren and the cause, and been borne out by instruments of no mean countenance.
> *Leatherhead.* Sir, I present nothing but what is licensed by authority.
> *Busy.* Thou art all licence, even licentiousness itself, Shimei!
> *Leatherhead.* I have the Master of the Revels' hand for it, sir.[29]

Busy's "good Banbury-vapors," as Knockem calls his diatribe, are not an inventory but a series of empty repetitions and comically negative lists. He tells us more about what he does not mean than he does about what he does mean. When he says "Assist me, zeal; fill me, fill me, that is, make me full," Busy has demonstrated almost perfectly the emptiness of his claims to plenitude. He achieves the effect of fullness through repetition and variation of the same thing. Leatherhead and he engage in a dispute over the meaning of the word "license"—freedom to do certain things. Busy accuses the puppeteer of being "all license, even licentiousness itself." But the authority for this license comes from the "Master of the Revels" or Dionysus himself, portrayed by a puppet and gifted (through Leatherhead's ventriloquy) with some irrefutable arguments in defense of the theater. The Fair is the place of freedom, and all those who seek to restrict it, whether they be puritan zealots or earnest constables, are forced to convert to its indeterminacy in the end. The play concludes with a banquet at Overdo's house, where empty enormities can be forgotten for the full bowl:

Quarlous. [To Overdo] Nay, sir, stand not you fixed here, like a stake in Finsbury to be shot at, or the whipping post i' the Fair, but get your wife out o' the air; it will make her worse else; and remember you are but Adam, flesh and blood! You have your frailty; forget your other name of Overdo and invite us all to supper. There you and I will compare our discoveries, and drown the memory of all enormity in your bigg'st bowl at home.[30]

Overdo's wife, who is ill, needs privacy. His own frailties, which are all men's frailties, need public acknowledgment. That is perhaps the reason why the puppet play will go on to its conclusion when the whole party arrives at the constable's house to banquet.

Even Shakespeare's problematic dark comedy *Troilus and Cressida* counters Troilus's disillusionment, hope for revenge, and final entry into the fray of battle with Pandarus's survival and further participation in society. In his epilogue, which Pandarus calls his legacy to other "good traders in the flesh," he makes an ambiguous appeal:

> As many as be here of Pandar's hall,
> Your eyes, half out, weep out at Pandar's fall;
> Or if you cannot weep, yet give some groans,
> Though not for me, yet for your aching bones.
> Brethren and sisters of the hold-door trade,
> Some two months hence my will shall here be made:
> It should be now, but that my fear is this,
> Some galled goose of Winchester would hiss:
> Till then I'll sweat and seek about for eases,
> And at that time bequeathe you my diseases.[31]

Pandarus speaks for and to a diseased society, but what he seeks is an ease from his efforts as actor; his "pains" can be relieved only by a receptive audience. Are the "brethren and sisters of the hold-door trade" panderers or actors? Pandar can bequeathe his pains to other players when they take up the burden of his play, discharge his discomfort on them, but his cure will come only through full audience participation in the theatrical collaboration that is the play. The epilogue of *Troilus and Cressida* is a variation on the same appeal for approval and grace that is made by Puck or Prospero or, for that matter, Face in *The Alchemist*, a rascal and go-between, like Pandarus, who nevertheless survives:

> Gentlemen,
> My part a little fell in this last scene,
> Yet 'twas decorum. And though I am clean
> Got off from Subtle, Surly, Mammon, Doll,
> Hot Ananias, Dapper, Drugger, all
> With whom I traded; yet I put myself
> On you, that are my country: and this pelf,
> Which I have got, if you do quit me, rests
> To feast you often, and invite new guests.[32]

Pandarus's diseases may not seem to be a very desirable legacy, but given aesthetic form, they may make a gift as entertaining as Face's banquet. The theme of fullness is as evident in a dark comedy, like *Troilus and Cressida*, as in a happier one. The epilogue is the clue. Neither Pandarus nor Face will change, for their characters as rogues are their dramatic roles. The play is a banquet to which the audience is invited or, when it describes the dying world of Troy, an inquest and reading of the will that at least offers the chance of legacy, a continuity accepted by one community as an acknowledgment of its tie to another. Thus even the themes of disease and absence have a different meaning in Renaissance comedy. It is the fullness of participation that transforms such isolating forces as disease and secrecy into erotic festival, so that Pandarus's venereal ailments and the degraded play of Hero and Leander and Damon and Pythias have a totally different value when they become part of the comic inventory of life.

In a totally different context, Gerald Bruns has distinguished between rhetorical and systematic criticism. "Method," he says, "tries to reduce rather than to amplify, for it wants always to determine what cannot be said in this or that case, and so by closure or the natural exclusiveness of its design it forbids all statements but those it can account for. As Descartes knew, method is a good way to reduce one's inventory of unnecessary ideas."[33] Interpretation and translation (that is, the reproduction of another text with embellishments, commentary, or interpolations) occur in an "open" place in a text which, Bruns says later, "the modern mind would figure as absence, the ancient as plenitude."[34] It is precisely this difference between absence and reductive method, on the one hand, and plenitude and invention, on the other, that distinguishes Renaissance comedy from Cartesian comedy or comedy of manners. In Jonson, Morose, Busy, and Overdo must be defeated because they are the anticarnivalesque spirit that must be exorcised from a world of carnival license. The boy dressed as a woman puts on a festive disguise that will allow plenitude to emerge and this absence—or miserliness and silence—to be filled with spending and noisemaking. Looking over the ruins of his city, his business, and his body, Pandarus still has something to give, something to embellish.

This distinction between method and invention is particularly useful as a means of accounting for Molière's position in the latter half of the seventeenth century. For all his influence on English comedy, it is clear that he belongs to a different world from Dryden, Wycherley, Farquahar, and Congreve. Theirs is a comedy of method that seeks to reduce aberrations to the lowest common denominator of currently acceptable social practice. It is the extravagant figure who is cast out and ridiculed, not the miserly one. Though he may seem to resemble Shakespeare's Malvolio, the fop or beau who is stripped of pretensions and disclosed in all his vacuity at the end of the play is a threat to the method of society, to its ways, not to its "cakes and ale." Malvolio is still quite anticarnivalesque. The fop, a sort of unsatisfactory clown, is a remnant of this outcast figure, a poor relative who lacks the verve and creativeness of the jester and the obsessive drive of a Morose, a Busy, or an Overdo. The Sir Fopling Flutters of Restoration comedy have none of the power that, for a moment at least, seems to make Malvolio a potentially disruptive and dangerous, if ridiculous, force.

Despite the frequent presence of a *raisonneur* or voice of good sense in Molière's mature comedies, in their essence his plays are neither comedies of method nor of manners. It is true, of course, that a piece like *Les Precieuses Ridicules* judges the pretentiousness of its absurd women characters who hardly seem much of a threat to any order except that of their own minds. But most of Molière's plays have a zany festive quality that makes *Le Médècin malgré lui* or *Le Bougeois gentilhomme* look closer to Jonson than to Etherege. The hypochondriac of *Le Malade imaginaire* is of the lineage of Morose, and Monsieur Jourdain is more like Christopher Sly or Bottom than like Mrs. Malaprop. In *Tartuffe* Molière's main thrust is perhaps most evident. Tartuffe can only survive if what he does is protected by the realm of the private—by religion and the four walls of one man's household. He is an astonishingly vigorous hypocrite, full of life and appetite, and all the more dangerous for his energy. The intervention of the king, at the end of the play, used to be criticized as arbitrary or as deploying a kind of *rex ex machina*, but its significance is obviously part of the medieval-Renaissance pattern. It is the public world that saves the private one from its own delusions and appetites.

Molière's *Le Misanthrope* offers the greatest problem, I think, for the argument that carnival and inventory are still at the heart of his plays. But his is a particularly original version of Malvolio and Morose—a man who is barely, if at all, ridiculous and who excites admiration and love in his friends despite his inability to reconcile himself to the ways of the world. His ambiguity as a character cannot disguise his ancestry; he disturbs the free-wheeling society around him in his passion for method and a purer order. As is always the case with such a *pharmakos*, he must be expunged or, in this instance, allowed to leave. He chooses solitude at the end—his desert place—over a world that has learned, in however makeshift a fashion, to tolerate its shortcomings. Alceste will not join the dance. Though he is the main figure in the comedy—and his position in it makes the play a daring variation on a very old theme—his disgust reveals only a lack of generosity that his "impure" friends display even in their weaknesses.

Molière's plays end too often in a dance or festive gesture to be thought of as true comedies of manners. They exploit disguise in a carnivalesque, often extravagant situation. The truth is, perhaps, that the French and the Italians—Beaumarchais, at least, and Goldoni—preserved the festive plenitude of comedy longer than their British contemporaries. *Le Mariage de Figaro* concludes with prosperity, generosity, and a final vaudeville. The atmosphere of the fair still prevailed in 1784. But Alfred de Musset's comedies, from the mid-nineteenth century, are another matter. In *Un Caprice*, the unappreciated wife is restored to her husband's embraces at the end, but the atmosphere is hardly that of *All's Well that Ends Well*. De Musset's play, like so many of his other comedies (one of them, *On ne badine pas avec l'amour*, ends with a death) concludes with a note of reduced activity and sober accommodation. By the end of the century, Chekhov's comedies—to choose an outstanding dramatist—can offer only a world of absence and loss that avoids the tragic through the ability of the protagonists to endure the restraints that hedge their joys, desires, and freedom at every point. This survey could be extended, of course, into an inventory of its own that would include German and Scandinavian dramatists and comedies—Grillparzer and Grabbe, *Leonce und Lena*, *Der Zerbrochene Krug*, Holbert and Heiberg—or the great Spanish dramatists, but though the tradition of Renaissance laughter survives longer in some traditions than in others, by the end of the Enlightenment it is barely evident anywhere. A list that is a mere survey lacks interest, comic or otherwise.

In modern comedy, then, copia is renounced and caution is embraced. The comic action is accommodated to a tragic plot of self-knowledge. Inventory yields to the way of the world. Perhaps the best instance of this shrinking perspective is to be found earlier, in a play about two witty and delightful but comically reduced protagonists that is generally acknowledged to be one of the finest comedies of manners ever written—*The Way of the World*. Both the limits and the greatness of Congreve's last play, first performed in 1700, are revealed by the insights of its fourth act, which depicts a world that has lost forever the sense of fullness and delight that characterize Rabelais's crowded lists.

After they agree to marry, Millamant and Mirabell continue the repartee that has characterized their conversation throughout the play:

> *Millamant.* —My dear liberty, shall I leave thee? My faithful solitude, my darling contemplation, must I bid you then adieu? Aye, adieu—my morning thoughts, agreeable wakings, indolent slumbers, all ye douceurs, ye sommeils de matin, adieu? —I can't do't, 'tis more than impossible.... —And d'ye hear, I won't be called names after I'm married; positively I won't be called names.
> *Mirabell.* Names!
> *Millamant.* Aye, as wife, spouse, my dear, joy, jewel, love, sweetheart, and the rest of that nauseous cant, in which men and their wives are so fulsomely familiar.... Let us be very strange and well-bred...."

Mirabell, who is not at all taken aback by her demand that they be "very strange" (reserved), considers her stipulations "pretty reasonable," but he is skeptical enough to wonder if she has "any more conditions to offer."

> *Millamant.* Trifles! —As liberty to pay and receive visits to and from whom I please; to write and receive letters without interrogatories or

wry faces on your part; to wear what I please; and choose conversation with regard only to my own taste; to have no obligation upon me to converse with wits that I don't like, because they are your acquaintance; or to be intimate with fools, because they may be your relations. Come to dinner when I please; dine in my dressing room when I'm out of humour, without giving a reason. To have my closet inviolate; to be sole empress of my tea table, which you must never presume to approach without first asking leave. And lastly, wherever I am, you shall always knock at the door before you come in. These articles subscribed, if I continue to endure you a little longer, I may by degrees dwindle into a wife.

Mirabell. Your bill of fare is something advanced in this latter account. Well, have I liberty to offer conditions—that when you are dwindled into a wife, I may not be beyond measure enlarged into a husband?

Millamant. You have free leave. Propose your utmost; speak and spare not.[36]

The amusing note that is struck in these contractual inventories is the way in which freedom is played off against constraint, the private against the public, the long list of conditions against the very notion of conditions.

Mirabell. I denounce against all strait-lacing, squeezing for a shape, till you mould my boy's head like a sugar loaf, and instead of a man-child, make me the father to a crooked billet. Lastly, to the dominion of the tea table I submit, but with proviso, that you exceed not in your province, but restrain yourself to native and simple tea-table drinks, as tea, chocolate, and coffee. As likewise to genuine and authorized tea-table talk—such as mending of fashions, spoiling reputations, railing at absent friends, and so forth; but that on no account you encroach upon the men's prerogative and presume to drink healths, or toast fellows; for prevention of which, I banish all foreign forces, all auxiliaries to the tea table, as orange brandy, all aniseed, cinnamon, citron, and Barbadoes waters, together with ratafia and the most noble spirit of clary. But for cowslip-wine, poppy-water, and all dormitives, those I allow. These provisos admitted, in other things I may prove a tractable and complying husband.[37]

Act 4 of *The Way of the World* is an original treatment of inventory on the verge of becoming restraint. From here it is but a step to T. S. Eliot's *The Cocktail Party*, a theological comedy of manners that, despite its obvious Christian tone and use of a classical plot, is more Cartesian method than carnival madness. Congreve's sophistication was perhaps too much for his original audience, who were unaccustomed to having their limitations so pointedly criticized. A not improbable guide to his world is in a book published some sixty years later—but set only a few decades into the century—*The Life and Opinions of Tristram Shandy*. In Sterne's country gentry, a great deal of the old mood is still alive: litanies of curses mingle with exhaustive lists of proposals and schemes, and Walter Shandy vainly applies the full encyclopedic range of his knowledge to insure that his son's head is not misshapen at birth. But the realm into which the unfortunate Tristram is born is always on the verge of a farcical tragedy. Restraints of all kinds hem him in, including even a possible castration. Long, repetitive stories about seven kings are begun and yet again begun without ever being fully told. Deaths in the family occasion displays of eloquence more than displays of grief. The work ends with a story of a sterile bull, suggesting a universe of proliferating verbosity that leads to the end of an era rather than to new life. As Rabelaisian and vigorous as its comic invention is, Sterne's book is about a society that is so overwhelmed by rules, provisos, gadgets, legalities, and words, words, words as to be close to paralysis. In its constant mocking of the Lockean principle of the association of ideas, *Tristram Shandy* seems to acknowledge, as it makes fun of, the inescapably Cartesian comedy of its era.

This is a world that Millamant and Mirabell hope to escape by being private. The public life can no longer provide forms that will allow them to be themselves. "Oh, horrid provisos! filthy strong waters! I toast fellows, odious men! I hate your odious provisos," Millamant proclaims. "Then we're agreed..."Mirabell responds. The way of the world that they would escape swarms with meaningless rituals which deform and stunt the natural growth of affections. Yet to marry means for the lovers to submit to and sustain the rules of a private world that sets them apart from the public fashions through which they must carefully navigate. The frankness and fun of the Shandy household conceals a certain isolation and reduction. Uncle Toby's miniature wars are the ritualized repetition of the one event—an ambiguous war wound that may have affected more than his leg—which has meaning in his life. Yet he cannot understand the body for what it is. He sees it as a field of battle—as the Widow Wadman discovers, to her disappointment—rather than as a field of love. Too gentle to harm a fly, Uncle

Toby seems to be incapable of moving beyond an obsession with his own maiming and a desire to replicate the past. For all his fine nature, he seems incapable of a genuinely social engagement. His warlike energies are of no use to him in his hapless assault on the Widow, and his inventory of weapons may well be lacking the one essential to his conquest.

Yet the habit of inventory, as we can observe in Congreve and Sterne, is not easy to kill. The very epilogues of Restoration and eighteenth-century comedy show an inversion, however, that begins to turn abundance into misery. At the conclusion of Sheridan's *School for Scandal*, Lady Teazle speaks of the fate that awaits her in giving up "the gay dream of dissipation":

> And say, ye fair, was ever lively Wife
> Born with a genius for the highest Life,
> Like me untimely blasted in her bloom,
> Like me, condemned to such a dismal doom?
> Save money—when I just knew how to waste it!
> Leave London—just as I began to taste it!
> Must I then watch the early-crowing Cock?
> The melancholy Ticking of a Clock?
> In the lone rustic hall for ever pounded,
> With Dogs, Cats, Rats, and squalling Brats surrounded?[38]

Lady Teazle, a less subtle, less appealing version of Millamant, knows that marriage is not a liberation, as it is in the older comedies, but an enslavement that forces her to "blow all one way" like a "tradewind" to "one old rusty weathercock—my spouse."

Perhaps inventorial exuberance cannot be recovered in the modern world except in the form of meaninglessness and the irrationality of dreams. Surrealism and the comedy of the absurd have begun to recover some of its elements in our century, but the hope they express is severe and limited in its quality. When the Dutch painter Piet Mondrian wrote of rejecting the "tragic," which for him as an artist was implied in representations of the natural world, he expressed the mystical desire of all post-Cartesians to simplify and schematize. Abstraction in art—from Kandinsky on often identified with the "spiritual" and the soul—appealed to his generation as a means of discovering a harmony and equilibrium that nature cannot provide. The "old kind of harmony" produced by nature exists as a "relative equilibrium." "In it, the typical 'repetition' of nature is dominant; it expresses an opposition, that is true, but not a permanent synthesis of the two terms." Mondrian saw the "new man" as bringing forth a new age and a new art that would go beyond the past, which is "characterized by the search for and will to the tragic" and which has its source in nature's domination."[39] Michel Seuphor notes that Mondrian means by the term "tragic" "every kind of fear of life, including the dread of the new, and sentimental attachment to the past."[40] But he seems to mean more than that. Like Goethe, he sought to avoid the tragic, but his primary means of transcending the natural world was in simple geometrical forms and the primary colors. It is a late form of Enlightenment optimism and of the comedy of method, brilliantly and heroically executed on canvas. Mondrian has his own inventory, as it were, recorded in variation after variation on the same basic theme. He is testimony to how much a great artist can draw from the severe restrictions of his moral world. But his art is not comic in the fullest sense; it avoids comedy as well as tragedy. Schopenhauer's refusal to draw back from his basic insight of the World as Will—and therefore his refusal to embrace a comedy that, for him, was an escapist illusion —stands behind Mondrian's Schoenmakerian mysticism. Nietzsche's solution of the eternal return, while rejected by Mondrian as tragic, nevertheless informs his art, which circles craftily about its limited resources in painting after painting. As Erich Heller says, "once a man is compelled to penetrate to that central point in all seriousness, then there is only one region left that stretches, for the European, beyond tragedy. Beyond Hamlet and the rest that is silence, there stands only Prospero...."[41] But Prospero's return to the hustle and bustle of Milan has seldom been a successful option for the modern artist, who finds a very different city upon his return.

In the modern world, then, the comic inventory is as fearful as tragic knowledge. It takes on a seductive aspect and its methodical or analytic version develops a taste for the hopelessly infinite. This, I take it, is the main theme of that prescient nineteenth-century artist Gustave Flaubert, who along with the Byron of *Don Juan*, Dickens, Dostoevsky, Gogol, and other select artistic company, grasped the significance of inventory as transmogrified by modernity. It is an appetite for the unusual, the new, the wonderful that emerges, provoked by words alone and the historical and scientific methods that allow them to be analyzed and catalogued endlessly. In Flaubert's *Bouvard et Pécuchet*, the *copia verborum* of the modern world stands in sharp contrast to the exuberant array of good things—*res et verba*—to be enjoyed in Rabelais's universe. Bouvard's name suggests both the bovine impenetrability of spirit of a Charles Bovary and the endless but inconsequential *bavardise* of a man who does not know when to stop talking. Flaubert's last book brings the act of narrating and the act of listing into intimate comic conjunction. It was unfinished when he died—appropriately so, one would think—and the conclusion is only partly clear from the outlines he left. Yet this work is the forerunner of such major achievements of twentieth-century inventory as Joyce's *Ulysses* and *Finnegan's Wake*, and it demonstrates that comedy, like tragedy in the nineteenth century, takes refuge in the printed word when it no longer has a place on the stage.

The plot of Flaubert's book is not particularly complicated. Two middle-class gentlemen decide to devote themselves to learning. Yet each of their endeavors to master an art or science ends in failure or, on occasion, public catastrophe. It is their thirst for absolute completeness that does in Bouvard and Pécuchet because they have the notion that an inventory can substitute for an experience. They are professional copyists by trade and lack utterly any inventive talents. They read *Les Epoques de la Nature* and *La Majestè de la création*, which are as astonishing to them as the creation they describe. Their heads swell; they are proud to think about such grand subjects. It is when they attempt to follow Buffon in his description of the bizarre events in nature that they fail. Desirous of providing new creatures—monsters, in fact—they attempt to mate incompatible animals. Their effort ends in farcical defeat as the goat and sheep they try to unite turn on them and drive them to experiment with less dangerous subjects, such as ducks and chickens. After many repeated trials and mistrials, they finally decide to return to their trade as copyists; but at the last they begin to accumulate entries for an enormous repertory of human stupidity called the *Dictionnaire des Idées reçues*. An inventory of the anticreative, it is a list of clichés, of words that no one will object to and that have no conceivable poetic value because the public these ideas satisfy will not allow a thing to exist unless it is familiar to the point of banality. Flaubert's book is the mock-epic of lists; it suggests that listing, in the modern world, has none of the creative power that it manifested in Renaissance comedy.

If Bouvard's name suggests the disease of *bavardise*—running at the mouth—perhaps Pécuchet's implies that this modern *copia verborum* is our world's *péché originel*, our original sin of abundant emptiness. We are empty because we have lost what Renaissance laughter stands for—the sense of man speaking in and to a community. The music of the list has vanished because the world is no longer informed by a point of view that gives inventory its telos. Even the nature that Ishmael celebrates in the long enumerations of *Moby-Dick* has lost its mystery. Flaubert's comedy, like Joyce's and Beckett's, is about the ability to endure in a world where plenitude evokes not wonder but paralysis. His two seekers come finally to understand that, whatever abundance the world may offer, one cannot suffer fools gladly, even if the number of fools is infinite.

Notes

1. Mikhail Bakhtin, "Rabelais et Gogol," in *Esthetique et theorie du roman*, trans. Daria Olivier (Paris, 1978), 477.
2. Gunther Anders, "Being without Time: On Beckett's Play *Waiting for Godot*," trans. Martin Esslin, in *Samuel Beckett: A Collection of Critical Essays*, ed. Martin Esslin (Englewood Cliffs, N.J., 1965), 144.
3. Thomas McFarland, *Shakespeare's Pastoral Comedy* (Chapel Hill, 1972), 18.
4. Erich Heller, "Goethe and the Avoidance of Tragedy," in *The Disinherited Mind: Essays in Modern German Literature and Thought*, expanded ed. (New York and London, 1975), 40–41.
5. Ibid., 62.
6. Donald Phillip Verene, *Vico's Science of Imagination* (Ithaca and London, 1981), 115.
7. Ibid., 114.
8. Jaako Hintikka and Unto Remes, *The Method of Analysis: Its Geometrical Origin and Its General Significance*. Boston Studies in the Philosophy of Science 25 (Dordrecht and Boston, 1974), xiii.
9. Ibid., xiv.
10. Ibid., xiii.
11. C. S. Lewis, *An Experiment in Criticism* (Cambridge, 1961), 79.
12. Roger B. Henkle, *Comedy and Culture: England 1820–1900* (Princeton, 1980), 12.

13. G. W. F. Hegel, *On the Arts. Selections from G. W. F. Hegel's Aesthetics or the Philosophy of Fine Art*, trans. Henry Paolucci (New York, 1979), 199. For an excellent summary of Hegel's theory of comedy, see Anne Paolucci, "Hegel's Theory of Comedy," in Maurice Charney, ed., *Comedy: New Perspectives* (New York, 1978), 89-108.

14. Gregor Malantschuk, *Kierkegaard's Thought*, trans. Howard V. Hong and Edna H. Hong (Princeton, 1974), 46.

15. Soren Kierkegaard, *Stages on Life's Way*, trans. Walter Lowrie (New York, 1967), 55.

16. Ibid., 231-32.

17. Ibid., 293.

18. Ibid., 335.

19. Genesis 11:10-14, cited from *The New English Bible, with the Apocrypha* (Oxford and Cambridge, 1970), 11-12.

20. For an account of the nature of lists, see Jack Goody, *The Domestication of the Savage Mind* (Cambridge, 1977), 80-111.

21. William Shakespeare, *The Tragedy of Macbeth*, act 4, sc. 1, lines 112-17, in *The Complete Signet Classic Shakespeare*, ed. Sylvan Barnet (New York, 1972), 1251.

22. Geoffrey Chaucer, "The Prologue of the Nun's Priest's Tale," lines 3958-60, in *The Works of Geoffrey Chaucer*, ed. F. N. Robinson, 2nd ed. (Boston, 1957), 198.

23. Geoffrey Chaucer, "The Knight's Tale," lines 2920-26, in *Works*, 45.

24. François Rabelais, *Gargantua and Pantagruel*, trans. J. M. Cohen (Baltimore, 1965), 173.

25. Ibid., 168-69.

26. Ben Jonson, *Epicoene, or The Silent Woman*, act 5, sc. 4, lines 168-72, in *The Complete Plays of Ben Jonson*, ed. G. A. Wilkes (Oxford, 1982) 3: 221.

27. Ibid., act 5, sc. 4, lines 207-16.

28. Ben Jonson, *Bartholomew Fair*, act 1, sc. 6, lines 61-69, in *Complete Plays* 4: 30-31.

29. Ibid., act 5, sc. 5, lines 1-14, p. 115.

30. Ibid., act 5, sc. 5, lines 86-92, p. 121.

31. William Shakespeare, *The History of Troilus and Cressida*, act 5, sc. 10, lines 46-55, in *The Complete . . . Shakespeare*, 1049.

32. Ben Jonson, *The Alchemist*, act 5, sc. 5, lines 158-65, in *Complete Plays* 3: 356.

33. Gerald L. Bruns, *Inventions: Writing, Textuality, and Understanding in Literary History* (New Haven, 1982), 1.

34. Ibid., 56.

35. William Congreve, *The Way of the World*, act 4, lines 163-85, ed. Kathleen M. Lynch (Lincoln, 1965), 85.

36. Ibid., act 4, lines 190-210, pp. 85-86.

37. Ibid., act 4, lines 235-52, pp. 87-88.

38. Richard Brinsley Sheridan, "Epilogue" to *The School for Scandal*, in *Sheridan's Plays*, ed. Cecil Price (London and New York, 1975), 299.

39. Piet Mondrian, "Natural Reality and Abstract Reality: An Essay in Dialogue Form," in Michel Seuphor, *Piet Mondrian: Life and Work* (New York, n.d.), 341, 351.

40. Seuphor, 352.

41. Heller, 41.

9

The Icon and the Spirit of Comedy: Dostoevsky's *The Possessed*

DENNIS SLATTERY

To place Dostoevsky's novels in the realm of comedy would seem to indicate, on the surface of it, a strange geography indeed. But failure to recognize the appropriateness of such a designation has led more than one reader to a distaste for what appear in the writings to be melodrama, loose structure, and unconvincing characterization. One such negative judgment was recently pronounced by a critic so otherwise astute as Vladimir Nabokov. In his disparaging remarks Nabokov maintains that Dostoevsky's major fiction neither sets up clearly nor resolves effectively any artistic or human problem. "He is not a great writer," Nabokov declares, "but a rather mediocre one—with flashes of excellent humor, but, alas, with wastelands of literary platitudes in between."[1]

What I should like to explore in *The Possessed*, the third of Dostoevsky's four major novels, is not Dostoevsky's humor, which Nabokov recognizes, but a totally different feature—his comic vision, of which apparently Nabokov is unaware. In response to Nabokov's accusation, I should like to maintain that in this strange and prophetic work at least (and I should say in his other writings as well) Dostoevsky does indeed create an artistic and human problem and resolve it effectively, the particular action that Nabokov believes is the platinum bar against which literary achievement must be measured and confirmed. Briefly put, the *problem* is Nikolay Stavrogin, the idol sponsored by the power-seeking revolutionaries in the provinces outside Petersburg: the *solution*, the Russian icon. The governing action of the novel is redemption, specifically that of Stepan Trofimovich and, by an implicit allegory generally present in Dostoevsky's plots, Russia. Stepan is Stavrogin's teacher, a foppish, serio-comic figure, the central character in whom the two antithetical forces come together. What Nabokov calls "wastelands of literary platitudes" derive from a Dantesque (and hence comic) view of a spiritual and political situation in which the prevailing powers of darkness must be purged.

Perhaps one should suggest at the outset that *The Possessed* may be understood as a successful attempt by Dostoevsky to reaffirm the relationship between comedy and sacrality. Such a suggestion has a partial basis in the comments of some incisive critics: Jacques Ellul has written that the conclusion of *The Possessed* offers "a reconciliation between the individual and the world, between man and the sacred"[2]; Robert Louis Jackson suggests that Dostoevsky expresses in the character of Stepan Verkhovensky "a transition from the aesthetic idealism of the 1840s, with its faith in the beautiful and sublime, to a faith in the Christian ideal."[3] The final action of the novel is, as they indicate, religious, and, as I hope to illustrate, comic. Although dominated by such demonic figures as Pyotr Verkhovensky, Nikolay Stavrogin, Shigalov, and others, *The Possessed* contains nevertheless a contrary and seemingly improbable impulse to reinstate the Orthodox icon, that holy image described by Saint John Climacus as "the daughter of hope and the denial of despair."[4] Dostoevsky uses the iconic image as both the instrument of education and a figure of hope. For even as the novel shows the sacred dimension of life to be under seige, with iconoclasts threatening the images that promise redemption for the Russian people, it depicts the icon as ever more certainly revealing in sacred figure the community's faith and endurance.

In Dostoevsky's work, as in Russian culture, the icon may be said to embody the people's sense of identity and their special calling as a people. For the icon is an image that, in capturing the dimensions of time, goes beyond the temporal to reveal the way in which eternity is embedded in time. Further, it is memorial: it reminds its viewer of a sacred past and teaches the way to reverence the physical order. The icon therefore promotes an awareness of the bond between earth and God and bears witness to a hope for redemption, while at the same time it dignifies the actual and the finite.

Hence the earth itself may be said to take on an iconic character through its constant process of nourishing and sustaining life. It becomes by this action a natural analogue of the maternal iconic image. In Russian thought the earth has traditionally been endowed with religious significance and regarded as holy in the way that icons are holy. The action of bowing and kissing the earth is a practice strongly rooted in the devotional life of the people. Sergei Hackel explains that, according to Russian Orthodoxy, when a person sins against another, he sins against the cosmos as well. He must seek forgiveness not only from the community but also from the earth.[5] Repentance reflects a change of heart, a *metanoia*, a fundamental transformation of one's outlook, or as the theologian Kallistos Ware expresses it, "a new way of looking at ourselves, at others, and at God."[6] The act of repentance, consequently, is a way for a person to reintegrate himself with the world and with the human family.

In *The Possessed* earth resonates with qualities of the icon. Just as the icon is distorted or violated, sometimes stolen or broken, so the earth is wrenched away from its normal order. It is muddy, messy, frequently clinging to individuals and covering those who fall and kiss its face. Earth and icon are the fundamental images of redemption in a community threatened by the demonic ambitions of anarchists, uprooted by their Western educations. For the world depicted in the novel is torn asunder. It is wildly fanatical and fragmented. In such chaotic surroundings it is little wonder that the community's most spirited young leaders have moved from the atheistic humanism of their immediate forebears to a nihilism that is no longer idealistic and speculative. The muddy earth and the violated iconic figures of the Madonna are mute victims of the rage of an essentially demonic energy. Against these powers of destruction is set the comic disposition.

The comic disposition, marked by imagination, hope, and remembrance, is a full acceptance of the relation of the mundane to the sacred.

Comedy recognizes the temporal limits of mortality: it embraces the finite and celebrates, as Lynch has written, "the pull of imagination toward heaven or toward earth."[7] It seeks to recall what Ellul characterizes the "incredible relation between mud and God."[8] In *The Possessed* comedy plays through the full range of human possibilities —from the scatological to the eschatological,[9] from the muddy earth in which Fedka sprawls to the diarrhea of Stepan Trofimovich;[10] from the grotesquely pious utterances of Marya Timofyevna to Stepan's reception of the Eucharist. The muddy earth and those figures to whom I shall refer as images of the "violated icon," specifically the icon of the Madonna, are set off against the pseudo-iconic idol of Pyotr Verkhovensky's demonic imagination, Nikolay Stavrogin. Both of these rebels are in a sense sons of Stepan Verkhovensky. This beloved though slightly ridiculous teacher is the sick man of the biblical parable that constitutes the epigram for the novel and delineates its entire action. And though the battle for Stepan's soul and the soul of the Russian people may seem at times to favor the demons, the image of the icon progressively emerges in the action of the novel, becoming the force that finally drives the demons out of the invalid into the swine and causes them to destroy themselves. At the end, the sick man is found healed and, as in the parable of Luke, "sitting at the feet of Christ."

To examine the iconic images that affirm the possibility for redemption even as the titanic Stavrogin surrenders to his own ennui[11] is to discover more fully the comic nature of the iconic. The word "icon" derives from the Greek *eikon*, meaning image or portrait. The Russian word is *obraz*.[12] As an image the icon "corresponds as well to the word of Scripture," according to the Russian theologian Ouspensky,[13] for as Scripture proclaims the words of the divine image, so the icon is an image of the divine word. In its aesthetic properties it fuses image to word, Scripture to image, and man to his supratemporal destiny. Hence the icon, as an aid to reflection, is rhetorical, mnemonic, and communal, embodying Scripture for a dominantly nonliterate people. But it also points toward the transfiguration of humanity and the entire visible world. As icons recall the past, the reality in history of Christ's sacrifice, they also look toward the future, to an eschatological fulfillment. Icons may be understood in this light as historical-teleological images of hope, embracing the entire temporal order. The two essential images in Eastern iconography are those of Christ, who became man, and the Blessed Virgin, the "first human being to attain deification."[14] These two central iconic images are present in *The Possessed*, although they appear under various guises. Together they develop a spiritually dynamic interplay of image and word, especially in the climactic figure of the gospel saleswoman, Sofya, who looks after Stepan Trofimovich just before his death.

The icon transmits visually the realization of the patristic formula: "God became man so that man may become God."[15] The distinction between image and likeness is important to a comprehension of the place of the icon both in Russian culture and in Dostoevsky's reflection of it in *The Possessed*. In Orthodox thought, the *imago dei* in humanity has become distorted because of the Fall; nonetheless, man is created in God's image. This *image* is a gift, bestowed with no effort from the recipient. To recover God's *likeness*, however, requires an action that, unfolding in time, is fulfilled in life. This action must be freely chosen in love if the interplay is to take place between image and likeness which Ouspensky sees as the movement of the soul toward its final destination in God.[16]

It is this journey of the soul toward its divinization that is the ultimate subject of comedy. More, it is the knowledge that man is potentially divine that creates the comic cosmos, be it in Chaucer's *Canterbury Tales*, Dante's *Divine Comedy*, or Dostoevsky's *Possessed*. Even at his most mediocre, comic man bears invisibly within him the divine image. At his best, the supernatural reality permeates the mundane in his actions and in his very being. In this light, a Tihon, a Marya Lebyadkin, or a Sofya is capable of being understood as an iconic realization of sacral reality in a comic mold.

Where this transformative process is end-stopped and the divine image is replaced by the merely human proclaiming itself absolute, what results is an idol rather than an icon. The idol, therefore, is always a signal of the infernal realm. In *The Possessed*, the regression from icon to idol is to be seen in the series of characters from Marya and Sofya to Kirillov, who attempts to become God by eliminating the fear of death, on to Nikolay Stavrogin, the prince of darkness destroyed by his own emptiness. In contrast to the "theology in image,"[17] of the icon, which expresses the reality of the God-man, the idol tends toward the realization of the man-God. Whereas the icon expresses spiritual beauty contained within physical beauty—"the beauty of holiness," according to Constantine Cavarnus,[18] the idol elevates a material creature into the realm of spirit and endows it with godlike qualities.

In its battle against the idolatry promoted by Pyotr Verkhovensky and his horde of followers, the icon assumes various forms, some of them incomplete and distorted, though nonetheless effectual. The result of the presence of a series of wounded, debased, and violated icons is the reeducation of Stepan—a reunification with earth, with the tradition of Russia, with the Madonna, and with the words of Christ. Within these images Dostoevsky affirms the critical connection between human embodiment and salvation, between the soil and memory, between tradition and the historical reality of Christ's presence. If these relations are lost sight of, the community might well give itself over to the construction and worship of idols, images of fragmentation that destroy form as well as the relation to past or future. Without the iconic earth as ground and as a place from which one begins, the iconoclasts would be able to violate all forms of holiness, to smash and disgrace all forms of the icon.[19] The moral character of a people, preserved in the power of the icon to impose a sacred order on reality, would be traduced and betrayed if the earth were not a participant in the iconic image.

The manner in which Dostoevsky answers the threat of the demonic rush toward anarchy is subtle but consistent, his method a continual poetic effort to wed word and image—word as creator of image, image as the embodiment of word. His poetic theology never wanders far from the image of woman and earth as the guardians of redemption. One of these figures is Marya Timofyevna Lebyadkin, the first of a series of abused iconic figures. An examination of her role in the novel provides an opportunity to explore the theme of poetic iconography and to understand its relation to comedy

Early in the novel Shatov and the narrator, Anton Lavrentyevich, visit the rooms where Marya lives with her brother, Captain Lebyadkin, a drunken officer of the military, now retired. The two visitors are at first astonished at the filth and squalor of the apartment: the walls are smoke-grimed, the wallpaper sooty and tattered; in fact, "everything was in disorder, wet and filthy; a huge soaking rag lay in the middle of the floor in the first room, and a battered old shoe lay beside it in the wet."[20] As if to counteract the sordidness around her, Marya uses powder and rouge excessively, paints her lips, blackens her eyebrows—all cosmetic decorations to hide her emaciated visage. Such an artificial masking enables her to tolerate more easily the squalid surroundings. But in spite of her extreme make-up, what remains most remarkable for Anton are her eyes. The description he offers calls to mind the presence of Orthodox icons, and Dostoevsky certainly draws on our familiarity with the iconic image when he describes both Marya Timofyevna and the light surrounding her: by the dim light of a thin candle in an iron candlestick the narrator sees in the face of the emaciated woman "soft, gentle grey eyes" which he considers remarkable. "There was something dreamy and sincere in her gentle, almost joyful, expression," he comments (119). "This gentle serene joy, which was reflected in her smile," astonishes Anton. His own heart is filled not with revulsion but with pity mixed with adoration. Shatov tells him that Marya will sit and dream for hours, even for days, with no sense of time. Her dream is always the same—a longing for her lost son, which the narrative makes clear she never had. Marya Lebyadkin could be called an iconic image of the Madonna without her child.

Later everyone learns that Marya is the wife of Nikolay Stavrogin, who married her as a gratuitous gesture some four and a half years before. This early incident shows something of Nikolay's disregard for convention, for the sacredness of marriage (since he abandoned her almost immediately), and for the family; he acts to satisfy the impulse of his own will and to alleviate the ever-present threat of engulfing boredom.

Marya, however, is important for two other reasons. First, it is through her that the way to redemption through the earth and through the Son of God is expressed. As a Madonna image of the wounded icon, she dreams of a son she has lost. What she weeps for most often is not the abuse she receives from her drunken brother but the loss of her son. She yearns for the child, remembering only that she took the infant to the woods without christening him. The child has not been blessed; the loss of her unblessed son implies an image which is incomplete, fragmented, and unredeemed. Marya and her absent child signify a first stage on the way to redemption that it is the large comic task of the novel to delineate.

The second reason for Marya's importance concerns not only how she appears (image) but what she utters (word); she relates to Shatov and Anton her comment about the earth to the Mother Superior in a convent, and in so doing serves as guide to an understanding of the relationship between earth and icon. She recalls that when she was asked about God she replied: " 'I think,' said I, 'that God and nature are just the same thing' " (122). And, shortly after, as she was leaving, a woman doing penance at the church stopped her to ask: "What is the mother of God?" to which Marya responded, "The great mother, the hope of the human race." "Yes," the old woman answered, "the great mother—the damp earth, and therein lies great joy for men" (122). The woman's words sink into Marya's heart. She has come to see that "the great mother" is both Virgin Mary and earth, the one born without stain, the other the dark soil. With this response Marya recalls the gesture of those suffering characters who seek contrition and forgiveness by bowing down, kissing the earth, and watering it with tears. It is the fullest act of humility (from the Latin "humus"), and the anticipation of redemption. Throughout the novel there occurs this ritual of human tears watering the earth and muddying the world, assisted constantly by the continuous rainfall which keeps the setting of *The Possessed* an appropriate place in which the swine may wallow, if we recall Luke's epigram to the novel. Muddy and messy, the earth pulls people toward her; she grounds their flight, forcing them to dwell more closely in her embrace. Some characters like Lizaveta actually fall to the earth, become muddy, and are transformed through their act of repentance. *The Possessed* is a novel of man falling back into the finite, the actual, concrete realm of human existence, the place of comedy.

This action of falling to the earth reaffirms one's mortality and illustrates the value of humility. All of these actions situate the drama of possible redemption within a community overrun by men possessed. Kirillov attempts to rise above the earth and become God by overcoming the greatest handicap of being mortal—the fear of death. Pyotr, an inverted figure of Saint Peter, wishes to affirm a grotesque Christ, a prince not of light but of darkness. Boredom replaces the comic interplay of man and world which rests always on hope, on wonder, and on mystery.[21]

The iconic dimension of the novel reconfirms the action of salvation through what is finite and concrete—images of the earth, water, the people, and of mother and son. Marya Lebyadkin, however mad and in-

The Icon and the Spirit of Comedy: Dostoevsky's The Possessed   203

firm, offers both the image and the word of redemption even while she is mocked by Stavrogin, abused by her brother, and eventually killed by Pyotr and his brigands. At one point, when Shatov questions Stavrogin about Marya's child, Stavrogin replies that though he has been married to Marya for several years, she is still a virgin. During this same conversation, Shatov pleads with Stavrogin, whom he understands as a man full of spiritual contradiction: "Kiss the earth, water it with your tears, pray for forgiveness" (216).

The earth, associated so closely with Marya Lebyadkin, through her earlier conversation at the convent, assimilates the iconic quality of the injured Madonna. Dostoevsky intensifies the association between icon and earth during the meeting between Shatov and Stavrogin by describing the earth's muddiness pulling on Stavrogin. He sinks "five or six inches" into the earth (196), and his feet slip in the mud (218) as he stumbles through the night after leaving Shatov. Locked in his own will, Stavrogin is unable to thwart the earth's attempts to trap him, for he is less possessed than he is *dis*possessed from the land, his people, even his own personal history. The earth's failure to encompass him reflects, I believe, the extent to which Stavrogin has already lost his footing in the world and has moved toward his own suicide.

In contrast to his isolation and impending death, other forces work to incorporate Stavrogin into community. Nature and grace, in their excessive conditions as the saturated earth and the heavily rouged Marya Lebaydkin, both embody the possibility of redemption. As images, both mud and rouge are imperfect examples of the power of transformation but, as in much of Dostoevsky's writings, exaggeration is necessary when the community is distorted and in flux. Only if exaggeration challenges distortion is the norm reinstated. In fact, exaggeration, distortion, and contradiction are all elements of a comic plot.

Shortly after his meeting with Shatov, Stavrogin seeks out the new accommodations of Marya Lebyadkin and her brother; they now live in a small wooden structure isolated from the rest of the town. When he enters the house, Stavrogin notices "in the corner there was an ikon, as there had been in her old room, and a little lamp was burning before it . . ." (230).

The play of image and word, the two dimensions of the iconic, is given another distorted treatment by the moral anarchists in response to the figure of a gospel saleswoman. Sofya enters the town to promote the word of Scripture, but she is met with malice by Lyamshin who, encouraged by a divinity student, surreptitiously places "obscene and indecent photographs from abroad" into the woman's purse (273). Later, when selling the Scripture, Sofya pulls from her purse the indecent images; she creates in the crowd a mixture of indignation and mirth. At this juncture the word contrasts with the obscene image; pornography consumes piety. The icon is again violated in its wholeness. The woman selling the word of Christ is another model of image and word, mother and son, Madonna and child. But once again, in a comic grotesque action, the image is debauched, cheapened, and exploited. Jacques Ellul writes that actions of this nature reveal the fact that modern man no longer believes in the sacred: "Man has tangibly profaned everything which previous generations had held sacred, and he is even consumed with a desire to desacralize all sacred objects."[22] Lyamshin is a buffoonish modern, a coarse disciple of Pyotr, and his action is one more in a series of raids on the holy in its deformation of both the woman and the word she wishes to share. The demonic elements revel in blasphemy; as iconoclasts they desire to debunk any sense of the life of the spirit or that which could redeem man. And yet their actions are self-defeating because they reveal pettiness of manner and simpleness of mind in their adolescent trickery. Suddenly these devils, when one recalls the demons of Milton, Marlowe, Shakespeare, or Goethe, appear as crude and ridiculous clowns. They are little more than comic imps.

However, they irritate without respite; they quickly expand their activities to steal the image itself. In front of the ancient church of "Our Lady's Nativity" is a large icon of Mary. One morning it is missing; in its place is a live mouse which occupies the space behind the grating in the wall (275). Ironically, the icon receives increased attention by its absence, for at all times of the day crowds of people surround the empty space. Each one who approaches it crosses himself and bows down to the absent figure. Many leave offerings, including Lizaveta Nikolaevna, who bows down three times to the iconic space and leaves her diamond earrings as an offering (276). She then rides off, muddied from the wet earth, a consequence of her act of worship. Diamonds and mud, icons and earth—the comic disposition leaves out nothing; it embraces all extremes in its inclusiveness and thrives on diversity and contradiction.

This scene is important because it gathers up several themes necessary to any discussion of *The Possessed*. In addition, it points to the distinction once again between icon and idol. What the iconoclasts in the novel fail to recognize in their theft is that the icon is not worshipped for itself. It is, in other words, not the same as an idol, whose worship goes no farther than itself. Rather, the iconic image transmits "a certain spiritual reality; it indicates man's participation in the divine life."[23] One does not worship the image, but *sees through* the transfigured surface of the image to the reality of eternity in time. The viewer sees by means of the finite, transformed image of the icon the infinite, transfigured body of redemption that the icon represents. If this awareness did not exist, if the true nature of the icon were not understood by the Russian people, they might begin to worship the live mouse. Instead, they continue to worship the space of the icon, made holy by the icon's presence, because they know that the icon is representative of a body transformed. Transformation is also at the heart of the comic. Comedy, in fact, is essentially a carrying away of death, "a triumph over mortality by some absurd faith in rebirth, restoration, and salvation."[24] But the sad parody that the demons wish the people to see—the icon of Mary transformed into a mouse—amuses no one. It stalls as a bad joke.

In contrast, the idol is an image that ends in itself. It points to nothing beyond its own one-dimensional reality. In its singularity and self-containment, its presentation must be worshipped or idolized for itself alone. It reveals no mystery, no sanctity, no sense of the divine; its persuasive force must begin and end in itself. No other world but the existing material reality in the present is implied. One might go so far as to say that the idol is tragic, the icon comic. The tragedy of idols is that they offer nothing transcendent, nor do they return the worshipper to the larger community of man. Contrary to the icon, which gathers up history as well as eschatology, the idol remains arrested in the present. Such is the import of Nikolai Stavrogin for his followers. Far from leading into visions of other worlds, the idol closes one's breadth of sight and limits perception. For Stavrogin, the end of his bifurcated existence is the eclipse of life by boredom.[25]

To return for a moment to Lizaveta's gesture in the space of the icon: her action toward the holy object's absence is doubly significant here because at the ancient church, whose name implies Christ's birth, she is soiled by the earth and so regrounds herself in the substance of the great mother spoken of earlier by Marya; and associated with the great mother is the tradition of Russia and her people. Liza's gesture is also a public action, on which the town passes no judgment. Absent, the icon, so strongly embedded in the popular mind, still serves its purpose, namely, to call to mind the historical action of revelation and the eschatology of redemption. This remembrance is the joy of the Christian imagination as well as the source for its vision of human life as comic.

How much richer, even in its absence, is the icon of Mary than is the bloated, yellow, decaying resident "saint and prophet," Semyon Yakovlevitch. A parody of holiness, he appears immediately after Liza's gesture of humility and contrition, sharpening the distinction between icon and idol. He also reveals that, in the absence of icons, some souls may gravitate toward the idols always present in a community. He is a bumptious pseudo-sacred double of Shakespeare's Falstaff. And his presence in the novel is humorous. He is an effective reminder of the human capacity to distort the sacred, and, in so doing, to reaffirm it. The comic disposition reveals in contradiction what is true and enduring. Yakovlevitch is an idol, like Stavrogin. Both signify an essentially good attribute carried to excess and so distorted.

But if Semyon Yakovlevitch is humorous, then the monk Tihon is comic. It is to his cell on the outskirts of town that Stavrogin journeys after his impassioned talk with Shatov. His home is a comic setting, for the dominant characteristic of Tihon's cell is balance amid diversity. Here are placed lavish gifts of "Bokhara rugs," finely finished tables, "exquisitely carved bookcases" beside ordinary, everyday household items. Engravings on the wall contain subjects both secular and mythological. In one corner is a "shrine holding icons gleaming with gold and silver, one of them an ancient piece containing saintly relics" (589). Dostoevsky portrays the world of his monk as containing objects and subjects which are "all too varied and of conflicting character" (589). Tihon is said to be a drinker; he receives no respect from the abbot of the monastery and is generally considered to be a man of little consequence. Yet nowhere in the novel is there a more compelling figure, one more grounded in both realms of spirit and the created world, than is this ignored monk. Living alone in his cell, Tihon embraces far more of life's fullness than do the figures flitting through the city creating disorder. His diverse possessions reflect his ability to make room for more of the world than any other character in the novel can encompass. Far from dividing the world, Tihon has a vision of reality that is broad and inclusive; seen as a holy fool by some, Tihon is a man comic in his playfulness, at home with paradox.

Tihon is comic, too, in that he enjoys the beauty of worldly objects while not being seduced by them. He remains faithful and sensitive to the world of souls. Moreover, he is wise. His observation on the consequences for a man who divorces himself from the earth, tradition, and the heritage of his people is that he will experience "boredom and a tendency toward idleness, even where there is a desire for work" (612). Stavrogin carries Tihon's judgment one step further. If, as he confesses, he has lost all ability to distinguish good from evil, then any sensational action becomes possible, even necessary, in order to stave off the terrible ennui which he feels engulfing him. Consequently, as he confesses to violating the young virgin, Matryosha, a deed which is a violation of the earth itself, he breaks a cross belonging to Tihon: "Stavrogin stopped at the writing table, and taking up a small ivory crucifix, began to turn it about in his fingers, and suddenly broke it in half" (610). The association between the broken crucifix and the suicide of Matryosha, who has despaired after Stavrogin's corrupting act, is intentional and appropriate. Stavrogin's own inability to forgive himself, his difficulty in distinguishing goodness from sin, and Tihon's distress at his blindness—all conjoin to show the tragic effects of moral degradation when one loses sight of the relation between earth and icon. Far from kissing the earth, Stavrogin's moral myopia no longer allows him even to see it.

The intention of Dostoevsky's poetics is to keep in dynamic equilibrium a contrapuntal movement of earth and icon, icon and word. Where one is exalted, so is the other. The image linking the two is the figure of the Madonna; Dostoevsky's method is first to show the series of wounded or violated images of the feminine while moving toward the final representation of word and image in Sofya, the gospel saleswoman. Her relation to Stepan Verkhovensky signals a fundamental reeducation back to the earthly present and to the transfigured eschatology contained in Christ's words. By means of Sofya, Stepan arrives at what might be called a poetic knowledge of Russia—that is, a knowledge which, feminine in form, is more a "communion with" than a detachment from what is known.[26] He engages in what Wylie Sypher has called an "unmasking," which allows clear vision into human action.[27] Furthermore, as much of the action of *The Possessed* reveals the mother weeping for her lost son (Marya Lebyadkin, Varvara Stavrogin, Marie Shatov, the earth herself), the figure of Sofya unites the mother and son through the intermediary of the earth.

The centrality of the Madonna and the earth is engaged once again in Stepan's complete disillusionment with his son Pyotr's ambitions and his rekindled interest in the Sistine Madonna. Her presence as his "ideal of humanity" increases his desire to speak about her at the Fete, the setting for carnival on a grand public scale. Image promises to become word. But Varvara Petrovna, disgusted with his old-fashioned aestheticism, rebukes his desire: "You've got that madonna on your brain. You seem bent on putting everyone to sleep" (218). Yet Stepan, a childlike man (both *puer* and *senex*), who laces his speech with sprigs of French, turns out to be the lost son of Russia, the Europeanized educator who is pulled back to earth and communion with Christ and the Virgin. This new interest in the Madonna begins a current of activity in opposition to the demons' work of desecrating the tradition that the community, albeit unconsciously, seeks to maintain intact and sacred. But even with the beginning of Stepan's reversal of attitude and his turn back to the earth and to the feminine presence of holiness, scattered outbreaks of iconoclasm continue.

Just at this time in the story the narrator recalls an incident in which a well-educated soldier, outraged at a reprimand by his superiors, suddenly began a series of strange actions. He had, for instance, "flung two ikons belonging to his landlady out of his lodgings and smashed up one of them with an axe" (296). While destroying these sacred images, the young sublieutenant, it was discovered, had collected a large horde of manifestoes and was intent on distributing them. Although the incident, like Stavrogin's breaking the crucifix, seems minor, the reader of Dostoevsky's writings soon learns that the small parenthetical actions are almost always models of a more enveloping concern. They serve as motifs to the grander symphonic plot. Taken together, these motifs reveal the world of *The Possessed* as one full of broken images, violent attacks on the holy, and insulted or violated women. Yet sacrilege, crazed outbursts, deformation, and destruction all find a place in comedy. Wylie Sypher has written that "in an artist like Dostoevsky the comic experience can reach as deeply down perhaps because the comic artist begins by accepting the absurd, 'the improbable' in human existence.... After all, comedy, not tragedy, admits the disorderly into the realm of art; the grotesque depends upon an irrational focus."[28]

Yet through it all, in *The Possessed*, the important dimensions of a human society survive and prosper. For the sacred, or iconic, dimension of the community is always sufficiently resilient to survive attack. At various times the image of the Madonna almost miraculously appears, to counteract anarchy and comfort those souls surviving among swine. One of the most articulate outpourings of the demonism in the community is contained in the social utopia proposed by Shigalov, a member of the group of five gathered around Pyotr. Shigalov intends to replace the current social organization with a system that begins with "unlimited freedom" and arrives at "unlimited despotism" (343). One-tenth is to enjoy absolute liberty and unbounded power over the rest of society. These plans for "depriving nine-tenths of mankind of its freedom and transforming them into a herd through the education of whole generations are very remarkable," the group is told, "founded on the facts of nature, and highly logical" (344). This is the way to primeval innocence, "something like the Garden of Eden" (344). Certainly Shigalovism is in direct contrast to the iconic imagination and to the disposition of comedy. The irony of course is that idolatry ends by attempting to restore a lost innocence through denying the human. For as the icon is the external expression "of the transfigured state of man,"[29] this transfiguration rests on living through one's fallenness toward the fullness of redemption. The icon does not deny the fallenness of man, nor does it imply that man can become God while on earth. Both Shigalovism and Kirillov's intention to kill himself are two predictable exaggerations of man's desire to perfect himself by becoming like God: Shigalovism promises an earlier state of innocence; Kirillov plans to become perfection itself by removing the fear of death—his slightly epileptic definition of God. The iconic image, in contrast, calls the person back into history, into the historical reality of Christ's nature, and to his suffering; it does not encourage an escape from human temporality, but rather enables life to be lived within the finite fullness of time. Further, iconic images are representations of holiness through bodies transfigured; they are not themselves holy bodies, but are witnesses to this possibility. Finally, Shigalov's notion of creating the earthly paradise (345) and Kirillov's fanatical idea to become God both evidence a wish to destroy mystery and for it to substitute rational clarity. The icon, on the contrary, seeks to maintain mystery as part of the form of salvation. The comic and the iconic share a common presupposition of faith and mystery. The gospel saleswoman, Sofya, will reveal how image and work unite to continue the dramatic eschatological action of redemption within time.

Stepan's resolution to pursue the image of the Madonna, to abandon his former fantasies, and to seek the earth as well as the Russian people, is hinted at in one small incident involving the icon's restoration. In an agitated state, dreading the coming fete, he confesses his fear of being disgraced by his speech on the Madonna. As he feverishly tells of his misgivings, suddenly his servant woman, Nastasya, enters and lights the lamp under the icon in the corner of his room. Anton registers his surprise at her action because, as he recalls, "there had never been a lamp there before and now suddenly it made its appearance" (364). Again, woman illumines the iconic, spiritual reality. To reinforce his new determination to speak about the Madonna at the fete (as if to replace through language the stolen image in the town's square) Stepan proclaims, while "he stretched out his arm to the lamp before the icon—*'cher*, I have never believed in this, but . . . so be it!' He crossed himself. *'Allons'*" (370). His action signals a change in the progression of the novel. The change involves a shift from the destruction and violation of icons to their restoration in the community. The most vivid example of the Madonna's presence and of her being united with the son is of course the return of Marie Shatov to her anarchist husband on the night she is to deliver her child. Occurring late in the novel, the birth of the boy is directly antecedent to Stepan's rebirth through the icon as he begins his quixotic journey across the land to rediscover Russia.[30] To seek the earth is a comic action, for by it one accepts limits, boundaries, and simplicity; the action allows a person to embrace human mortality.

The icon's presence, evident when Shatov's wife Marie, who had run away with Stavrogin, returns to her husband, appears most fully at the birth of her son. The child's birth transforms all of those who participate in its mystery. It is the peripety of the novel. In fact, the event is a rebirth of mystery and miracle which enchants all who rush to secure the infant's survival. The child's coming infuses the air with carnival, play, and a dissolution of social boundaries; humanity rushes forward to preserve new life. The birth of man and of mystery is described by Anton as sacramental in its effect; it transforms the midwife Anna Prokhorovna's attitude; it promotes the greatest outpouring of charity and generosity in Kirillov, who becomes like a generous child himself; it fills Shatov with complete joy. Arina's brusque biological explanation of the child's birth—"it's simply a further development of the organism, and there's nothing else in it, no mystery" (510)—only sharpens Shatov's declaration of its ineffable design: " 'the mysterious coming of a new creature, a great and inexplicable mystery; and what a pity it is, Arina Prokhorovna, that you don't understand it.' " (510). The mystery of the newborn brings with it a rapture which transfigures both Marie and Shatov. This event, the birth of a human being, again shared by the entire community, is an action both comic and antithetical to the death of young Matryosha at the hands of Stavrogin—a death in solitude amidst squalor and shame and remorse. With ironic appropriateness, Stavrogin is also the begetter of life in that he fathers Marie Shatov's child. Dostoevsky describes the birth of Marie's child in lyric fashion:

> Everything seemed transformed. Shatov cried like a boy, then talked of God knows what, wildly, crazily with inspiration, kissed her hands: she listened, entranced, perhaps not understanding him, but carressingly ruffling his hair with her weak hand, smoothing it and admiring it. He talked of how they would now begin a 'new life' for good, of the existence of God, of the goodness of all men. . . . She took out the child again to gaze at it rapturously. (511)

The scene reminds us of the holy family in offering an image of that moment in which Christ entered the world to transform it, "to raise up the dead," as Alexey Karamazov explains in a context not unlike the one described here. Amidst the "monstrous doubles"[31] of Pyotr, Stavrogin, Shigalov, and others appears this birth which reaffirms the endurance of man, the wonder of God, and the preservation of mystery. Joy and comedy conjoin to celebrate human existence. Clearly this is the effect on Shatov, who gazes in ecstasy at an infant adulterously engendered by a murderer and Shatov's own wife. The moment is a comic one, for it draws together several contradictions: he who recognizes no purpose in life spawns life; the betrayed husband is no longer betrayed, for he recognizes that not infidelity but life itself is reconfirmed; the woman taken in adultery becomes the Madonna. These transformations occur in a moment of grace. Shatov celebrates goodness and innocence once again entering the world; for him Marie and her child are iconic prototypes of Madonna and Christ—together they transform the anarchist, fill him with hope for the future, and inspire in his soul a yearning for a new life in love. In its mystery Shatov regains his belief in salvation and in the goodness of creation, whereas until now he had been full of brooding resentment toward men through his association with nihilists. Suddenly he is offered and accepts a new image to offset the manifestoes from his printing press. He gives up the secular word for a sacred image, that of the family. He is offered grace in the image of the newborn boy. In a sense, Shatov buries the word of the anarchists when he hides the printing press under the earth. Like the icon, the image of the mother and son imparts to Shatov a sense of grace. The image reeducates him into the mystery of God and redemption. It is at this moment that he resolves to break his alliance with the group. Joy replaces disgust, and cynicism gives way to festival. The icon has assumed flesh and dwells in the lives of those who have witnessed the infant's birth.

Perhaps Stepan's journey into the Russian countryside has many similarities with Shatov's transformation at the sight of his wife and child. Stepan's wanderings complete the themes of earth, icon, lost son, and redemption. His journey expresses what Aldous Huxley, in speaking of comedy, has called "The Whole Truth." In the light of the Whole Truth, all reality is play.[32] Stepan's wanderings are in the spirit of play. He leaves his comfortable, well-ordered world of dependence on Varvara Stavrogin, who has been like a mother to this "child," a sobriquet attached more than once to Stepan, and journeys toward the earth, what Marya Lebydkin earlier called "the great mother." On the road Stepan's consciousness is both heightened and transformed.

The land affects him like an ether: "Logical reasoning or even distinct consciousness was unbearable to him at this moment.... He did not even notice either how he threw his bag over his shoulder, nor how much more comfortably he walked with it so" (553). His whole attitude and posture exhibit a playfulness, a meandering action of both discovery and recovery, of wandering and wondering. He may be compared to that other traveller, Odysseus, who seeks in his wanderings to return to his origin and his heritage.

As he returns to the earth, Stepan meets a peasant couple who offer him a ride in their cart. He accepts their invitation but continues to walk beside them: "'How wonderful it is,' he thought to himself, 'that I've been walking so long beside that cow, and it never entered my head to ask them for a lift. This 'real life' has something very original about it'" (547). The cow, of course, being a real source of life for the peasants, is another emblem of the land, of nourishment and fertility.

Like a child wandering in the world, or like a foreigner in a strange land, highly conscious of the ordinary customs and habits of a people, Stepan wonders at the ways of the common folk. He returns to the earth. In the figure of the peasant woman is the other side of Russia which the men of intellect have either missed or chosen to ignore. She is the life of Russia, the Madonna who is robust, enduring, sturdy with even, white teeth, rosy cheeks and a warm smile (546). Earth and icon together lead Stepan to the eucharist. The action of his journey is comic in its playfulness and in its concreteness, for within this action the finite reality is extolled, diversity is respected and encouraged, and the ordinary is elevated.

Dostoevsky persuades us to see Stepan as a child with childlike feelings and thoughts; the last scenes, in which his wandering is occasioned by a continuous wondering at life around him, promote such an image. His association with the peasants, whom he wishes less and less to leave, and with the reality of the grange, the damp earth and constant drizzle, assumes the disposition of a child's world when the three of them reach town. Here the peasant couple and their newly acquired "child" enter a cottage owned by a Russian family. Certainly Stepan's joining the couple suggests a coming together of the family.

After seating himself in the corner of the room in order better to observe the folkways of the people, Stepan smells the aroma of pancakes coming from the kitchen: "The delicious fragrance of hot pancakes with which the woman of the house was busy at the stove tickled his nostrils. With a childlike smile he leaned toward the woman and asked for a serving with tea" (549). The charity with which Stepan is treated by the peasants is abundant. After all of his earlier esthetic harangues, Stepan, a man of some knowledge and little experience, finds his greatest happiness in being served hot pancakes from a peasant's kitchen. The ordinary becomes extraordinary. The folk and not the intelligentsia confirm Dostoevsky's belief that each of us is responsible for all. Charity and responsibility are both emblematic actions of comedy. With Sofya's arrival, the two perspectives of the icon begin to congeal: image and word conjoin. She approaches Stepan to sell him the Bible: "he raised his eyes and to his surprise saw a lady—*une dame, et elle en avait l'air*, somewhat over thirty, very modest in appearance, dressed not like a peasant, in a dark gown with a grey shawl on her shoulders. There was something very kindly in her face which attracted Stepan Trofimovitch immediately" (550). With their meeting the image is increased: first, there is the relation of Mary and Christ in the Gospels themselves; second, the relation of Sofya to the gospels, for she guards, protects, and dispenses Christ's words; third, the relation of Sofya as a nurse to the invalid Stepan, who exclaims, "Blessed is he to whom God always sends a woman...." (555); and fourth, the continuing relationship between Varvara Stavrogin and Stepan, now a wayward youth pursued by his mother. She finds him, however, in delirium on his deathbed. Stepan, forever an incurable pedagogue, promises to help educate the peasantry into the words of the Gospel. He has no notion of when to stop.

The presence of the family is felt once again as a unit of order. For he and Sofya travel to a cottage nearby where Stepan will die. The room he occupies is the secular equivalent of Tihon's cell, for its synthetic gathering of disparate images of reality promises a community whole and complete. The walls of the room "were covered with old and tattered yellow paper, and had horrible lithographs of mythological subjects on the walls; in the corner facing the door there was a long row of painted icons and several sets of *brassones*" (557). This link between mythic and iconic images was made in Tihon's cell as well. May not Dostoevsky be suggesting that mythic models served pre-Christian communities in the same way that iconic images serve a Christian people? "The whole room," he tells us "with its strangely ill-assorted furniture was an unattractive mixture of the town element and of the peasant traditions" (557). Mythic figures are iconic prefigurements; mythologies are like the histories of those represented in icons, for they ask that a people remember the past such that the future has direction and purpose. The essential difference, however, is that mythic images contain nothing of eschatology; icons of course are, as transfigured bodies, a promise of an eschatological reality.

In Stepan's room is a microcosm of the complete Russia, both pre-Christian and Christian; in the presence of the icon Stepan confesses to Sofya, whom he refers to as "my savior" (560). Here the icon's image urges man toward God's likeness through serving others. Her actions and words guide Stepan toward communion. Sofya reads him the story in Luke of the swine who receive the devils of the sick man, a figure who contains "all the sores, the foul contagions, all the impurities, all the devils great and small that have multiplied in that great invalid, our beloved Russia" (563). The novel becomes overtly allegorical at this point, when the reader is made to interpret Stepan as the sick man, his son and his associates as all of the poisons infecting a people's soul. But the action is comic when Stepan receives communion. For comedy "is both a sacrifice and a feast."[33] The sacrifice of Christ, the central action which makes iconography possible, and the feast of the Eucharist congeal in Stepan's death. His final hours, however, are marked by Sofya's presence; for as Saint Sophia, she is not only the voice of wisdom but also, as Karl Stern writes, "the she-soul of Eastern Christendom." Sofya unites the word of the gospel to the tradition of the people. In her action is the original meaning of icon, meaning "to happen, to become true."[34] As a figure of wisdom Sofya guards the word of Christ just as His earthly mother guarded His mortal development.

As she reads the gospels to Stepan, Sofya bears the word of Christ into the world; she delivers the word, reanimates it, and assists in the rebirth of beatitude, mystery, and redemption. Mother and son unite in Stepan's dependence on Sofya. She takes responsibility for him in his sickness. She is shocked when, toward the last hours of his life, and after a particularly agonizing bout with the summer cholera, he gets out of bed and "thinking of nothing, fell on the floor at her feet"

(560). Instead of falling to the earth to seek contrition, Stepan falls at the foot of woman. The analogical connection between woman, icon, and earth is complete.

The iconography of mother-son ends in the figure of Sofya and the word of the gospels. While Stepan's fascination earlier with the Madonna promoted his movement back to the earth, the humble gospel saleswoman brings him from the earth to revelation. The words of the gospels are images, ways of seeing, as the icon is a word, a way of knowing. Words create images, remembrances of sacred figures of the past—their images ask to be recalled. The words create images. Icons are image words, a Scripture in image. This is the realization Dostoevsky embodies in the last scenes of the novel. As the earth is a repository of the dead past, so is the word an embler of the eschatological reality of rebirth and redemption. Image and word, earth and heaven, these are the unities which allow a people to continue, to endure, to hope, and to love. In such action is a comic attitude toward human life and eternity which is iconic: "'My friends,' Stepan said, 'God is necessary to me, if only because He is the only being whom one can love eternally'" (570).

After Stepan's death, Sofya returns to live with Varvara Stavrogin. Varvara even suggests that the two of them might sell the gospels together; "I have no one in the world now," she declares (572). To Dr. Salzfish's reminder that she has a son, she snaps out: "I have no son!" a remark that, we are told, is "like a prophecy" (572).

At the end of the novel the swine have been purged, the group of anarchists broken up, and Stavrogin destroyed by his own hand. But what remains for the community is wisdom, a sense of what is durable and lasting, and the paradigm of the mother-son relationship, which is the original experience for man so that he might learn to love. Stavrogin ends in suicide; his action reveals the danger inherent in a preoccupation with image which seeks nothing but its own gratification. His end is tragic, for it denies life. Comic action, on the other hand, resides in a fuller dimension of life which acknowledges and worships the eternal through what is incarnate. Human embodiment is not the end but the beginning of love, for the icon reveals the body transformed, redeemed, and so fills the spectator with a feeling of hope and promise. One writer has suggested that "the terms of Christian comedy must include hope. Irony is the logical tone of Christian comedy."[35] Existing in time, the icon points to the realm which is the fulfillment of time. Such a disposition places one at the center of Christian comedy in a way similar to Dante the pilgrim's journeying through the regions of the soul after death. His final meeting there is also with the virgin mother, an image of hope which promises through her son the possibility of redemption. The Christian comic imagination can embrace the world of swine, mud, disease, man's finitude, his mortal frame, and yet move on to communion, resurrection, transfiguration, and redemption. Here exists the whole truth, implied within the image of the icon. In this spirit the Christian comic vision suggests that all is play.[36]

The icon maintains and preserves mystery while promoting the physical order—but the body imaged in icons has already been transformed. Thus, the icon asks that we remember our humanity while it reveals a promise of transfiguration. Stavrogin destroys others and himself because he cannot believe in the power of forgiveness. He refuses, moreover, to remember what it means to be mortal. Tragedy refuses to remember.[37] Stavrogin's demonic imagination sees the truth of life composed of three stages: birth, struggle, death. The iconic imagination understands human life moving through the same three steps, but adds a fourth—resurrection. As the fullest image of the comic spirit, the icon is an interlude between God and man in the same way that the mother is the interlude between man and world.

The earth is the ground from which we begin our mortal existence. The Madonna gives birth to Christ, *the* image of salvation which begins our transfigured existence. Taking our cue from Dostoevsky's notebooks, we realize that the icon reinstates the family: "We can have neither family nor familial virtues without the earth. A family is destroyed the very moment it is severed from its native land."[38] In addition, as he continues to speak of Stavrogin, Dostoevsky observes that "the prince does not believe in God because he does not believe in his soil or in his nation."[39] In short, he cannot love. To be attached to the earth, to be part of the soil, is to accept the limits of being human; it is also to have the capacity to love and be responsible for all men, for they are of the earth, which, we are promised, will itself be transformed in the fullness of time. To have such knowledge of the spirituality of matter is to have the iconic imagination and to live within the disposition of comedy.

Notes

1. Vladimir Nabokov, *Lectures on Russian Literature*, ed. Fredson Bowers (New York, 1981), 98.
2. Jacques Ellul, *The New Demons*, trans. C. Edward Hopkin (New York, 1975), 36.
3. Robert Louis Jackson, *Dostoevsky's Quest for Form: A Study of His Philosophy of Art* (Pittsburgh, 1978), 148.
4. St. John Climacus, cited in Sergei Hackel, "Paths to Reconciliation: Some Ways and Byways from the Orthodox Past," in *Sobornost: Eastern Churches Review* 2, No. 1 (1980): 20.
5. Hackel, "Paths to Reconciliation,", 15.
6. Kallistos Ware, "The Orthodox Experience of Repentance," *Sobernost: Eastern Churches Review* 2, no. 1 (1980): 21.
7. William F. Lynch, *Christ and Apollo: The Dimensions of the Literary Imagination* (Notre Dame, 1968), 105.
8. Ellul, *The New Demons*, 34.
9. John Crossan, *Raid on the Articulate: Comic Eschatology in Jesus and Borges* (New York, 1976), 27.
10. Edward Wasiolek, ed., *The Notebooks for* The Possessed, trans. Victor Terras (Chicago, 1968), 398. Diarrhea originally meant a flexing of the belly or womb, or (Greek) a passing through. It is, I believe, the central metaphor for the entire action of *The Possessed*. Purgation takes place on several levels simultaneously.
11. Rene Girard, in writing of Stavrogin as a "monstrous double," suggests that "when violent hysteria reaches a peak, the monstrous double looms up everywhere at once." *Violence and the Sacred*, trans. Patrick Gregory (Baltimore, 1972), 161. Stavrogin assumes the role of a grotesque reflection of Christ and an incarnate image of sin.
12. Robert Louis Jackson's book cited above offers an excellent discussion of the *obraz* and Dostoevsky's understanding of beauty.
13. Leonid Ouspensky, *The Meaning and Language of Icons*, trans. G. E. H. Palmer and E. Kadlvinlsky (Boston, 1952), 37.
14. Leonid Ouspensky and Vladimir Lossky, *The Meaning of Icons* (Boston, 1952), 32.
15. Ouspensky, *Meaning and Language of Icons*, 37.
16. Leonid Ouspensky, *Theology of the Icon* (Crestwood, 1978), 184.
17. Ouspensky, *Theology of the Icon*, 164.
18. Constantine Cavarnos, *Orthodox Iconography* (Boston, 1977), 42.
19. In speaking of Hercules in Hades, James Hillman writes that iconoclasm is the first move of murder, by not recognizing the divine power in images. *Dream and the Underworld* (New York, 1979), 115.
20. Fyodor Dostoevsky, *The Possessed*, trans. Constance Garnett (New York, 1959), 119. All references to the novel will be indicated by page numbers in the text.
21. Geoffrey Clive, *The Broken Icon: Intuitive Existentialism in Classical Russian Fiction* (New York, 1972), 75.
22. Ellul, *The New Demons*, 34.

23. Ouspensky, *Theology of the Icon*, 195.
24. Wylie Sypher, "The Ancient Rites of Comedy," in George Meredith, *An Essay on Comedy* (New York, 1956), 221.
25. George A. Panichas, *The Burden of Vision* (Grand Rapids, 1977). Panichas continues by suggesting that Stavrogin is in severe contrast to any romantic archetype of Satan as a fiery rebel or "a composite of a Typhon and a Prometheus, denying divinity for the sake of oppressed humanity." Important in this connection also are Josef Pieper's remarks on boredom as the antithesis of leisure, celebration, prayer, all elements of comedy. (*Leisure: The Basis of Culture*, trans. Alexander Drew [New York, 1963], 59.)
26. Karl Stern, *Flight from Woman* (New York, 1971), 54.
27. Sypher, "The Ancient Rites of Comedy," 220.
28. Wylie Sypher, "Our New Sense of the Comic," in *An Essay on Comedy*, 201.
29. Ouspensky, *Meaning and Language of Icons*, 39.
30. "Precisely because he is face to face with the Inexplicable the comic hero is eligible for 'rescue,' like Don Quixote, who is mad to the degree of pouring curds over his poor head but who dies, like a saint, in a state of grace." (Sypher, "Guises of the Comic Hero," in *An Essay on Comedy*, 238.) Stepan and Don Quixote have much to tell one another.
31. Girard, *Violence and the Sacred*, 161.
32. Cited in Crossan, *Raid on the Articulate*, 28.
33. M. Conrad Hyers, ed., *Holy Laughter: Essays on Religion in the Comic Perspective* (New York, 1969), 113.
34. Ouspensky, *Theology of the Icon*, 117.
35. Hyers, *Holy Laughter*, 113.
36. Crossan, *Raid on the Articulate*, 30.
37. Hyers, *Holy Laughter*, 35.
38. Waisolek, *Notebooks*, 123.
39. Ibid., 180.

10

Faulkner's Bachelors and Fertility

MARY K. MUMBACH

IT is a commonplace of criticism that marriage is a frequent subject of comedy. But, rather surprisingly, the figure of the unmarried male is nearly as prominent in the comic genre as is the husband. A striking number of lifelong as well as short-term bachelors—prospective husbands, playboys avoiding permanent commitment, misogynists, and celibates of various sorts—are common figures in comedies. Their prominence in no way contradicts the overarching femininity of the comic world. Indeed, far from being unaffected by the women whom they avoid marrying at least for a time, the bachelors are often excessively aware of the presence of the opposite sex, exhibiting an acute sensitivity that for one reason or another makes them maintain an essential inner separateness. But the higher sorts of bachelors, more numerous than one might expect, are those who take seriously the mystery of femininity and devote themselves to its service. They become fathers and lovers in the spirit, guardians of those around them. Paradoxically, a study of sexuality in comedy may actually begin with a study of bachelor figures.

In no work of literature has the theme of sexuality been more prominent or the bachelor characters more numerous than in the Snopes trilogy, Faulkner's large work depicting the totality of the comic movement. One has come to expect marriage to be the symbol of the continuation of life "in motion," yet the Snopes novels are peopled with bachelors, characters who live a life without changing their state. His representation of many different masculine archetypes and the resulting variety of their encounters with women indicates clearly that Faulkner is not treating sexuality per se but rather giving an account of the motion toward wholeness, which is the life of the human spirit revealed in its encounter with the world. The most telling evidence of the spiritual meaning of sexuality in this work is that many of the central characters, both masculine and feminine, follow a pattern of renunciation of sexuality in a narrow sense, revealing thereby some aspect of its meaning in a more complete context. Clearly at the center of activity in the three novels is Eula Varner, the full focus of femininity who represents to society its underlying continuity—created nature itself—upon which each successive stage of civilization must build. After her death much of the discussion in the novels ranges around the destiny of her daughter Linda, with the constant issue being whether Linda is a true heir to Eula's riches. These two central women characters are "doomed" to live outside marriage as it is conventionally defined. Eula's marriage to Flem Snopes is a mockery of the institution. Linda's marriage to Barton Kohl lasts only about six months; she must spend the rest of her life as a widow. Both of these wives are in fact frequently referred to as "virgins," and they are surrounded by masculine figures called "bachelors," "monks," and "priests."

The central bachelors in the novels can be judged by their treatment of these women, as well as by their relationship to the community as a whole. Jody Varner and the schoolteacher Labove try to ignore or suppress their attraction to the femininity of Eula. Hoake McCarron and Manfred De Spain view her quite directly as an object of their natural passion. Flem Snopes, though he marries her, is impotent, a perfect mismatch to her overwhelming fertility. But the action of the novel is redeemed, indeed even these two women are redeemed, by the action of two other bachelors, Gavin Stevens and V. K. Ratliff. Though Eula commits suicide and Linda becomes a card-carrying communist, they are nevertheless saved by coming to participate in lives of genuine sacrifice, lives they could have discovered and come to desire only through the influence of Stevens and his companion-in-arms Ratliff. It is this redemptive process that constitutes the general action of comedy.

The single state of all six bachelors surrounding Eula Varner is given a religious significance of a sort. All of them, as already mentioned, are called either priests or monks or both, except Hoake McCarron, who is, however, given a cultic role. In *The Hamlet*, Jody Varner is a "seething eunuch priest" (*H*, 115);[1] Labove is the "virile anchorite of old time" (*H*, 118). Hoake McCarron is ironically like the bridegroom of the Canticle of Canticles. Manfred De Spain, Charles Mallison says in *The Town*, was "born a generation too soon," or "he would have been by acclamation ordained a high priest in that new national religious cult of Cheesecake" (*T*, 14); but Gavin and Ratliff are different. They are the two familiar complementary figures of comedy, like Don Quixote and Sancho Panza, Tom Sawyer and Huck Finn; but in the particular metaphorical structure Faulkner has established in his Snopes comedy, they represent two possible religious responses to value, distinct but related, both demanding celibacy: priest and monk. Both renounce the fallen world that is passing away for the sake of the redeemed world that is ever so precariously being born from it. Ratliff is said explicitly to have "that hearty celibacy as of a lay brother in a twelfth-century monastery—a gardener, a pruner of vines, say" (*H*, 43). But Gavin, though he usually performs a more sacerdotal role in the community, has at times the agonized spiritual intensity of an ascetic. Ratliff tells Gowan Stevens that Gavin has taken Montgomery Ward Snopes to war with him as a "hairshirt" and is explicit in his comparison of Gavin to one of the desert fathers: "Likely your cousin taken the same kind of proud abject triumphant submissive horror in keeping up with his doings that them ole hermits setting on rocks out in the hot sun in the desert used to take watching their blood dry up and their legs swivelling" (*T*, 115). Much of the conflict in the society arises from the presence not only of high priests participating in various pagan cults honoring Eula under the titles of Venus, Semiramis, and Lilith, but of celibates who in a dangerously debased world, practice the Christian virtue of chastity within the ambience of the splendid Helen of Troy.

The separation of these characters from ordinary sexual roles indicates their mysterious significance within the trilogy. The virginity of Eula, "that ungirdled quality . . . of being at once corrupt and immaculate, at once [virgin] and . . . [mother] of warriors and of grown men"

(*H*, 113), is an attention to a motion within: she appears "to exist in a teeming vacuum in which her days followed one another as though behind sound-proof glass, where she seemed to listen in sullen bemusement, with a weary wisdom heired of all mammalian maturity, to the enlarging of her own organs" (*H*, 95). Linda's virginity, in contrast, is an attention to a world not within but beyond. She is

> the young pointer bitch, the maiden bitch of course, the virgin bitch, immune now in virginity, not scorning the earth, spurning the earth, because she needed it to walk on in that immunity: just intent from earth and us too, not proud and not really oblivious: just immune in intensity and ignorance and innocence as the sleepwalker is for the moment immune from the anguishes and agonies of breath. (*T*, 132)

The virgins and the bachelors devoted to them have renounced the world in some way, in order to witness to a life that is invisible to those who are caught up in purely domestic concerns. Their renunciation of "motion" as it is ordinarily understood is paradoxically a recognition of the spiritual motion which is its source.

Faulkner defines the roles of the sexes primarily through the relationship of a hierarchy of masculine archetypes to the splendid Eula Varner. Eula is a visitation of divinity, a last revelation of the glory of creation, thrust upon the tiny village of her birth, Frenchman's Bend, then upon the nearby town of Jefferson, and, after her death, upon the world at large. The bachelors who surround her vary in their relationships with her according to the kind of society which each represents. Her sameness in the midst of their variety manifests a phenomenon described by the Jungian psychologist Erich Neumann:

> There is a broad resemblance between the mother figures of primitive, classical, medieval, and modern times; they remain embedded in nature. But the father figure changes with the culture he represents. Although in this case, too, there is in the background an indefinite archetypal figure from a spiritual father or creator god, it is an empty form; it is only filled out by the father figures that vary with the development of culture.[2]

Eula remains a constant presence, apparently unchanging, while she is surrounded by bachelors who represent the responses of different kinds of society to her presence. Each of her titles—Venus, Semiramis, Helen, and Lilith—is determined by the encounter of a particular bachelor with her, expressing at any one time only certain aspects of her being. Each man's encounter with Eula determines his total identity and indicates the fate of the society he represents. Neumann has noted that

> the woman's consciousness is inhabited by a multiplicity of masculine spirit-animus figures, contrasted with the single Janus-faced soul-anima figure in the unconscious of man.... The cultural diversity of ... the numerous father-husband images known to humanity, has left a deposit in the unconscious experience of woman, just as is the case with the uniform mother-wife image in the unconscious experience of man.[3]

Though Eula seems unchanged by the actions of different men with her, there is evidence that she does not forget what each encounter has been. She emerges, finally, as a character, a person, not simply a feminine archetype; therefore her actions as well as her meditations actually do change according to the way she is being treated, though only a discerning eye could notice the change—until, of course, that final change, her death. Eula's suicide is a crisis threatening the very existence of society. It is one thing for a bachelor to commit suicide for Semiramis, as Maggie Mallison in *The Town* tells her son Charles that men by nature do. It is quite another for Semiramis, as the primeval source of life in a society, deliberately to die for the sake of preserving respectability for a daughter. The meaning of Eula's act remains the center of concern even after her death, as the action of the trilogy widens to a consideration of the whole of history and of the Western world.

If it is she who is the source of motion in society, the center of honor and devotion, must her death mean a cessation of that motion? Her presence in memory rather than in person will demand positive effort on the part of all members of the society to be faithful to her. Her death betokens a different relationship. The guardians of the culture are responsible for seeing that what remains of her, not only in memory and in lineage but in spirit, still informs the culture itself.

It becomes clear in the study of sexuality in all of the Snopes novels, but particularly as manifested in *The Mansion*, that Faulkner's understanding of motion on earth corresponds with Dante's and with at least a large part of the comic tradition in literature. In that comedy, motion, or the quest for wholeness, is initiated by the appearance of a feminine figure whose very being is a call to man to recognize his own incompleteness and to move toward communion. In both Dante's *Commedia* and Faulkner's *Snopes*, motion at its fullest is a struggle away from isolation and toward community and, finally, toward the life of grace already at work transforming the universe. It is, in turn, an acknowledgment of the origins of this motion and an offering of the universe back to its source. The "bachelors," or the celibate priestly and monastic figures in the trilogy, represent and direct, or at least try to direct, this motion of transformation and offering. Their action is directed and inspired by the appearance of women whose virginal qualities witness, in turn, to divine action in creation. The dedicated masculine and feminine characters, celibate and virginal, are in different ways and degrees in service to a mystery which is invisible to those caught up in the daily life of society; they are witnesses to that life of the spirit which tends to be forgotten in the course of ordinary domestic concerns.

According to Allen Tate in his essay "The Symbolic Imagination," Dante presents two kinds of peace as sources and goals for two kinds of motion in the world. One kind is the stillness of God, the Source of Light and motion at the proper center of the universe. The other is the stillness of Satan, who in the early part of Dante's journey appears to be at the center of the cosmos. Tate says that even at the end of the *Paradiso*, however, "Dante is *still moving*." He explains the spiritual meaning of motion in the Dantesque cosmology: "Everything that moves, says Dante the Thomist in his letter to Can Grande, has some imperfection in it because it is, in the inverse degree of its rate of motion, removed from the Unmoved Mover, the Triune Circles, God." Tate says that if one considers a lack of motion to be an attribute of the Unmoved Mover, God Himself, which it is, then one can reason to the "specious" conclusion that "Satan himself has no imperfection: he too lies immobile . . . as the Still Point in the Triune Circles is immobile." On the other hand, "If Dante's will is turning like a wheel, he is neither damned nor saved; he is morally active in the universal human predicament. His participation in the love imparted as motion to the universe draws him toward the Triune Circles and to the immobility of peace at the center, as it draws all creatures; but a defection of the will could plunge him into the other "center."[4] The analogues in

Faulkner's *Commedia* are apparent: Flem Snopes represents that "stasis of final spiritual death," but Eula Varner is a revelation of the divine Still Point as it can be comprehended through mortal creation. Strangely, the two are wedded. Between the two still centers is a hierarchy of bachelors, who participate in different degrees in the wheel-like motion, which is an outward sign of man's relationship to the spirit, his participation in life.

Bachelorhood, a renunciation of domestic life, is for Faulkner always a position within motion, directed toward one of these sources of future peace, the divine peace or the Satanic peace. It may signify the action of rejection of society, an orientation toward spiritual death, which leads after a lifelong struggle to an independence from the feminine, from fecundity, and from all communal life. This stasis or calm is rest in oneself, a refusal to acknowledge the radical "otherness" of the divine as it is manifested in the world. On the other hand, bachelorhood may signify renunciation of the world as fallen, as it weighs one down, in order to seek and to work for the world redeemed. The renunciation of the world as fallen, especially of the world represented by the distorted relationship with the feminine, in order to witness to the world as it is being redeemed and completed (by motion) involves not the loss but the interiorization of the fullest communal life, and the containment in oneself of a balance of masculine and feminine characteristics, which is a likeness to the life of God Himself. The bachelor expresses at his highest that androgynous character which psychologists say is natural to man's soul.

Faulkner has in common with Dostoevsky, James, Conrad, and others the rediscovery in the modern world of these celibate and virginal figures as archetypal masculine and feminine presences and sources of communal life. Their distancing of self from the world is wholly unlike that of the *isolato*, the isolated figure who rejects society and is consequently a threat to it. Like *The Brothers Karamazov* the Snopes trilogy is in many ways the playing out of the contest between the solipsist and the solitary, who renounce two different worlds for two different reasons. The prize for this contest is no less than the world itself. In *The Brothers Karamazov*, Father Zossima articulates the terms of the same battle that is being fought in *Snopes*, asking his listeners:

Which is most capable of conceiving a great idea and serving it—the rich man in his isolation or the man who has freed himself from the tyranny of material things and habits? The monk is reproached for his solitude, "You have secluded yourself within the walls of the monastery for your own salvation, and have forgotten the brotherly service of humanity!" But we shall see which will be most zealous in the cause of brotherly love. For it is not we, but they, who are in isolation, though they don't see that.[5]

Dostoevsky and Faulkner, like Dante, juxtapose two opposing kinds of peace and oneness with oneself which indicate the two possible poles toward which Tate says man may move in the world. The monk Dostoevsky describes, whose life is one of "working for the whole," is the principal sign of what Faulkner would call "motion." His heart does not rest in the present, making idols of the world as it is in its fallen state. Instead, he is about the work that Faulkner insists is necessary, taking "the trouble and sin along with us and curing it as we go."[6] Though the "work" seems to be giving up the world, he is really gathering the whole world in and moving it forward toward its end. The two states of peace, one resulting from idolatry, which is resting in the images presented in a fallen world, the other resulting from a dependence on the redeemed world of the future, toward which one's actions in the present world must constantly be directed, in turn correspond to those extremes in the *Commedia* which Tate describes in his essay.

In comedy, bachelors or celibates are traditional symbols of the two extremes in the quest for perfection. For instance, in the realm of the sodomists Dante meets Brunetto Latini, with his purely masculine notion of education and of life. But the last "bachelor" Dante encounters is Saint Bernard, who leads him to the Virgin herself. Dostoevsky, too, presents pairs of bachelors who move toward opposite extremes. In *The Brothers Karamazov* he makes evident the contrast between the life of the fanatic hermit Father Ferapont and that of the wise and loving Father Zossima, and again between the cynical, worldly seminarian Rakitin and the dedicated spiritual man Alyosha, destined to live "like a monk in the world." Shakespeare presents in *Measure for Measure* a fairly exhaustive account of bachelorhood, all the way from Lucio, who boldly assumes the bachelor privileges of using women for his own pleasure and then abandoning them, to the deputy Angelo, whose pretended self-sufficient virtue reveals itself as a cold self-centeredness, avarice, and unfounded self-righteousness. They are both revealed in the end as men who, like Flem Snopes, would accept death by execution over a life of commitment in society, through marriage. In contrast, the bachelorhood of Duke Vincentio is a sign of a whole personality. He has "ever loved the life removed," he assures Friar Thomas; and his eccentric temporary retirement from public life is not a reaction to a private passion, but a concern for the general welfare.

In *Snopes* one tendency of bachelorhood is toward a "completeness," a masculinity achieved by eliminating from the personality and from one's world all that does not fit into a certain singular purpose, either of utility or of pleasure. It is an individualism which is fundamentally anti-communal and finally impotent, opposed to the fruitful bachelorhood which is a singular dedication to the renewal of life through selfless love.

Faulkner shows that the literal term "bachelor" has numerous analogous meanings. Though the bachelors have in common a renunciation of the feminine, in particular a renunciation of the splendid Eula Varner, they prove to be as unlike each other as Brunetto is unlike Bernard in the *Commedia*. The significance of the comparison of each bachelor with the others is introduced at the very beginning of the trilogy, with the comparison of the bachelorhood of Jody Varner, the lowest bachelor on the scale of being, to that of V. K. Ratliff, who represents the completion of personality possible in bachelorhood. Ratliff's bachelorhood is similar to Jody's only in an analogous way:

> With his lean brown shrewd face, in his faded clean blue shirt, with that same air of perpetual bachelorhood which Jody Varner had, although there was no other resemblance between them and not much here, since in Varner it was a quality of shabby and fustian gallantry where in Ratliff it was that hearty celibacy as of a lay brother in a twelfth-century monastery—a gardener, a pruner of vines, say. (H, 43)

The term "bachelor" is an astonishingly suitable one for the roles of all these men. The most ancient meanings of "bachelorhood" are gathered in and the word itself redefined in the Snopes novels. According to the *Oxford English Dictionary* (*OED*) the word probably originated with the Latin word for cow, *vacca*, and was applied to a man who tended cows on a "grazing farm," as the "assistant of a *colonus* who had not a *mansus* of his own." In a comic and figurative sense, Faulkner echoes this ancient meaning in two characters through whom the masculine role is studied, Ike and Mink Snopes, who are both in attendance on cows that do not entirely belong to them.

In the hierarchy of medieval knighthood the word "bachelor" refers to "a young knight, not old enough, or having too few vassals to display his own banner, and who therefore follows the banner of another; a novice in arms" (*OED*). Manfred De Spain, described as "the Jefferson Richard Lion-heart of the twentieth century," is said to have worn "that mantle well." No, Faulkner continues, "it wasn't a mantle: it was a banner, a flag and he was carrying it, already out in front before Jefferson knew we were even ready for it" (*T*, 13). Gavin Stevens, on the other hand, fights all his life for Eula and Linda Snopes, but his primary complication in battle is that he is never equipped to fight under his own banner. For most of his life, he has no home of his own (though late in life he surprisingly acquires a mansion). His brother-in-law Charles Mallison reminds him constantly what a novice-in-arms he is, as he loses battle after battle with Manfred De Spain and Matt Levitt: "it aint that he dont want to make trouble: he just dont know how . . . he just dont know how to make the kind of trouble a man like Manfred De Spain will take seriously" (*T*, 58).

The word "bachelor" has also been used to refer to "a junior or inferior member, or 'yeoman' of a trade-guild, or City Company" (*OED*), a usage applicable to what Gavin ironically calls his "apprenticeship to holocaust" (*T*, 133.). This apprenticeship includes his acquisition of academic degrees, including a bachelor of arts from Harvard. Bachelorhood defined only as a rejection of community or of life in society is actually a debased and incomplete definition of the word or, rather, of the experience of the single life. Faulkner restores it to its full significance as a period of preparation for the future. As a state of humility and of service to something not one's own, it is a voluntary assumption of the life of the poor, the dispossessed, in anticipation of future glory. Seen in the fullest light, bachelorhood is the state of the poor in spirit and of those who mourn, but who will, in the end, win the Kingdom of Heaven. Thus the bachelor is both an agent and a sign of the motion toward the future which Faulkner calls "life."

The Snopes trilogy presents an entire spectrum of love and its consequences in the person of the bachelor. But no bachelor is completely satisfied with his state in life. Each of Eula's lovers undergoes a degree of agony, whether or not he understands or accepts his suffering. Eula proves herself at least their match in her capacity for endurance, and in fact she surpasses most of them by deliberately sacrificing her life.

When Gavin Stevens announces that he himself will conduct Eula Varner's funeral service, his married twin sister retorts, "Gavin, at first I thought I would never understand why Eula did it. But now I'm beginning to believe that maybe I do. Do you want Linda to say afterward that another bachelor had to bury her?" (*T*, 343-44). If Eula's death is really caused by the bachelors who surround her throughout her essentially vital existence, one is tempted to assume that she ended her life in despair of ever finding love or even a helpmate for her parental tasks. But, surprisingly enough, the contrary proves true. By the end of *The Mansion*, Eula's suicide, though caused in one sense by the bachelors, is depicted as a free act of sacrifice for another and a declaration of the inviolability of the human person.

Whatever she may do, Eula cannot help being what she is; and she clearly belongs to another world than Frenchman's Bend: "she seemed to be not a living integer of her contemporary scene." In fact, as Faulkner tells us many times, she is a goddess. Before she was thirteen, "her entire appearance suggested some symbology of the old Dionysic times—honey in sunlight and bursting grapes" (*H*, 124). V. K. Ratliff sees her as a goddess who has come to "a little lost village, nameless, without grace, forsaken, yet which wombed once by chance and accident one blind seed of the spendthrift Olympian ejaculation and did not even know it" (*H*, 149).

Eula is something that the community could never have produced even with its most fervent Protestant industry. She herself is aware that she does not belong to the village and is even detached from her own body, which draws so much male attention. She possesses "a ruthless chastity" impervious to the excitement around her; she is at once "chaste and inviolate," essentially virginal and maternal. She is identified always with the earth, which appears as silent and fertile, emanating the light by which all things are to be discerned.

The bachelors of her native village, Frenchman's Bend, the first to encounter Eula, are completely unable to rise to the occasion of her appearance in their society. Instead, they frantically try to confine her within their own narrow laws, not seeing that she is closer to a revelation of divinity than any of their current customs may be. They are representative of a culture that is puritanical and materialistic and indeed death-bound. Therefore, in them, the "motion" which Eula inspires in Frenchman's Bend is revealed primarily as physical violence and force. Interpreting the power that Eula exudes as purely physical, they blame her for their own reaction to her. The bachelors of Frenchman's Bend wish to possess Eula, failing to understand that any relationship is possible other than one of absolute power over her. But they discover that physical possession too is impossible.

As a measure of the inadequacy of the masculine force, Eula's extravagant beauty is only a source of scandal to the niggardly villagers such as her brother Jody Varner, who finds himself her unsuccessful guardian. Eula is left in the care of her brother, "who emanated a quality of invincible and inviolable bachelordom" (*H*, 6). He assumes responsibility for his sister just as he has done for the other Varner enterprises, considering her to be part of the family property. He is what the schoolteacher Labove sees as "the jealous seething eunuch priest" (*H*, 115). Instead of recognizing her divinity, Jody treats his sister as less than human, viewing her as a dog or as "a blooded and contrary filly too young yet to be particularly valuable" (*H*, 98). Jody's bachelorhood is a quality that pervades his entire life, a quality uncreative, against nature, as is the usury he learns from his father. He is so intent on keeping his sister from the rest of the community that he fails to recognize her splendor. We are told that Jody will one day be "an old man who at about sixty-five would be caught and married by a creature not yet seventeen probably, who would for the rest of his life continue to take revenge upon him for her whole sex" (*H*, 324). He will be a January cuckolded by May and will lose that which he seems to have preserved by not giving himself in love.

In bringing his sister to school, Jody delivers her to another bachelor, the teacher Labove. Labove has left his father's farm, not to be a merchant and owner like Jody, but to be a scholar. Unlike Jody he leads a life of renunciation rather than of ownership. But in the debased society, even asceticism takes on the character of a simple power struggle. Of his face the narrator says,

A thousand years ago it would have been a monk's, a militant fanatic who would have turned his uncompromising back upon the world with actual joy and gone to a desert and passed the rest of his days and nights calmly and without an instant's self-doubting battling, not to save humanity . . . for whose sufferings he would have had nothing but contempt, but with his own fierce and unappeasable natural appetites. (*H*, 106)

The violent containment with which Labove keeps order in his classroom corresponds with the order he keeps within himself. In the same way he finds his eremitic desert in the library, "where he would be sitting over the books which he did not love so much as he believed that he must read, compass and absorb and wring dry" (*H*, 111). Actually Labove is not giving himself to his studies; he is conquering them bit by bit. He attains his law degree because of "his hill-man's purely emotional and foundationless faith in education, the white magic of Latin degrees, which was an actual counterpart of the old monk's faith in his wooden cross" (*H*, 118).

When Eula enters the class, Labove sees that she not only does not need to be taught by him but that her entrance means an end to the order he has forced on the class. He watches for two years, "still with what he thought was only rage" (*H*, 116) at the destruction of his classroom order, believing himself immune to the passion that has destroyed it. He finally realizes his own weakness, seeing that the law degree he had dedicated himself to attaining was only an attempt to escape holocaust. Recognizing that she is what his books are about, he is nevertheless afraid to accept her as the proper object of his education. A symptom of Labove's failure to synthesize the forces within himself is represented in the quality of his desire for Eula: he wants her not as a wife, but as someone to possess just one time, as a man wants the axe-stroke which will sever a gangrened limb (*H*, 120). But Eula has absorbed more of Labove's teaching than he dreams. He sees her as a character from his books, and she reciprocates. When he does finally attack her, she pushes him away, replying with a particularly apt comment—a literary allusion she has learned from him—calling him "You old headless horseman Ichabod Crane" (*H*, 122). In his search for wholeness by amputating a troublesome limb, Labove has in effect severed his head. The denial of an essential part of his personality results in madness. Even a moment's imaginary submission to Eula has destroyed his self-containment. He must now recognize his bachelor state as the lonely, injured, incomplete condition it is. But in contrast she can refuse his unworthy advances by means of the literary teaching he had not dreamed she had absorbed.

Labove despairingly foresees that someone like Flem Snopes will fall heir to all Eula's riches and take his place in her life: "He could almost see the husband which she would someday have. He would be a dwarf, a gnome, without glands or desire" (*H*, 119), and in the recognition of that waste he compares her to an abundant field whose fullness can never be owned. Unlike Jody, Labove reaches a state of reverence for the grandeur of Eula and even for the land which he had left to win an education. His admission of failure is attended by a prophetic vision of Flem Snopes, the man who will seem to have won Eula.

But not all the impotence of Eula's bachelors ends in total repudiation. Eula does at last, for a time, accept suitors whose bravery makes them seem more worthy than the first two bachelors she has known early in life. Hoake McCarron and Manfred De Spain are the bachelors specifically mentioned by Gavin Stevens in connection with Eula's suicide, the men whom he says she tried to love but who were no match for her capacity to love. They differ from Jody and Labove in that they are more public figures; each represents a whole community of men.

McCarron is new in town. His interest in Eula rouses to action a group of a half dozen young bachelors who band together to protect their territorial rights to the local fertility goddess, swarming about her like garter snakes. McCarron routs the unwanted suitors, breaking his arm but winning the favor of Aphrodite. As Ratliff later interprets the story of Eula's courtship, the McCarron boy was not sufficient by himself to win Eula: "It taken all six of them even to ravage that citadel, let alone seed them loins with a child " (*M*, 122). Motion, for them, is reduced to an attempt to serve the fertility goddess in her role of procreation, to continue the life force.

This purpose is accomplished in Eula's union with Hoake McCarron, who is at least brave and heroic enough to court her alone and risk his life to win her. Eula, as a fellow stranger in the village, seems to recognize in him a kind of heroism. In fact, her very active part in the fight with her lesser suitors and her willing cooperation with Hoake indicate that she is far more than the natural principle they consider her to be.

In *The Mansion*, Ratliff sees the union of Eula and McCarron as splendid and turbulent but incomplete. The end of *The Hamlet* includes a marriage and the birth of a child, in comedy traditionally signs of the renewal of the life of society. But the marriage is a betrayal, and the child a bastard. There is no celebration of Eula's nuptials with Flem, who never courts her but simply makes a bargain with her father: he will provide respectability for Eula, asking that she be only a nominal wife in return for a name for her illegitimate child. Thus Eula as a young woman is made to assume the feminine roles of wife and mother without having that change of status, that "motion," properly acknowledged.

Flem finds great profit in an unfaithful wife, who is better currency than money would be when he moves her to the town of Jefferson. The mayor of the town, Manfred De Spain, willingly gives Eula's "husband" all that he asks in return for her favors. Manfred, who besides being brave enough to attempt a union is strong enough to sustain it, looks like an older, more sophisticated brother of McCarron. The community of Jefferson to which he belongs is likewise more sophisticated, representing a higher civilization than Frenchman's Bend. He too represents the aspirations of an entire community of men: Chick says in *The Town* that all members of the town are "accessory to that cuckolding" (*T*, 15). Publicly its citizens cannot condone the affair. Privately they share with Manfred the thrill of "the divinity of simple uninhibited immortal lust" (*T*, 15).

If Flem is the "crippled Vulcan to that Venus," as Labove had said, Manfred De Spain must be the war god Mars, who seems the rightful match for her. He has the reputation of being a war hero. Like Labove, he is seen wielding an imaginary axe, but he uses it on society, not on himself. Chick Mallison, Gavin's nephew, says that the town was wondering what axe De Spain would use "to chop the corners off Jefferson and make it fit him" (*T*, 11). Actually the instrument he uses is mockery of the law and of marriage. After his affair with Eula has begun, he publicly ridicules Gavin for his attempt to defend Eula's honor and sends him a corsage with a contraceptive device in it to provide a more painful source of evidence for anguish. De Spain boasts thereby that their union is completely sterile.

Though McCarron's love was creative in that it produced a child, it could not be sustained in a personal union with Eula. Manfred's love, on the other hand, produces a long-lasting union, but its sterility is a scandal to the community. Not only does it produce no child; it keeps its participants from growing to adulthood. Ratliff says clearly that De Spain's strength is the strength of a natural force, as is MaCarron's, and that neither Hoake nor Manfred is a real rival of Gavin's cherishing and intensely personal love. The division in the realm of bachelorhood clearly separates Hoake and Manfred from Gavin and Ratliff. The motion each attends seeks different poles. Ratliff, too, is capable of loving Eula selflessly and is similar in some qualities of his bachelorhood to Gavin Stevens, yet Gavin's service in the roles of lawyer, teacher, and public man define a different calling. His life of turmoil is the result of the priest-like nature of his renunciation. Gavin's and Ratliff's differently motivated relinquishments of the world fit well the description which the theologian Louis Bouyer gives of two kinds of religious vocations:

> The monk, in becoming a monk, can have no immediate objective other than his complete liberation from all earthly ties to be wholly Christ's. The priest, in accepting the priesthood and more particularly the charge of souls, equally consecrates wholly himself to Christ, but, directly and by that very fact, to Christ in his brothers and especially in those to whom he is sent.[7]

He continues, "All kinds of political, social, cultural, and moral problems should attract his attention, which should not do so were he vowed only to that 'search for God' . . . to which the monk is consecrated."[8] Both Ratliff and Gavin take on an aspect of Christian heroism analogous to that traditionally represented by dedicated celibates in Christian cultures. Seen in this light, they fulfill complementary tasks in the community. Ratliff's life is more completely contemplative than his friend's. Gavin's is more directly devoted than Ratliff's to the spiritual lives of those around him. Ratliff's dedication to Eula is absolute but for the most part invisible. In contrast, Gavin is required by his vocation to take direct obvious action for her sake, though his behavior may at times be awkward. Ratliff mourns her loss quietly, lamenting his inability to save her, but Gavin must more openly bear the knowledge of his inadequacy to fulfill his task as his failures are made publicly evident.

V. K. Ratliff, the mysterious character who in *The Mansion* gives the final evaluation of the drama surrounding Eula, is also the most complete bachelor of all the characters. His role seems so secret and puzzling as to be irritating to his best friend Gavin as well as to readers of the novels; yet Ratliff's vision of the events of the trilogy is essential to a full understanding of their significance. Instead of being a sign of separateness and incompleteness, Ratliff's bachelorhood represents a life of communion and abundance. He is able to move freely among both men and women. In fact, his traveling between them is essential to the life of the community. Among the men he is known for his loquaciousness, among the women for the acuteness of his hearing:

> still doing the talking apparently though actually doing a good deal more listening than anybody believed until afterward—among the women surrounded by laden clotheslines and tubs and blackened wash pots beside springs and wells, or decorous in a splint chair on cabin galleries, pleasant, affable, courteous, anecdotal, and impenetrable. (*H*, 13)

More than sewing machines, he trades all kinds of merchandise, more than merchandise,

> retailing from house to house the news of his four counties with the ubiquity of a newspaper and carrying personal messages from mouth to mouth about weddings and funerals and the preserving of vegetables and fruit with the reliability of a postal service. (*H*, 13)

Not only complete in himself, he is a way of bringing to completion the life of the community. But he maintains a secret life that his fellows do not understand.

Ratliff knows more about the women of the village than do any of the husbands. But his attempts in *The Hamlet* to convey his knowledge to his fellows end in dismal failure. The men already know that Mrs. Littlejohn will disapprove of their exploitation of the idiot Ike Snopes' love for Houston's cow. Mrs. Littlejohn does know and disapprove, but she remains silent. Ratliff combines her womanly disapproval of their unnatural pleasure with courageous and manly action.

In his story of the Negro woman who pays Flem for her groceries by submitting to his desires, he attempts to warn his unheeding fellows of the inhumanity of Flem's actions, tying together the sins of usury and prostitution. The men likewise ignore his attempt to arouse in them sufficient indignation to defend Mrs. Armstid from Flem Snopes. In this dark stage of comedy, they have been permeated by the selfish spirit represented by the sterile bachelorhood of Flem. In a later talk with his friend Bookwright, Ratliff announces that he will no longer help those who refuse to help themselves.

Because of this remark, we cannot think that Ratliff tries to find the buried treasure of the Old Frenchman's Place as purely a project of philanthropy undertaken in order to help the Armstids' financial situation. Neither is his motive the avarice that is symptomatic of the rest of the community's disorder. But his freedom from the typical vice of the community does not mean a total immunity from fault. In *The Town*, Ratliff admits that his motive was an inordinate curiosity. He is the first to recognize that the property has a mysterious value related to the value of Eula. Both Eula and the estate seem wasted on a poor and ignorant community such as Frenchman's Bend. Ratliff is frustrated in his attempts to discover the nature of that value and attributes it to a literal buried treasure.

Ratliff's character as a "pruner of vines" gives him a unique relationship to Eula, whose "appearance suggested... the writhen bleeding of the crushed fecundated vine beneath the hard rapacious trampling goat-hoof" (*H*, 96). The pruner does not do violence to a plant but helps it grow. He is not so much interested in taking the wine as he is in encouraging it to flourish. Though Ratliff himself would never have courted Eula, he alone in Frenchman's Bend recognizes the awesomeness of her waste in marriage to Flem Snopes:

> That would never have been for him, not even at the prime summer peak of what he and Varner both would have called his tomcatting's heyday. He knew that, without regret or grief, he would not have wanted it to be... and he even thought of the cold and froglike victor without jealousy.... What he felt was outrage at the waste, the useless squandering; at a situation intrinsically and inherently wrong by any economy... as though the gods themselves had funnelled all the concentrated bright wet-slanted unparadised June into a dung-heap, breeding pismires. (*H*, 161–62)

The comparison of Ratliff to a monk is seriously meant. He seems to have taken a vow of chastity as apparently he has of poverty. In *The Town*, Gavin and Eula puzzle over Ratliff's life of renunciation, concluding at first that under the initials "V. K" Ratliff hides his royal Russian name "because how could anybody named Vladimir hope to make a living selling sewing machines or anything else in rural Mississippi?" (*T*, 322). But immediately Gavin realizes that the assignment to Ratliff of solely monetary motives is wrong and suggests that, on the contrary, if everyone had known Ratliff's Russian name, he would be a millionaire by now (*T*, 323). The concealment of his name is associated with a renunciation of the world. His names are in fact the names of the early monks who were apostles to the Russians and to the Slavs, Saint Vladimir and Saint Cyril. Their mission resulted not only in a transferral of religion but of a culture which is its medium.

Ratliff recognizes the splendor not only of the possible wealth he is sacrificing but also of love; he is admittedly the kind of man who would prove attractive to women. His chosen state of life is a mystery even to Gavin, who decides not to carry the question of his relation to women further. There is no provision in the modern Southern town for a public declaration or explanation of the life of poverty, chastity, and obedience. But even the Gospel gives no obvious explanation in Matthew 19:12, saying only that "there are eunuchs who have made themselves so for the kingdom of heaven. Let him accept it who can." The argument of this statement is explicitly against assuming such a life for expedience and comfort or even because of disillusionment with the world. Ratliff's way of life is chosen before the discouragements he faces in *The Hamlet*, and he seems to be the only man who, while knowing and appreciating Eula, has no sense of regret at not possessing her. In fact, his lack of regret is based on a profound humility in the face of her worth.

Ratliff's place in the culture is that of the monastic, who has been traditionally the preserver of culture in dark times. He witnesses to all that has happened and carries from one order to another the history that has gone before. His is not a scribe like his predecessors in the Dark Ages, but he carries in memory to the town the tale of what has happened in *The Hamlet*. He is a sign of continuity between the two orders, recognizing even the values that he cannot yet explain or understand.

* * *

In his relinquishment of the world Ratliff is similar to Gavin Stevens, although, as earlier indicated, the two have different callings. An early Faulkner sketch, "The Priest," elaborating a character with startling likenesses to Gavin, indicates the author's long-standing interest in the priestly vocation as an analogue for the dedicated life. A shorter version of this sketch, published in 1925 in *The Double Dealer*,[9] presents in a more concentrated lyric form the meditations of a young man the night before his ordination, the last night of his novitiate. As he is about to take the vow of celibacy, his thoughts are drawn to images of the feminine presence to whom he is about to dedicate his life, the Virgin Mother of God, and to images of the world of the flesh, lovely and dark, which does not yet recognize why it is restless and dissatisfied. He joins his own sorrow at his renunciation with that of the "little silver virgin, hurt and sad and pitiful, remembering Jesus' mouth upon her breast."

The more extended version of this sketch, published only recently,[10] reveals even more distinct parallels with the experience of Gavin Stevens. In the long story, the young man recalls that after entering the seminary, he had thought that his renunciation of the world would bring him peace. But instead, he has remained in a state of suffering. His celibate life will not be a simple surrender of life, which darkens and lessens the world around him, but a shedding of light on that suffering world, which will, in turn, bring him more suffering. The priest, like Gavin, believes that real dedication to human love is finally a dedication to the future, to "tomorrow." Each in his separate situation must acknowledge the goodness of that way, though he cannot choose it. The night before his final relinquishment to Eula, Gavin Stevens watches the spring darkness full of lovers. He thinks of the fullness of human love as "not the first day at all, not Eden morning at all. . . ." It is instead the "sum of all the days: the cup, the bowl proffered once to the lips in youth and then no more; proffered to quench or sip or drain that lone one time and even that sometimes premature, too soon" (*T*, 317). Gavin is acutely aware of what his life of sacrifice has prevented him from enjoying.

The young priest and Gavin Stevens are similar, finally, not simply in the complexity of their acts of renunciation of the world, but also in the complexity of their assent and consecration to the feminine. The image of the Virgin Mother to whom the priest gives himself, like that of Eula (the virgin and mother of warriors, "at once corrupt and immaculate"), is the embodiment of the fullness of human love: the novice meditates, "something beautiful and fine meant to him a Virgin not calm with sorrow and fixed like a watchful benediction in the western sky; but a creature young and slender and helpless and (somehow) hurt . . . a little ivory creature reft of her first born and raising her arms vainly upon a dying evening." The Virgin, he says, is a child made into "a symbol of man's old sorrows," just as he too will become such a symbol in his loss, a "child reft of his childhood." It is in this priestly sense that Gavin's "holocaust" must be understood. As Saint Thomas has written in his study of the religious life, the life exercised in charity is a sacrifice, but that exercised under religious vows is a holocaust, an offering of oneself as a sacrifice for all, out of a love which leaves nothing of the lover unconsumed.[11]

Not many critics have understood the peculiar nature of Gavin's bachelorhood.[12] It is of a different nature from that of the most of the others because, as Ratliff points out, it was Gavin's doom to have been born "into that fragile and what you might call gossamer-sinewed envelope of boundless and hopeless aspiration" (*M*, 128). His mode of being is hopelessness but not hardened hopelessness, not so much a separateness as a vulnerability, an endless yearning for a union he cannot achieve. Though it marks the highest reach of comedy, it is a state accompanied by anguish and suffering that will leave him open to the mystery of another person. He has no rivals in the suffering he endures for love: for there can hardly be competitors in a submission which requires the embarrassment that would have destroyed Jody, Labove, Hoake, and Manfred. Gavin tells Ratliff that his bachelorhood is a condition beyond his control: "Marriage is constantly in my life. My fate is constantly to just miss it or it to, safely again, once more safe, just miss me" (*T*, 351). Though Gavin attributes safety to the state of bachelorhood, it actually compels a state of danger, because for him it is a sacrifice for the sake of another. At the end of *The Mansion*, while waiting for a call telling him whether there is danger of Mink Snopes carrying out his mission in killing his cousin Flem, Gavin Stevens muses on his more than five decades of single life:

> His life had known other similar periods of unrest and trouble and uncertainty even if he had spent most of it as a bachelor; he could recall one or two of them when the anguish and unrest were due to the fact that he was a bachelor, that is, circumstances, conditions insisted on his continuing celibacy despite his own efforts to give it up. (*M*, 391)

Gavin emerges as the one bachelor in the trilogy who would have liked to marry and is even given the chance to marry, but who says that because of external conditions he has been forced (if he were less modest, he would say "called") to forgo marriage for many years. He is the one bachelor of the trilogy who finally does contract an apparently happy marriage, much to the relief of the friends and relatives who think that as a husband he will be less "dangerous." By the end of the trilogy Gavin seems used to that state of danger, which he realizes is a quality inherent in his whole way of life and not to be ameliorated by marriage.

The rest of Jefferson seems to consider Gavin's bachelorhood to be a threat to its own existence. When Gavin begins his crusade to "save" Eula from Manfred De Spain, Maggie feels he ought to have married in order to preserve himself. His attempt to redeem Eula's reputation seems to achieve nothing but to make Gavin himself look ridiculous. At the Cotillion Ball, Charles Mallison says, his uncle was not trying to hurt De Spain but "simply defending forever with his blood the principle that chastity and virtue in women shall be defended whether they exist or not" (*T*, 76). After the fight only Maggie seems to understand its meaning, and she concludes by protesting indignantly that the women of the town "don't deserve you! They aren't good enough for you!" (*T*, 77).

Gavin is astounded when, after he has attempted to implicate De Spain in the brass-stealing incident, Eula comes to Gavin's office and offers herself to him; he tries to guess which of the two men she is trying to protect by her apparent bribe. He dismisses the possibility that it is Flem whom she wishes to save, because it would be too unbearable to think that she cares for Flem; and he realizes further that she has no need to protect Manfred from him. But Gavin's dreariest realization is expressed in his comment, "So you came just from compassion, pity;

not even from honest fear or even just decent respect. Just compassion. Just pity." He reacts in disappointment at this knowledge, not alone because of his own humiliation but because of the absence it shows in Eula. However, even greater than this hurt is the recognition of a further motive: "Not just to prove to me that having what I think I want won't make me happy, but to show me that what I thought I wanted is not even worth being unhappy over." Humiliated, he asks her, "Does it mean that little to you? I don't mean with Flem: even with Manfred?" The only thing that could be worse for the courteous, honorable lover than his unrequited love would be the acquiesence of the lady to his current wishes, which would necessarily mean that she was not even true to another love. Few readers understand Gavin's desperate refusal of Eula's offer. Eula, accustomed to the completely natural love of Manfred De Spain, at first chastises him somewhat: "You spend too much time expecting.... You just are, and you need, and you must, and so you do. Don't waste time expecting." Still he refuses her, in saying that could he merely do what he desired, "I wouldn't have been me then" (*T*, 94). She considers him to be afraid, and indeed Gavin here seems to believe that he acts as less than a man.

Instead of accepting the offer that he naturally wants as much as any of the other bachelors, he cares sufficiently for Eula to reprove her, not for her unlawful adultery but for her infidelity to her own identity; her casual offer of herself reveals a profound ignorance of her own worth.

Gavin cannot comprehend that his actions have any effect upon Eula, but even during the conversation she suddenly begins to understand his motives. If he had refused to expect and so had attained what Manfred has possessed, then, he says, "I wouldn't have been me." But Eula offers another explanation, "Maybe it's because you're a gentleman and I never knew one before" (*T*, 94). Gavin replies in self-deprecation that Manfred and Hoake McCarron were also gentlemen: "All three gentlemen but only two were men" (*T*, 95). Whereas the other bachelors are self-conscious about playing their masculine role, Gavin abdicates even that vanity. Not only will he refuse her in spite of his normal desires and emotions, as Labove once tried to refuse her; but he will refuse even at the risk of seeming less than a man, a risk which Eula recognizes that Manfred would never take. Finally Gavin decides that if Eula has not come for Manfred's sake, she must have come for

Flem after all; in other words, she must have submitted to a force worse even than the one Manfred De Spain represents. She is living according to expediency, providing a home for her child as well as enjoying her love affair. He reprimands:

> You told me not to expect: why don't you try it yourself? We've all bought Snopeses here, whether we wanted to or not; you of all people should certainly know that. . . . But nothing can hurt you if you refuse it. . . . And nothing is of value that costs nothing so maybe you will value this refusal at what I value it cost me. (*T*, 95)

He can help save her from Snopes only by refusing to take her. However, only she can really protect herself from Flem. But Eula has had a new experience in being protected from Snopes by someone who accepts responsibility for Snopes.

Gavin's sister Maggie tells her nephew Gowan that Gavin could never marry Eula: "You dont marry Semiramis: you just commit some form of suicide for her" (*T*, 50). Later Ratliff elaborates on the nature of this "suicide." He sees that if Manfred is fated to be Eula's lover on the natural level, Gavin is destined never to possess her on that basis. But this deprivation is attributable to a higher power than fate, since Gavin's love for her is more than a natural force. Ratliff perceives as well Eula's silent appreciation of Gavin: "And he never did realize that she understood him because she never had no way of telling him because she didn't know herself how she done it" (*T*, 101). He sums up their relationship, which Ratliff can see is reciprocal after all, observing "that one dont really ever lose Helen, because for the rest of her life she dont never actively get rid of him. Likely it's because she dont want to" (*T*, 102).

Gavin's next dangerous venture is his adoption of Eula's daughter Linda. When he returns to Jefferson after his long sojourn in Europe, he sees the girl as he walks one day with his nephew Chick Mallison. He muses that she is "like the young pointer bitch, the maiden bitch of course, the virgin bitch" (*T*, 132). He wonders why Eula's power could not have produced another exactly like herself, but he realizes that there would have to be time before Nature could produce fresh fodder to replace what Eula "had exhausted, consumed, burned up" (*T*, 133). Apparently the "fodder" is that which calls forth the masculine yearning in the men who had pursued her, which, however, was not completely exhausted; for Gavin, thinking himself a part of that fodder, is reminded by it of his "apprenticeship to holocaust."

Gavin's meditation on the parentage of Linda leads him to decide that it is better to consider Linda a bastard and Eula promiscuous than to have to believe that Eula has actually loved Flem and has had a child by him. Furthermore, if Eula's mate is in reality the heroic human spirit dedicated to her honor, he concludes, "that girl-child was not Flem Snopes's at all, but mine." He feels himself in this way united to Hoake McCarron. Instead of considering himself a proxy father for the absent Hoake, it is as though Gavin considers Hoake to have acted as a proxy for himself, engendering the child so that Gavin might be given her. Unlike Hoake's momentary violent battle, Gavin's battle is one of remaining, surviving, living on, and suffering.

The community has its own anguish over the relationship of the county attorney with an adolescent girl. Maggie worries for a time but then decides that their relationship is like the one Gavin had several years before with Melisandre Backus, based on his desire to "form her mind." The town, including even Gavin's twin sister, has trouble defining a relationship based on friendship and a common concern, such as Gavin's and Linda's. Gavin tries to show his pupil the world of poetry because he realizes that she has no model for love in her life. He concentrates on studying John Donne's poetry, but he goes further and actually lives the life of the poetry. He describes the empty and lonely aspect of his bachelor life as creative: the "damned-fool poet's Nothing, steadily and perennially full of perennially new and perennially renewed anguishes for me to measure my stature against whenever I need reassure myself that I also am Motion" (*T*, 135). His adoption of Linda is a creative act, from Nothingness, since on the natural level their relationship is nothing; yet his anguish fills that nothing with motion and life. His problem now is not a matter of curbing his natural feelings, but of expressing the love of teacher for student without the town's thinking that he has wicked designs on her. He must behave in a manner older than he feels and again much more cautiously than he would like, lest Linda's reputation be ruined.

Gavin's service to Eula and his guardianship of Linda are culminated in a final interview with Eula, after Flem has exposed her affair with Manfred De Spain. Many years after their first encounter, he feels unequal to any task she might ask him to perform. He judges himself to be so far inadequate in all that he has attempted and wonders, "*Why dont you let me alone? What more can you want of me than I have already failed to do?*" (*T*, 318). Gavin seems unaware of the change in Eula's character that his own devotion has wrought. She tells him that his well-intended gift to Linda—the possibility of going away to school—has been used by Flem to "twist her arm" and to gain power over her. When Eula informs him matter-of-factly of her own shameful situation, Gavin assumes that she intends to follow Manfred's plan for elopement. Eula inserts hints of her own perception of the situation, revealing a moral sensibility approaching Gavin's own. When she speaks of Flem's impotence, for instance, it is she who assumes the superior role, warning Gavin to beware of pitying Flem, as he had once warned her of doing.

Gavin takes no notice of Eula's growth in stature, expressed in her complete lack of self-pity. She has called him not to ask for comfort, compassion, or advice but to provide for a daughter whom she herself can no longer protect.

When she asks Gavin to marry Linda, he believes that her request is merely to supply a name for the girl about to lose one when her mother elopes. She finally asks him to swear, not necessarily to marry Linda but to care for her, and admits that Gavin's relation to Linda is radically open. She here seems to recognize the reality to which Gavin has been trying to bear witness with his life of devotion, the existence of love not dependent on any particular legal relationship or on any personal gratification to be gained. Gavin assumes that Eula will follow Manfred's plan of action. He ignores her tone of acceptance and finality, merely asking about the facts of the case.

When Gavin drives Eula home, he makes his final commitment to her that night before her suicide, perhaps at the same moment she makes her own resolution final. She has him swear a third time that he will be Linda's guardian. He watches her pass through the door into the house, as Chick Mallison notes in *The Mansion* that it is Gavin's bachelor vocation to watch women do. This particular door does not lead to a new state of maturity or to marriage, however, but to suicide. As usual, Gavin remains behind. Remembering the scene, he describes her passing from his life as a dimension less, then a substance less, then the sound of a door and then, not *never been* but simply *no more is* since always and forever that *was* remains, as if what is going to happen to one tomorrow already gleams faintly visible now if the watcher were only wise enough to discern it or maybe just brave enough. (*T*, 334)

Though Gavin does not realize that Eula will commit suicide, he does know that this is the last moment he will ever see her, and for him that "was" remains "always and forever, inexplicable and immune, which is its grief." This moment when Eula crosses the threshold from light to darkness, from is to was, carries immanent within it the "gleam" of "what is going to happen to me tomorrow." His meditation shows that what is lost does not pass away but becomes full and portentous with meaning, however much the loss may cause suffering. Though Gavin indicates that normally one is not "wise" or "brave" enough to see his own involvement in the moment of passing away, nevertheless Eula's passage "into the shadow" has the effect upon him as of a death and its finality intensifies the sense of his irrevocable bondage to her and to her daughter. His service is of course to that woman, who, like the Virgin Mother in "The Priest," represents the fullness of mortal beauty and love.

Gavin's decision to offer himself up permanently to the service of these women will mean a relinquishment of himself, so that there will be no further decision to make, no matter what his situation. His spiritual "dimension" will be lost to his own use and will be dedicated completely to their service. He sees, as he meditates, that he will be "better off for having lost it. . ."

> who had nothing in the first place to offer but just devotion, eighteen years of devotion, the ectoplasm of devotion too thin to be crowned by scorn, warned by hatred, annealed by grief. That's it: unpin, shed, cast off the last clumsy and anguished dimension and so be free. (*T*, 335)

* * *

This is the moment of "holocaust" for which Gavin's previous life has been the "apprenticeship." It marks the highest point in the life of the comic hero: Dante reaches this stage in preparation for the coming of Beatrice at the summit of Mount Purgatory; Prospero reaches it in *The Tempest*; Lambert Strether in *The Ambassadors*. It is a complete donation of the self; but even in this act Gavin makes light of the flimsy part of himself that he is sacrificing. It is worthless in itself, only making him vulnerable to anguish. But giving up, "unpinning," his "ectoplasm of devotion," is his perpetual vow of service. No longer will his devotion be his to offer: it is already given and it cannot be given again, much less withdrawn. After this decision Gavin loses the self-consciousness characteristic of his previous behavior. One part of him can serve and act, no matter what he feels personally.

At this point Gavin believes that Eula is already lost, and that by her leaving with Manfred she has lost her daughter too. He can no longer have grand notions of changing their lives. He has submitted to the will of another out of disinterested love, not even because he hopes to accomplish any particular task. Only after Eula's death can he recognize that he has not simply submitted to her will, but that their wills have, after all, been one. Both of them have that night made a discreet and courteous but drastic sacrifice, each lacking even the satisfaction of believing that the other recognizes the nature of his devotion. Both have the solemn yet self-deprecating, almost cavalier attitudes of martyrs, which in a sense they are. But according to the judgment of Jefferson that moment of failure confers on Gavin the title of "the bereaved, the betrayed husband forgiving for the sake of the half-orphan child" (*T*, 342). Like the priest in the sketch, Gavin joins the lady in her sacrifice of the state of marriage and becomes the father of a child not his, a child entrusted now to both of them. Gavin has "unpinned it now," has "cast off the last anguished dimension," and so is free. After this relinquishment, Gavin is never again in a quandary about his decisions. The fury of his activity in preparing Eula's funeral and her gravestone does not stem from a lack of certainty of purpose, but only at times from an error in choosing the particular means for fulfilling his aim. His knowledge of what service he must perform is set, though he should be expected to have even more reservations than ever about cooperating with Flem. He springs into utterly unselfconscious action, preparing Eula's funeral and then the monument Flem wants built for her. Though he acknowledges all the complications and the danger of sending Linda to Greenwich Village, yet he has no doubt that sending her there is a risk he must take, however foolish he may look in doing so. She must leave the place where her mother committed suicide.

Gavin's service to women has all the complexity and outward uncertainty, but also all the absoluteness, of any dedication to an institution whose members behave scandalously at times. Because he lives a life of commitment to motion, his actions will not be revealed in their completeness at any one moment. But his eyes are on the object of his dedication, and about that object he no longer has any choice to make.

The paradoxical position of the bachelors is revealed in his part in the death of the lady. She reveals in her death his inadequacy and the poverty of mortal existence. Early in *The Town*, when Gavin Stevens is contemplating the parenthood of Linda, he says that she could not have been fathered by Flem Snopes because Eula Varner "owed that much at least to the simple male hunger which she blazed into anguish just by being." He contemplates the nature of that anguish: the splendor is unbearable because mortal:

> And that single *one* doomed to fade; by the fact of that mortality doomed not to assuage nor even negate the hunger; doomed never to efface the anguish and the hunger from Motion even by her own act of quitting Motion and so fill with her own absence from it the aching void where once had glared that incandescent shape. (*T*, 132-33)

Eula's fading from light to dark, Gavin indicates here, is really the transmutation to another kind of presence; she is present in her absence after death in the "aching void where once had glared that incandescent shape." As the life principle within a society, her very fertility has required her death. If she is to bring life more abundantly to others, she must, like a grain of wheat, submit to the darkness of earth. Both the splendor of her life and the emptiness caused by her death are part of Motion. Her mortality causes a void like "the poet's Nothing, perennially full of perennially new and perennially renewed anguishes for me to measure my stature against" (*T*, 135). Gavin's continuing in motion is the acknowledgment of his own inadequate, so far incomplete, service, which must be fulfilled. Both Ratliff and Gavin must acknowledge the significance of Eula's death and honor her, each in his own way. Neither possessed her; both are worthy of her only in their bachelorhood, which allows them an unlimited love. Ratliff will build a private shrine to her memory in his house. Gavin will arrange for the public monunent on her grave and will care for the daughter she has given him. The paradox of such a death within comedy is that it brings forth fruit among whose who remain in motion: in this case Eula's child, Gavin, Ratliff, and the society as a whole are the beneficiaries. Flem chose better than he knew when he selected the text for her headstone:

> A Virtuous Wife Is a Crown to Her Husband
> Her Children Rise and Call Her Blessed

Notes

1. All citations of the three novels constituting the *Snopes Trilogy* will be indicated in the text by first initials and page numbers in parentheses and will refer to the following editions: *The Hamlet* (New York: Modern Library, 1956); *The Town* (New York: Random House, 1957); *The Mansion* (New York: Random House, 1959).

2. Erich Neumann, *The Origins and History of Consciousness*, trans. R. F. C. Hull (Princeton, 1954), 172.

3. Ibid.

4. Allen Tate, "The Symbolic Imagination," in *Essays of Four Decades* (Chicago, 1968), 438–39.

5. Fyodor Dostoevsky, *The Brothers Karamozov*, trans. Constance Garnett (New York, 1950), 377.

6. James B. Meriwether and Michael Millgate, eds., *Lion in the Garden* (New York, 1968), 131.

7. Louis Bouyer, Cong. Orat., *Introduction to Spirituality*, trans. Mary Perkins Ryan (Collegeville, Minn., 1961), 224–25.

8. Bouyer, 226.

9. "The Priest" was originally published in *The Double Dealer* (January–February 1925) as part of a series of sketches entitled "New Orleans." This version is reprinted in *New Orleans Sketches*, ed. Carvel Collins (New York, 1958), 4–5.

10. A more extended version of "The Priest," probably written in 1925 as part of the "Mirror of Chartres Street" series for the *Times-Picayune* and probably rejected for publication, is published by James B. Meriwether from a typescript in the New York Public Library's Berg Collection in the *Mississippi Quarterly* 29 (Summer 1976): 445–50.

11. Saint Thomas Aquinas, *The Religious State*, trans. and ed. John Proctor, O.P., (St. Louis, 1903), 49. Saint Thomas here is glossing Saint Cyril.

12. In general the character of Stevens in this work as in previous ones is greatly misunderstood. Many see him to be an ineffectual and ridiculous figure who comes under criticism for his habitual abstraction. Even notable critics like Brooks (*Yoknapatawpha Country*, 194-204) and Millgate (*Achievement*, 237-244; and "William Faulkner: The Problem of Point of View," in *Patterns of Commitment in*

American Literature, ed. Mouston LaFrance, [Toronto, 1967], 181-92) are extreme in their misreading of the character. To Brooks (203), like the medieval courtly lover described in Denis de Rougement's *Love in the Western World*, Gavin is in "the neo-Platonic-Gnostic-Puritan tradition"; for Millgate (241), "There can be no question of Stevens's inadequacy for life." Their comments are representative of the negative interpretation of the character.

There have been many favorable analyses of the character of Gavin Stevens, seeing him as representative of an ethical truth; generally, however, critics reserve their assent to him in saying that his action can have little or no effect in the world of the novel. See in this regard John L. Longley, Jr., "Galahad Gavin and a Garland of Snopeses," *Virginia Quarterly Review* 33 (Autumn 1957): 627-28. The most valuable insights into Stevens's character and role in the trilogy are those of Beck, in *Man in Motion* and in his essay-review of *The Mansion*; that of Vickery in *The Novels of William Faulkner*, 182-92 ff; two excellent essays by Arthur Mizener, a review of *The Town*, *Kenyon Review* 19 (Summer 1957): 484-88, and "The American Hero as Gentleman: Gavin Stevens," in *The Sense of Life in the Modern Novel* (Boston, 1964), 161-81; and Eileen Gregory, "A Study of the Early Versions of Faulkner's *The Town* and *The Mansion*," (Ph.D. diss., Univ. of South Carolina, 1975), 74-100 ff.

Index

Abartis, Caesarea, 141
Abraham, 42, 43, 45-49
Abundance, 163, 164, 170, 176, 178, 181, 183, 186, 191, 192
Action, purgatorial, 19, 20; tragic, 43
Adam, 42-43, 45-47
Adamo, Maestro, 95
Adrian V, Pope, 96
Aeschylus, 10, 67, 71, 78-79
Alceste, 12, 142, 185
Aldobrandesco, Omberto, 98
Anders, Guenther, 164, 192
Angelo (*Measure for Measure*), 229
Antigonus, 126, 132, 134
Apocalyptic, 65-66, 70, 76-77, 82, 84
Aquinas, Saint Thomas, 241, 250
Argenti, Filippo, 96, 108
Aristophanes, 1, 10, 13-15, 20, 61-87, 100, 165, 168; *Acharnians*, 69-72, 74, 76, 82, 84; *Birds*, 14, 77, 80-83, 86; *Clouds*, 82, 100; *Frogs*, 77-78; *Knights*, 82; *Lysistrata*, 69, 74-76; *Peace*, 69, 72-74, 77, 79, 82, 84; *Wasps*, 82, 84
Aristotle, 3, 7, 8, 17, 57-58, 67, 75, 107, 167, 170; *Poetics*, 17, 58
Arlecchino, 115-20
Armstid, Mrs. Henry, 238
Athene, 24, 35-37
Auden, W. H., 120, 123, 151, 162
Auerbach, Erich, 91, 108
Augustine, Saint, 97, 101; *The Confessions*, 97
Austen, Jane, 13
Autolycus, 136, 138

Babel, 46-48
Bachelors, 221-22, 224, 226-27, 229-32, 237, 243, 249
Backus, Melisandre, 245
Bakhtin, Mikhail, 7, 17, 64, 85-86, 144-47, 150, 152, 155-57, 161, 162, 163, 164, 168, 172, 192

Barber, C. L., 135, 141, 144, 146, 161, 164
Barth, John, 172
Basileia, 14, 81, 82, 87
Baudelaire, Charles, 17, 68, 101, 108-09, 115, 174; "On the Essence of Laughter," 17, 101, 108, 122
Beatrice, 14, 36
Beaumarchais, 185; *Le Mariage de Figaro*, 185
Beck, Warren, 251
Beckett, Samuel, 2, 13, 41, 163, 164, 172, 173, 192; *Waiting for Godot*, 163, 177
Belmont (*Merchant of Venice*), 14
Benengeli, Cide Hamete, 149, 161
Berek, Peter, 141
Bergson, Henri, 17, 48, 59, 164
Bernard, Saint, 229
Bible, 41-43, 57-58, 172, 173, 214; Deuteronomy, 45; Exodus, 52, 91; Genesis, 42, 43, 45-48, 52, 53, 56-58, 65, 193; Psalms, 10; Proverbs, 55; Song of Songs, 10, 54, 223
Biggens, Dennis, 141
Blake, William, 12, 105; "London," 12
Blisset, William, 141
Bonaventura, Saint, 100
Boniface VIII, Pope, 96
Borges, Jorge Luis, 172
Bottom (*Midsummer Night's Dream*), 16, 18, 82
Bouyer, Louis, 236, 250
Bovary, Charles, 191
Bradbrook, Muriel, 61, 64, 85
Brigella, 113, 118
Brooks, Cleanth, 250-51
Bruns, Gerald, 183, 193
Buechner, Frederick, 48, 59; *Leonce und Lena*, 186
Buonconte da Montefeltro, 97-98
Byron, George Gordon Lord, 190

Cacciaguida, 101, 102
Callimacho (*Mandragola*), 11, 168
Camillo, 127-30, 132-33, 137, 139, 140
Can Grande della Scala, 90, 91, 226
Capitano, 117, 119, 120
Caputi, Anthony, 144, 146, 161
Carnival, 64, 67, 135, 143-48, 150, 153-61, 164, 175, 184, 208
Catharsis, 3, 84, 111
Cavarnos, Constantine, 200, 218
Cervantes, Miguel de, 13, 84, 143-62
Chaucer, 12, 13, 15, 199; *Canterbury Tales*, 174, 199; "Nun's Priest Tale" (Prologue), 193
Chekhov, Anton, 13, 185
Childers, D. T., 141
Childs, Brevard, 57, 59
Christ, 36, 56, 91, 92, 199, 201, 204, 208, 210-11, 214-15, 217
City, 10, 14, 27, 29, 43, 56, 62, 65, 66, 68-69, 74, 76-85, 101, 173
Climacus, Saint John, 196, 218
Clive, Geoffrey, 218
Close, A. J., 162
Cloten (*Cymbeline*), 12
Clown (*Winter's Tale*), 138
Clytemnestra, 5
Coghill, Nevill, 3, 17, 91, 97, 108, 141
Comedy, biblical, 41-42; dark, 84, 107; infernal, 10-11; New, 1, 3; of Manners, 3, 41, 164, 166, 178, 184; Old, 41, 62, 63-64; paradisal, 13-14, 80; purgatorial, 13, 80; Restoration, 12
Comic terrain, 8, 10, 14-17, 77-82
Commedia dell'Arte, 111-22
Communal space, 153
Communitas, 119, 135-40
Community, 2, 10, 11, 13, 16, 26, 43, 62, 74, 118-21, 126-27, 130-31, 134, 136, 138-41, 145-47 155 159, 196-97, 203, 209, 214-16, 229, 237
Congreve, William, 184, 187, 189, 193; *The Way of the World*, 186, 187, 193
Conrad, Joseph, 227
Contrats rompus, 113
Covenant, New, 46, 53, 55, 56; Old, 55, 56

Cook, Albert, 3, 17, 115, 123
Corinthia, Everbe, 14
Cornford, F. M., 126, 141, 161
Crane, Ichabod, 233
Crashaw, Richard, 173
Criticism, Italian Renaissance, 3
Crossan, John, 218, 219

Dante, 1, 7, 10-11, 14-17, 20, 36, 39, 47, 70, 77, 83-84, 89-109, 166, 199, 217, 225, 226, 228, 247; *Commedia* (*Divine Comedy*), 16, 41, 47, 83, 90, 95, 98, 102, 107, 226-29, 237; *Convivio*, 108-09; *Divine Comedy*, 91, 93, 100, 106, 165, 199; *Inferno*, 77, 83, 92-93, 95-97, 100; *Purgatory*, 77, 97, 98
Dapper (*The Alchemist*), 179
De Spain, Manfred, 222, 230, 233-36, 241-46, 248
Deception, 12, 14, 16, 32, 38
Descartes, René, 166, 167, 183; *Discourse of Method*, 166, 167
Dickens, Charles, 105, 190
Dido, 53
Dikaiopolis, 11, 70-72, 82
Dionysus, 61-64, 66, 70-71, 78-80, 82, 143, 180, 181
Disguise, 12, 14, 24-25, 32, 114, 153, 160
Doctor (pedantic), 116, 119-20
Dodds, E. R., 86
Don Juan, 190
Don Quixote, 143-62, 223
Donati, Corso, 106; Forese, 106; Piccarda, 106
Donne, John, 1, 10, 245
Dostoevsky, Fyodor, 13, 84-85, 190, 195-19, 227, 228, 250; *Brothers Karamazov*, 227, 250; *The Possessed*, 13, 195-19
Dover, K. J., 87
Dryden, John, 184
Duchartre, Pierre Louis, 112, 116, 122
Dulcinea del Toboso, 152, 155, 161

Eden, 10, 209, 240
Egan, Robert, 141

INDEX 255

Elijah, 46, 55
Eliot, T. S., 12, 13, 187; *Cocktail Party*, 187
Ellul, Jacques, 196, 204, 218
Elohim, 45, 58
Else, Gerald F., 59
Epic, 2, 7, 8-10, 58, 91
Esau, 47, 49
Etherege, George, 184
Euripides, 71, 78-79
Eve, 42, 43, 45-47, 53

Face (*The Alchemist*), 11, 182, 183
Falstaff, 206
Fantasy, 10, 15, 67-69, 77, 80, 83, 153
Farinata degli Uberti, 95
Farquahar, George, 184
Faulkner, William, 13, 14, 84-85, 221-51; *The Hamlet*, 223, 237, 239; *The Mansion*, 225, 231, 235, 237, 241, 246, 250; "The Priest," 240, 247, 250; *The Reivers*, 14; Snopes Trilogy, 13, 221, 227, 229, 231, 237, 250; *The Town*, 223, 235, 238, 249, 250
Feast, 38, 42, 215
Femininity, 221, 225, 226, 241
Ferapont, Father, 228
Fergusson, Francis, 8, 17, 97
Fertility, 64, 80, 126, 144-45
Festival, 38, 67, 70, 72, 136, 146, 149, 164, 210
Fielding, Henry, 13
Finn, Huck, 223
Flaubert, Gustave, 12, 191, 192; *Bouvard et Pecuchet*, 191; *Dictionnaire des idees recues*, 191; *Madame Bovary*, 12
Flavio, 113
Florizel, 136-38
Flutter, Sir Fopling, 184
Forest of Arden, 14
Francesca da Rimini, 94
Frazer, Sir James George, 161
Freud, Sigmund, 17, 146
Frey, Charles, 141
Frye, Northrop, 3, 17, 43, 52, 59, 65, 86, 101, 105-6, 109, 123, 164

Gabrielli, Scapino, 119
Gadamer, Hans-Georg, 58, 59
Garden, 10, 43, 45, 209
Gilbert, W. S., 173
Girard, Rene, 95, 218, 219
Goethe, Johann Wolfgang von, 19, 165, 166, 169, 180, 204; *Faust*, 165; *Iphigenie*, 165; *Tasso*, 165
Gogol, Nikolai, 12, 84, 163, 173, 190; *Dead Souls*, 12
Goldoni, Carlo, 185
Gongora, Luis de, 173
Goody, Jack, 193
Gozzi, Carlo, 112, 113
Grabbe, Christian Dietrich, 186
Gregory, Eileen, 251
Grillparzer, Franz, 186
Guido da Pisa, 92

Hackel, Sergei, 197, 218
Hadas, Moses, 63, 85
Hagar, 47, 53
Haggard, Stephan, 116, 122
Hannah, 54, 55
Happy idea, 75, 81, 168
Harcourt-Reilly, Sir Henry (*The Cocktail Party*), 12
Hegel, G. W. F., 13, 18, 98-108, 170, 171, 193; *Lectures on Aesthetics*, 99-101 103-05 107-08 171; *Philosophy of Fine Art*, 18; *Philosophy of History*, 99
Heiberg, J. L., 186
Heidegger, Martin, 23
Heilman, Robert, 17
Helen of Troy, 53, 223, 244
Heller, Erich, 165, 190, 192
Henderson, Jeffrey, 86
Henkle, Roger, 169, 170, 192
Herbert, George, 56
Hermione, 126-34, 139, 140
Hero (*Much Ado About Nothing*), 133
Hesiod, 45, 58; *Theogony*, 45
Hildebrand, Adolf, 8
Hillman, James, 62, 85
Hintikka, Jaako, 167, 192
Holberg, Ludvig, 186
Hollander, Robert, 90, 108

Homer, 10, 15, 19-21, 24, 34, 41, 64, 66, 172, 173, 175; *Iliad*, 19, 20, 172; *Odyssey*, 13, 19-40, 41
Hope, 27, 167, 169, 196, 198, 216
Horace, 3
Humors, 97
Huxley, Aldous, 212
Hyers, M. Conrad, 219

Iachimo (*Cymbeline*), 12
Icon, 195-200, 204-05, 208, 210-12, 214-17
Idol, 196, 199, 200, 205
Image, 198, 199, 203, 209, 212, 216; comic, 2-4, 7, 15, 64-66, 85, 120, 121, 134, 140; iconic, 196-98, 201, 202, 205, 209, 210; *mundus imaginalis*, 9, 85; mythic, 215; of a world, 8, 16, 150, 152; of man, 9, 121, 140, 150
Imagination, Christian, 206, 217; Greek, 58; Hebrew, 58; iconic, 217; symbolic, 226, 250
In exitu Israel, 91
Isaac, 42, 45-49
Isaiah, 55
Ishmael (*Moby-Dick*), 192
Israel, 43, 50, 52-55
Itinerary of the Soul Toward God, The, 100

Jackson, Robert Louis, 196, 218
Jacob, 42, 43, 45-47, 49, 50, 52, 53
James, Henry, 13, 14, 227; *The Ambassadors*, 247
Jansen, J. Gerald, 57, 59
Jeremiah, 55
Jesus, 46, 56
Jezebel, 55
John the Divine, Saint, 66
Jonson, Ben, 2, 12, 91, 97, 164, 165, 178, 179, 184, 193; *Alchemist*, 12, 179, 182-83, 193; *Bartholomew Fair*, 179, 180-82, 193; *Epicoene*, 178, 179, 193; *Volpone*, 12, 165, 179
Joseph, 45, 46, 50-53, 57
Jourdain, Monsieur (*Le Bourgeois gentilhomme*), 184

Joyce, James, 85, 172, 173, 191, 192; *Finnegans Wake*, 191; *Ulysses*, 191
Judah, 50, 52
Judas, 43
Judges, 54, 55
Julia (*The Cocktail Party*), 12
Jung, C. G., 65, 86
Justice, 14, 16, 91, 94, 95, 133

Kandinsky, Wassily, 189
Kalypso, 14, 22, 29
Karamazov, Ivan, 84; Alexey (Alyosha), 211, 228
Keats, John, 10, 174
Kerenyi, Carl, 62, 66, 85, 86
Kierkegaard, Soren, 49, 171, 172, 193; *Fear and Trembling*, 49; *Stages on Life's Way*, 171
Kirillov, 199, 202, 209-11
Knight (*Canterbury Tales*), 174
Knight, L. C., 164
Koch, Klaus, 86
Kohl, Barton, 222

Laban, 47, 50
Labove, 222, 232-35, 241, 243
Langer, Susanne, 2, 3, 8, 17, 18, 119, 123
Language, 20, 39, 68-69, 82-83, 114, 122, 128, 130, 144, 147, 150, 158
Latini, Brunetto, 95, 228, 229
Laughter, 2, 3, 6, 84, 94, 101, 118, 163, 164, 172, 174, 192
Laventyevich, Anton, 200-02, 211
Lazzi, 120, 121
Leah, 42, 45, 47, 50, 53
Leatherhead, Lanthorn (*Bartholomew Fair*), 180
Lebyadkin, Captain, 200; Marya, 199-03, 206, 208, 212
Leontes, 126-39
Lewis, C. S., 19, 20, 24, 168, 169, 192
Ligurio (*Mandragola*), 12
Lindenbaum, Peter, 141
Littlejohn, Mrs., 237
Littlewit, John (*Bartholomew Fair*), 180
Locke, John, 188

INDEX

Longley, John L., Jr., 251
Love, 1, 10, 11, 14, 15, 27, 76, 81, 82, 92, 94, 95, 121, 169, 239, 240
Lovely Lady (pretty girl, beautiful woman), 11, 12, 14, 72, 96
Lucio (*Measure for Measure*), 12, 228
Luck, 10
Lucrezia (*Mandragola*), 168
Luke, Saint, 198, 202, 215
Lyamshin, 204
Lynch, William F., 42, 45, 59, 198, 218
Lyric, 7-9, 15, 90, 174

Machiavelli, Nicolò, 12, 168; *Mandragola*, 12, 168
McCarron, Hoake, 223, 233-36, 241, 243, 245
McFarland, Thomas, 164, 192
McKee, Kenneth, 113, 114, 122
Mak (*Second Shepherds' Play*), 11
Malantschuk, Gregor, 171, 193
Malaprop, Mrs. (*The Rivals*), 184
Mallison, Charles (Chuck), 223, 230, 235, 242, 244, 246; Maggie, 225, 242, 244, 245
Malvolio (*Twelfth Night*), 184 185
Mamillius, 126, 133, 134, 141
Marino, Giambattista, 173
Maritain, Jacques, 9, 10, 18
Marlowe, Christopher, 204; *Hero and Leander*, 181, 183
Marmeladov, Sonya (*Crime and Punishment*), 14
Marriage, 12, 16, 39, 42, 221
Marx, Karl, 108
Masculinity, 222, 225, 226, 229
Mask, 119, 120
Matryosha, 207, 211, 297
Matthew, Saint, 239
Medvedev, Pavel, 7, 17
Melville, Herman, 14, 173
Mercy, 16, 92, 133, 139
Meredith, George, 11, 17, 55, 59, 164
Meriwether, James B., 250
Milford Haven (*Richard III*), 14
Millamant, 186-88
Millgate, Michael, 250-51
Milton, John, 10, 92, 204

Mirabell, 11, 186-88
Miranda (*The Tempest*), 14
Miriam, 43, 53, 54
Mizener, Arthur, 251
Moby-Dick, 192
Molière, Jean-Baptiste Poquelin de, 12, 142, 163, 178, 184, 185; *Bourgeois Gentilhomme*, 184; *Le Médècin malgré lui*, 184; *Le Misanthrope*, 142, 185; *Les Prècieuses ridicules*, 184; *Tartuffe*, 11 184-85
Mondrian, Piet, 189, 190, 194
Morose, 178, 179, 184, 185
Mosca (*Volpone*), 11
Moses, 43, 46, 53, 54
Murray, Gilbert, 86, 87
Musset, Alfred de, 185; *Un Caprice*, 185; *On ne badine pas avec l'amour*, 185

Nabokov, Vladimir, 172, 173, 195, 218
Neumann, Erich, 224, 250
New Jerusalem, 10, 56, 69, 82
New Testament, 41, 42, 53, 54
Newton, Isaac, 167
Nicholas III, Pope, 96
Nietzsche, Friedrich, 80, 169, 170, 190
Nikolaevna, Lizaveta, 202, 204, 206
Nino de' Visconti, 93
Noah, 42, 46, 47

O'Connor, Flannery, 13, 84; *The Violent Bear It Away*, 13; *Wise Blood*, 13
Oderisi da Gubbio, 98
Odysseus, 1, 14, 20-40, 213
Oedipus, 169
Old Testament, 12, 13, 41, 42, 45, 46, 53, 55, 57
Opora, 72, 74, 80
Ortega y Gasset, Jose, 149, 162
Otto, Rudolf, 66, 86
Otto, Walter, 62, 85
Ouspensky, Leonid, 198-99, 218, 219
Overdo, Adam (*Bartholomew Fair*), 179, 182, 184

Pandarus (*Troilus and Cressida*), 182-84
Panichas, George A., 219
Pantagruel, 175-78
Pantalone, 113, 115-17, 119, 120
Panurge, 176, 177
Panza, Sancho, 152, 153, 156-59, 223
Paolucci, Anne, 101, 108
Paradigm, 1, 10, 14, 16, 20, 77, 102, 106, 226
Parker, Douglas, 75, 86, 87
Parody, 150, 158
Paul, Saint, 43, 46, 56, 93
Paulina, 12, 130, 131, 137-40
Peace, 67, 69-71, 74, 76, 80, 106
Pécuchet, 192
Pedrolino, 118
Peisthetairos, 80-82
Perdita, 134-37
Petrarch, Francesco, 174
Petrovna, Varvara, 208
Philokleon, 82
Physis, 15, 70, 178
Pieper, Josef, 219
Pier delle Vigne, 95
Piers Plowman, 12
Plato, 3, 68, 86; *Philebus*, 3
Polixenes, 127-29, 132-34, 136-38
Poneros, 20, 69, 75, 78, 83
Porter, Katherine Anne, 13
Portia (*Merchant of Venice*), 14, 116
Prokhorovna, Arina, 211
Prometheus, 58, 219
Prospero (*The Tempest*), 182, 190, 247
Proteus, 21-31
Puck (*Midsummer's Night Dream*), 182
Pulcinella, 118, 120

Quevedo, Francisco, 173

Rabelais, François, 84, 163, 175, 186 191, 193; *Gargantua and Pantagruel*, 144, 175-78, 193
Rachel, 43, 45, 50, 52-54
Ratliff, V. K., 12, 222, 223, 229, 231, 235-41, 244, 249, 250
Rebekah, 42, 45, 48, 49, 53, 54

Redemption, 43, 105, 196, 197, 202, 212, 217, 222
Remes, Unto, 167, 192
Reynolds, Barbara, 7
Romance of the Rose, The, 174
Romans, Epistle to the, 56
Rougemont, Denis de, 251
Rowland, Christopher, 86
Rowley, H. H., 86
Ruggieri, Archbishop, 95
Ruth, 54, 55

Samuel, 54
Sapia, 98
Sarah, 42, 43, 45-46, 48, 53-54
Satan, 219
Satire, 2, 67-69, 99, 101, 149, 150, 173
Sawyer, Tom, 223
Scapegoat, 126, 134, 141
Schless, Howard H., 108
Schopenhauer, Arthur, 169, 190
Scribe, Eugene, 171
Sebastian (*Twelfth Night*), 133
Second Shepherds' Play, 105
Senex, 45, 49, 58, 208
Seuphor, Michel, 190
Shakespeare, William, 1, 5, 6, 10, 12-15, 85, 91, 97, 125-42, 144, 146, 150, 170, 182, 184, 193, 204, 206, 228; *All's Well that Ends Well*, 185; *As You Like It*, 142; *Hamlet*, 5, 6, 117, 128, 190; *Macbeth*, 174, 193; *Measure for Measure*, 228; *Merchant of Venice*, 6, 116; *The Tempest*, 6, 14, 247; *Troilus and Cressida*, 12, 182, 183, 193; *Twelfth Night*, 128, 133; *The Winter's Tale*, 13, 125-42
Shandy, Toby, 188, 189
Shatov, 200, 202, 203, 206, 211, 212; Marie, 208, 210-12
Sheridan, Richard B., 189, 194; *School for Scandal*, 189, 194
Shigalov, 196, 210, 211
Ship of Fools, 13
Shylock (*Merchant of Venice*), 12
Sign (signifier-signified), 21, 23-26, 28, 29, 31, 33, 35, 36, 39

INDEX

Singleton, Charles, 92, 95, 102, 108
Sly, Christopher (*Taming of the Shrew*), 184
Snopes, Flem, 12, 84, 222, 233-35, 238, 242-45, 249; Ike, 230, 237; Linda, 14, 222, 224, 230, 231, 244-46, 248, 249; Mink, 230, 241; Montgomery Ward, 223
Societas, 135
Socrates, 100
Sofya, 199, 204, 207, 208, 210, 214-16
Solomon, 43, 54
Solomos, Alexis, 63, 64, 66, 85
Sophocles, 10, 71, 73
Spenser, Edmund, 84
Spitzer, Leo, 108
Stavrogin, Nikolay, 196, 198, 199, 201, 203, 205, 207, 208, 211, 217, 219; Varvara, 208, 212, 214, 216
Stern, Karl, 215, 219
Sterne, Laurence, 84, 173, 183, 189
Stevens, Gavin, 12, 222, 223, 230, 231, 233-37, 239-51
Strepsiades, 82
Strether, Lambert (*The Ambassadors*), 247
Sullivan, Arthur, 173
Swift, Jonathan, 12, 150; *Gulliver's Travels*, 12
Sypher, Wylie, 208, 209, 219

Tate, Allen, 226, 228
Taylor, Mark, 100, 108
Teazle, Lady (*School for Scandal*), 189
Theory, comic, 4, 13, 16, 92, 163, 166; neoclassical, 3
Tihon, 199, 206, 207, 214
Tillyard, E. M. W., 141
Timofyevna, Marya, 198
Tinkler, F. C., 141
Tragedy, 2, 5-11, 13, 19, 20, 46, 52, 58, 62, 67, 78, 79, 90, 91, 98, 100, 107, 126, 164, 165, 166, 168-70, 174, 186, 189, 190, 205, 207, 209, 217
Tristram Shandy, 188
Truewit (*Epicoene*), 179
Trygaios, 72-74, 80, 82
Turner, Victor, 135, 141, 162

Twain, Mark, 14
Tylor, Sir Edward, 161
Typhon, 219

Ugolino, 95

Varner, Eula, 222-27, 229-34, 236, 238, 240-50; Jody, 222, 223, 229, 232, 241
Venus, 223, 224, 234, 235
Verene, Donald Phillip, 166, 167, 192
Verkhovensky, Pyotr, 196, 198, 200, 202, 203, 208, 209; Stepan, 196, 198-200, 207-08, 210, 212-16
Vico, Giambattista, 166, 168
Vincent of Beauvais, 91
Vincentio, Duke, 229
Viola, 128, 133
Vionnet, Mme. (*The Ambassadors*), 14
Virgil, 10, 19, 70, 90, 92-96
Virgins, 222-24
Virgin Mary (Madonna), 56, 197-99, 201, 203, 204-10, 212-14, 216, 217, 240, 241, 247
Vyvyan, John, 141

Wakefield Mystery Plays, 48
Ware, Kallistos, 197, 218
Wasiolek, Edward, 218, 219
White, Hayden, 98, 99, 108
Whitman, Cedric, 11, 18, 68, 69, 83, 86, 87
Wimsatt, William, 3, 17
Wordsworth, William, 92
Wycherley, William, 184

Yahweh, 45, 58
Yakovlevitch, Semyon, 206
Yossarian (*Catch-22*), 11

Zeal-of-the-Land Busy (*Bartholomew Fair*), 180, 184
Zerbrochene Krug, Der (Kleist), 186
Zossima, Father, 227, 228

www.ingramcontent.com/pod-product-compliance
Lightning Source LLC
Chambersburg PA
CBHW032104090426
42743CB00007B/228